SPRING · NEW WRITING FROM BATH SPA

With a Foreword by Caroline Dawnay, Head of Books at PFD
and an Introduction by Professor Richard Francis

An Artswork Book published by the Bath Spa University Presses

This is an Artswork Book, published by the Bath Spa University Presses, Newton Park, Bath, BA2 9BN, United Kingdom, in March 2007.

ISBN   978-0-9545648-4-1

British Library Cataloguing in Publication Data.

A catalogue record for this book is available from the British Library.

10 9 8 7 6 5 4 3 2 1

Designed at Other Rooms.
Cover photography reproduced with the kind permission of Peter Gowland.
Printed and bound in the UK by APB Colour Print, Bristol.

First edition

CONTENTS

ACKNOWLEDGEMENTS

We should like to thank everyone involved in the production of this anthology. In particular:

- Graphic designers Kellie and Matthew at Other Rooms, without whose vision and production expertise this book could never have taken its present form;
- Tim Middleton, Head of the School of English and Creative Studies at Bath Spa University for his much-valued support, both directional and financial;
- Paul Meyer, Managing Editor of the Bath Spa University Presses, for his inexhaustible patience, commitment and enthusiasm;
- Richard Kerridge, Course Leader and intellectual benchmark of Bath Spa's postgraduate writing programme;
- Caroline Dawnay, for taking time out of her busy schedule to read our work and write our foreword;
- Professor Richard Francis, for his inspiring introduction;
- Loulou Brown, our proofreader;
- Tessa Hadley, Gerard Woodward, Richard Francis (again!) and all of our lecturers at Bath Spa for their direct and indirect involvement in, and influence on, our writing.

The Editors

Amethyst Biggs, Sally Hare, Lucy Hewitt, Rachel Knightley, Kate McEwan, Madeleine Tobert (copy-editors);

Val Bridge, Neil Callender, Stephanie Cage, Tara Diamond, Lindsay Flynn, KM Kernek, Emma London, Thea Martin, Jennifer Russell

FOREWORD

by Caroline Dawnay

Sometimes I'm asked: when are you going to write *your* novel? Perhaps I'm asked this because I'm a literary agent and my interlocutor thinks I somehow must know all the secrets: that my observations over nearly thirty years of representing writers will have accumulated so valuably as to give me the little gold key that opens the door to the perfect story, the one that publishers would fall on in ecstasy; that the Best First Novel prizes would all be mine and that the Man Booker dinner party is just over the horizon.

But those twin oxen, talent and will, have never been yoked together in my plough. Might I have the talent if I dig for it? Even now I can picture myself like the author of the French novel I read long ago, battling to perfect that first sentence, trying it over and over again and getting nowhere. Do I have the will? I should be more likely to hoover the entire house, pay my bills and plant my hyacinth bulbs.

I know imaginative, visionary, intelligent people who, I feel sure, possess the talent yet have no interest in writing books; every week, as an agent, I read people's work which demonstrates by contrast that the will is there ('I have written four novels and two screenplays; would you like me to send them by post or by e-mail?') but for whom, most often, alas, the talent is weak.

What is exciting about the work of the Bath Spa University students Peters Fraser & Dunlop has got to know over the years since the PFD Prize began is the realisation that the talent and the will are already harnessed and in action. The extracts in this anthology bear witness to a marvellous range of inventiveness, enthusiasm, subtlety and fresh thinking. Some of these are commercial successes in embryo and some of them are not. But they all have value in their different ways. What is wonderful about the plaudits and the good publishing deals that have arisen out of the MA course over the last years is that they have enabled it to continue, grow, flourish and get better every year. I'm proud and gratified to have been allied with it from the start and – who knows? This anthology makes it look so easy, perhaps I'll try writing that novel after all.

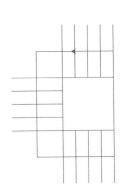

INTRODUCTION

by Richard Francis

No, you can't teach creative writing. I'm not sure you can teach anything much, come to that. Maybe in some data-heavy subjects you can heft lumps of knowledge into the waiting arms of students. But if you're hoping to help people think and use their imagination, the last thing you want is to impose your own thoughts and imagination on them. It would be a contradiction in terms.

So the students themselves provide the essential teaching resources and course materials. The first requirement is for them to bring their own flair and originality into the room with them. As you will see when you read this anthology, the ones on our MA in Creative Writing at Bath Spa have done so in abundance, this year as in years past (as have those on the sister course, the MA in Writing for Young People, which now has its own anthology). Sometimes I feel rather threatened by the talent out there, surging towards us in annual waves.

The job of teachers is to help direct that flow and energy, to ensure the students make their writing as powerful and well-crafted as possible; to be creative readers in response to our creative writers. As you turn the pages and read the work engendered by the MA, I hope you'll agree we must be doing something right. In case that sounds like hogging the credit, I should add that every member of a workshop becomes a teacher. *We* means all of us.

A creative writing workshop can be an amazingly complete experience, a matter of giving and receiving, reading and writing. As the year goes on we all become more sensitive to each other's narratives, in the personal as well as the literary sense. We learn something about the intentions, objectives, needs, ambitions, of the other members of the group, and, as a kind of bonus, about our own. Because that's the point. It may be impossible to teach creative writing, but it *is* possible to learn it, and in some mysterious way learning becomes contagious. And so, by the end of the year, people have almost always produced work that's markedly better, sometimes astonishingly so, than they could have done at the beginning. They've learned something about themselves, about what they want to achieve, and about how to achieve it.

What the MA offers, then, is a context, an environment, a built-in audience. True, a writer must serve his or her own muse, but that muse isn't some sort of self-projection, a posturing ego. It's more like an embodiment of the ultimate autonomy of art. The task is to identify the part or aspect of oneself that can be made sufficiently portable: endowed with meaning and resonance so that it no longer belongs just to the writer but is available to others.

The contributors to this anthology will all have experienced moments of disappointment, pain, fear, as they've gone about their work. In trying to define to new students the most productive tone and atmosphere for creative writing workshops, I often suggest they should try for a middle course between mutual congratulation and blood on the carpet, but in fact the former is sometimes inevitable precisely because the latter is an occupational hazard. It's a testing and difficult experience but a rewarding one, both week by week as work develops, and at the end of the course, when a project is approaching completion. For one student the reward will take tangible form with the PFD Prize for the most promising piece of fiction that, in the opinion of the judges, has been produced on the course. Peters, Fraser and Dunlop have been loyal supporters of our creative MA courses for a long time now.

Every year several of our graduates have work taken up by agents and ultimately published. This in itself is quite an achievement, if you think of the odds against finding a publisher faced by the average writer in the street (or garret). Often there's a slow burn too: a number of our graduates will discover that the experience of the MA has in fact been an apprenticeship, and they will get some success later on. And most if not all will have the satisfaction of having produced work that's the very best they can do for now, their springtime as writers.

We believe in craftsmanship, and that extends to having a professional attitude towards the presentation of work, both to the publishing world and the public at large. The annual collection of MA writing provides a good example. The students themselves are responsible for the editing, production and marketing of this anthology. I hope you'll agree this is a case where form does justice to the quality of content.

CHICKEN SALAD

from the novel by Jessica Barnecutt

I ran a bath. The bubbles grew and the smell of lavender steamed into the room. I undressed in front of the mirror. I looked at my legs. The sight of them always disappointed me. The muscles were unfashionable. It was the speed-walking around restaurants, up and down escalators, always in a hurry to get out of the Underground, to get the next thing done, to get the day over with. My breasts were swollen and heavy. My period was due. I looked at my pale skin and heard my sister.

'You're so pasty. I can see the veins in your neck! Get a tan for goodness sake.' She said it every time I saw her. She meant well.

Stepping into the deep hot water was a precious escape. Easing my back into the water and feeling the warmth rising up the back of my neck made me hold my breath as the hairs on my arms stood on end. I couldn't stop yawning – after-sex tiredness was bewildering. Everything was shaken up again. I replayed the sensations and images. I wanted it again.

The imbalance of hormones was upon me. For the next three days everything would be difficult. Looking at my husband would make me want to scream. He pretended to be a bit of a geezer. But he was soft around the edges, cuddly. Jerome's body was solid. The problem with Charles was he didn't have a life outside of cooking. He was awkward at parties, stiff, smiling and nodding appropriately. Drink didn't work on him; it brought on his tiredness. He spent his days off making bread or reading biographies of famous chefs and eating fish fingers and beans on toast – giving his taste buds a break.

In the beginning his fastidiousness was mysterious. I remember thinking: who is this arrogant man, Charles Jackson? Who does he think he is, shouting at me like that?

'Watch it. Don't stick your fucking thumb in the *jus*,' was the first thing he said to me. 'You're not in Cornwall any more.'

He didn't know my name for a month. I couldn't look at him.

'Fucking waitresses, they don't give a shit. Yeah that's right, wobble the plates, fuck it up,' I heard him say.

I wished he wouldn't layer up the food. The sprig of parsley or whatever it was balanced on top of the fillet of sea bass or lamb chop blew off as I kicked open the double doors. I was shaking by the time I got to the table.

As soon as the hotplate light was switched off and his apron discarded, he removed this façade, like it was a thick layer of congealed skin on his hollandaise sauce. What was left was someone who said he'd be at this party or that staff gathering, or a Sunday session at the pub, but never turned up.

What was it behind that passion for cooking, for getting it right? Every day, lunch and dinner, every dish he sent across his pass, the pass of perfection, had to be approved. The precision could be achieved every time he put on the finishing touch – with that swirl of oil around the scallops or the handful of chopped parsley scattered across the lemon sole.

Every day he got it right.

The cat came into the bathroom. I sat up, stroked his head and then reached for the hot tap. I lay back and watched the steam rise. Closing my eyes, I could feel the temperature change start at my feet. When it reached my shoulders, I turned it off. Closing my eyes again, I saw myself, leaning against the coffee machine, steaming milk for cappuccinos, watching the talented young chef. It was 1987. My first year in London, finally free from my parents' opinions. What did I look like, my hair dyed blonde, permed and stuck up with hairspray?

In the early days, I watched him as I frothed the milk, falling in love with his concentration, his delicate spoonfuls of sauce, and the way he leaned in close to the dish as he assembled it, as if he was short-sighted.

I was too nervous to work on the floor so I ended up staying on the coffee machine for a while. I got to look at him. He caught me once. He spotted a plate coming back in the opposite direction, as he often did, with too much left on it. Over he went to the wash-up area. As I looked on in disbelief, he used the customer's knife and fork to eat what they'd left, prodding at it, tasting noisily.

'Nothing wrong with that,' he said to himself. He pushed it to one side and on returning to the hotplate, he looked up. I was staring – my mouth gaping.

'Don't worry. I've been doing it for years. I've got a strong immune system.'

'Oh, good,' I said and felt my face return to its former expression.

Opposite the hotplate, I was caught in the glare of the lights and heat of the oven. All the orders seemed to come at once. Double espressos, decaf single shot latte, Assam, Darjeeling and peppermint tea, and Canarino – I'd never heard of it – hot water and lemon.

'You don't know what a Canarino is? Tut tut. It's good for digestion,' the head waitress said. Her big brown eyes glared at me. She dressed for work in dark make-up and dangly beaded earrings. The collar on her stiff white shirt was always turned up and her short hair was styled to perfection. She was Asian but had a perfect English accent. It was a huge surprise to me when I first heard her speak. (That's what Cornwall did to me.) As we folded napkins together, she talked about the books she was reading at university. I hadn't heard of any of them. I hadn't even done A-levels. I tried to line up the seams of white linen. She could fold two to my one.

Charles was wrapping all his ingredients with cling film and putting them in the fridge. He did it quickly, fiercely tearing the plastic from the jagged edge. When he finished, I was in the middle of making an Irish coffee. (Nowadays it's such a naff drink.) I could feel sweat resting under my eyes and above my top lip and see my red frowning reflection in the chrome coffee machine. I could see Charles's reflection too.

'Wouldn't make me a coffee would you?'

'I'm a little busy right now. But yes, in a minute. I wouldn't drink coffee at this time though, it's nearly midnight.' Wiping loose strands of hair out of my eyes I ended up with grains of coffee on my face and double cream in my hair.

'Just a black coffee,' he said. I could feel him watching me.

'OK.' I was shaking up the double cream in a plastic bottle. It had to be thickened to sit on the coffee. I'd already messed one up so I was shaking it really hard. Suddenly I couldn't see properly. Charles and I were both sprayed with white spots. My manager came in.

'What a mess,' he said raising one eyebrow. 'These people have been waiting nearly twenty minutes for their coffee. It's not good enough, Rosie.' Christopher, his name was. He was from Paris. I hated him. That was before I found pleasure in everything French.

'She's a right messy one, isn't she,' Charles said, wiping the cream off his face.

'Yes, she's dirty, I bet. And wouldn't you like to know,' Christopher said.

All the chefs laughed. Christopher looked very pleased with himself.

'You better go to the bar and get another whisky,' he said.

My hands were shaking as I poured the cream. I watched it sink into the black coffee for the second time. Eva snatched the jug out of my hand and took over. I made Charles his espresso.

'Here you are.' I put it down on the hotplate.

'Not there,' he said. I moved it to the side. 'What's your name?' he said.

I got out of the bath and dried off. I felt a bit sore inside. I'd forgotten about Jerome for a while. I got into bed and tried to read the newspaper. It was more of the same: the threat of terror on the increase, more vigilance on public transport required. Since 9/11 it was always the same. As the headlines drifted around in my head I kept remembering the smell of Jerome, the feeling of him inside me. I put my hand between my legs. It was as if that part of my body quickly got used to being touched.

I slept for a while and when I woke I was hungry. What did I fancy to eat? I went to prepare myself a salad. I stared into the fridge, downing a glass of water. There was half a smoked chicken left.

I tore the white breast meat off the carcass and ate the first few bits. I toasted some cashew nuts, picking at them in the pan; made a dressing with honey and soy sauce and sesame oil; chopped some nearly-dead coriander; squeezed over some lime juice and tossed it all together with some iceberg, sliced spring onion and cucumber. I was so hungry I began shoving spoonfuls into my mouth straight from the salad bowl.

I could cook perfectly well. I didn't need him in the kitchen peering over my shoulder. It was going to be crunchy and spicy, sweet and fragrant.

I'd made enough for two and considered ringing David or Sophie, the ex-head chef at Green's. But I decided I didn't want to listen to anybody, or my own voice. I might have been tempted to tell them where I'd spent the night. I'd learnt very early in life that if you really didn't want the wrong person to find out a secret, it was best not to tell anyone, not even your own sister.

I picked up my wonderful creation and made my way upstairs. Clutching my knife and fork and glass of white wine (it was my day off) in one hand, I stared at the salad in the other. My appetite was shrinking away.

Almost at the top of the stairs I caught the sole of my slipper on the step, stubbing my toe. With no hands to break my fall, I dropped the plate and the glass of wine. The whole thing made an awful noise. The glass smashed on the wooden stairs and the plate slid all the way down to the bottom. White wine cascaded over the steps and I realised I was bleeding. I'd landed on the glass, cutting the palm of my hand. I wiped it on my pyjama bottoms. The soy dressing dressed the wall. My arm ached where I'd wrenched it, grabbing hold of the banister as I fell.

After a few minutes of wallowing on the landing, I reached for my handbag and found a plaster. In my purse I had nearly ten pounds. I grabbed my coat, checked I had my keys and left the house.

Goldhawk Road. When I first arrived in London, I lived above a shop next door to the best fish and chip shop. I used to comfort myself with a portion of chips on what became known as Suicidal Sundays. Don't get me wrong; I was happy, but Sundays were strange. I should have put up with that shitty flat for longer. I was only there for six months before I moved in with Charles.

Joining the queue, I could smell the vinegar. What had I been doing having a salad on the fourteenth of February? Valentine's Day was a disaster for so many women. But from now on, it would be a day on which I'd love myself. And my daughter. This would probably be the last year she'd spend her birthday with Charles and me.

I was the only woman in the queue. Golden Fry was one of the only establishments in the street without hearts in the window. I ordered cod, chips and mushy peas.

'Take away or eat in, love?'

'Eat in, please.'

The chips were soft and actually possessed a texture of potato without being soggy or anaemic. This was achieved by frying them in at least two stages. The batter wasn't perfect – it never was – but I loved every mouthful.

It had never occurred to me to eat in before. At home in Cornwall our local chippy was called Bridge End. It had one of those small rides that Dad had to put five pence in and I sat on and got rocked back and forth while he waited. Anna would stay at home and warm the plates in the bottom oven of the Rayburn and lay the table with ketchup and white pepper and rounds of soft white sliced bread, with a thick layer of butter. I loved those short journeys to the chippy. It was one of the rare times it was just me and him. It meant nothing to him – he was just picking up the dinner. Me demanding to go along for the ride was probably a nuisance.

'Excuse me?' I said. The grease-stained bloke looked over at me and stopped stirring the hot fat.

'I don't suppose you've got a bit of bread and butter?'

'Yep.'

'And a mug of tea, please.'

I tucked into my fish and chips and sipped my tea. One of those perfect, comforting combinations. The tea somehow cuts through the grease, like good Chianti with Spaghetti Bolognese. I tried to remember when I'd first drunk a cup of tea – or first really enjoyed one – but I couldn't.

I hadn't felt so full and satisfied in a long time. I watched a bus pull up. A stream of people continued to emerge from the middle doors. The pavement was getting fuller and fuller. It was nearly four o'clock. The people getting off put on gloves and hats and scarves. When the bus pulled away, it was almost empty. My feet were cold. I didn't want to go back out there. I wiped my plate with another piece of bread. I used to watch my father put the butter on very thick and then fold the slice in half. One of his elbows would go up on the table. Then he'd start mopping up the grease and remains of tartar sauce from the plate until it was clean. Halfway through he'd stop for a slurp on his tea. The news was always on. It went on forever, while I waited for cartoons. He and Mum would talk. It was always about work – how much money he was making and how useless his staff were. Then he'd put his knife and fork together and go back to the pub.

Sitting there, feeling that sense of happiness from eating my fish and chips, it didn't seem possible that I could be tearful again. None of it mattered though. I wasn't a daughter any more. I was a mother. Using my sleeve, I blotted away a tear in the corner of my eye. Why couldn't fish and chips just be that – fish and chips? Everything was always more than it was.

I thought of the mess I'd left at home. Victoria would have discovered it.

I walked slowly up Goldhawk Road, looking at the ground. Doorways were full of takeaway food cartons and plastic drink bottles and newspapers. The pound shops sold absolute rubbish but they were always busy. The pavement was black and covered in chewing gum and cigarette ends. I looked up at the small trees that lined the road and then at the sky. I tried to slow my breathing. It was easy to forget that the sky was there at all.

THE WORLD'S END

a short story by Amethyst Biggs

> *Somewhere at the side of the rough shape*
> *your life makes in your town,*
> > *you cross a line,*
> > *perhaps*
>
> *in a dusty shop you pause in, or a bar*
> *you never tried, and a smell*
> > *will do as well;*
> > *then you're*
>
> *suddenly very far from what you know.*
>
> – Glyn Maxwell, *The Nerve*

Elliott often thought of Kansas – the storms, their towering thunderheads and broad streaks of purplish cirrus clouds behind dark profiles of barns and silos. He envisioned oceans of blonde wheat, sunflowers, distant, looming farmhouses with their tiny, unblinking windows, and bobbing oil wells, like herds of cattle, along the lonesome stretches of I-70. Or the low, hazy blue-brown arc of the sky, and how, as it met the earth at the end of his father's fields, the horizon seemed to bow. It was that flat. As a child, he often pretended the end of their land was the end of the world, and if he went any further, he would fall off the edge into nothing. He did not like to remember; it seemed he never thought of Kansas unless something bad was happening. Something he was trying to block out, make un-happen. Like when two young men – one short and broad, the other tall, sinewy and quick – were standing on either side of him and shoving him backwards towards the side of a building. Like now.

But this was only the start of it; he knew there would be more. He felt the hard brick of the building graze his shoulder blades as he stepped back. The tall man continued to advance. He stopped a few inches from Elliott, then jabbed his fingers into Elliott's shoulders. The short man stood and watched, his thick arms folded tightly across his chest. He said nothing. A streetlight shone down into the alley and cast its light across his body at an angle; his head, swathed in darkness, was nearly invisible. For a moment Elliott thought of the Headless Horseman. He imagined a pumpkin head and almost laughed.

'The hell you smilin' for?' the tall man said. He was called Pete. He wore a thin white T-shirt and baggy cargo pants. He was dark-haired and pale and looked like a handsome, frightening child. He grabbed Elliott by the arms, pulled him away from the brick wall and swung him around.

The first thing he noticed, once he'd got off the train and began wandering, was the goddamn Hard Rock Café: a stately-looking building stamped with a garish neon sign in the shape of a guitar. A short queue of bored-looking girls and their dates loitered outside the door, smoking cigarettes, free hands resting casually on cocked hips. They wore the same low-rise jeans and strappy tops with long, belted sweaters. Like mannequins, he thought. Elliott stuffed his hands into his coat pockets, lowered his head and walked fast. He lit a cigarette and veered right down a narrow thoroughfare smeared with more neon, ducking through the crowd. It seemed as though everyone in town was out, and all going the opposite direction. Typical for New Year's Eve, he supposed.

He was not sure why he'd come here – he'd wanted a break from Rebecca, but that didn't seem reason enough – and after only a few minutes in the city, Elliott decided he hated Manchester, and perhaps even the whole of England. He couldn't understand why Rebecca liked it so much. The last thing she'd shouted at him before he slipped out the door was, 'Happy fucking New Year to you too!'

They'd met during his second year of college in New York. Rebecca was from Iowa – close enough to Kansas to give them an instant rapport – and, like Elliott, had escaped to the city to be a writer. The relationship subsisted on pot, bottles of red wine, discussions about books and occasional sex. When Elliott received an e-mail inviting him to come visit her in England, they hadn't spoken in two or three years. The invitation felt like a windfall; the chance to get out of New York for a while was too good for Elliott to pass up. He sent her a reply and booked the tickets. Now, three days into his visit, he remembered why they'd never had a proper relationship – the drugs and alcohol must have played a major role in all of the fun he'd recalled them having. Even sex wasn't worth it any more. His return flight was in ten days.

Elliott tossed his cigarette on to the damp pavement and it went out with a quick hiss. He noticed a McDonald's and realised he was hungry. He darted inside, ordered two cheeseburgers without pickles, and carried them outside. Then he continued down the street, eating the cheeseburgers without really tasting them. He was cold and bored. He decided to find somewhere that wasn't too crowded and have a drink.

The name of the place – The BierKeller – sounded homely enough. Another in the string of dimly-lit, smoky English pubs Elliott had seen since he'd arrived in the country. He descended a narrow flight of stairs and pushed through the heavy door. Thick wooden pillars, like tree trunks, held up the low ceiling, and machine-generated fog billowed and mixed with cigarette smoke. A handful of kids in shiny black pants and combat boots shuffled back and forth on the dance floor to what sounded like Nine Inch Nails. Not what he'd been expecting, but it would do.

Elliott ordered a beer and sat down on one of the long, wooden picnic-style tables in a dark nook. He sipped from the bottle and watched the people dancing. In the far corner, a lone kid with rowdy Robert Smith hair bobbed his head like a pigeon as he stepped forwards, then back, forwards, then back. His eyes were closed. His mouth was slightly open and his arms swung and flapped like misshapen wings. When the song changed, he carried on dancing the same way, the same tempo, no rhythm, out of time. Elliott sipped and watched. He got up and bought another beer. The Robert Smith kid was still dancing. Then Elliott noticed a girl.

She had planted herself in the centre of the dance floor, moving unselfconsciously with the music, as if she were alone in her bedroom. She paced around a bit, keeping the rhythm, before dipping again into her little personal dance – all fluid hips and rolling shoulders. The coloured lights shone vividly on her frizzy blonde hair, turning it red, then pink, then blue. Elliott couldn't get a good look at her face, but he could see she was wearing thick smears of black eyeliner and dark lipstick. Her top was see-through; the nipples on her smallish breasts were covered with star-shaped stickers. She bent over, resting her hands on her knees, and started swinging her head around. Elliott watched her. She wasn't beautiful; in fact she seemed to him a bit trashy, but nonetheless interesting.

When the song ended, the girl stopped dancing and made her way to the bar. Elliott continued to watch as she ordered a glass of wine, then carried it over to a table on the other side of the club and sat down alone. She drank the wine in quick little gulps and gently nodded her head to the beat as she watched the others dance. Elliott knocked back the dregs of his beer and got up to get another. Then he walked over to the girl's table. She continued gulping and nodding and watching; she did not look up or seem to notice him at all.

'Excuse me,' he shouted over the music.

The girl turned her head sharply and raised her eyebrows.

'Mind if I sit with you?'

'OK,' she said, and shrugged.

'You by yourself?'

'Sort of,' she replied, then shrugged again. 'I know everyone here.'

Elliott sat down. 'I'm not bothering you, am I? I'll leave.'

'Nah,' she said. She looked down into her wine glass and smiled. It was an odd, crooked half-smile, as if one side of her mouth were paralysed.

'I'm Elliott.'

'Star,' she said.

'Your name is Star?'

'Yeah.'

'Cool name.'

'Not really,' she said. Another shrug. Though it was still too dark to see properly, Elliott noticed she was even less attractive than he'd thought, and younger. She looked about eighteen or nineteen.

'Out for New Year's then?'

'I reckon I am. Come here most nights anyway though. You?' She punctuated every pause with a quick, nonchalant shrug.

'Yeah. Figured I might as well do something.'

She looked at him. 'You're American.'

'Unfortunately,' Elliott said, then gave a quick laugh.

'I like Americans. All the ones I've met were nice.'

'How many have you met?'

'Two maybe.'

'Including me?'

'Three then.'

'I didn't vote for Bush or anything.'

'OK.'

'You want another?' Elliott pointed to her empty wine glass.

'Sure,' she said. 'It's the house white.'

Elliott got up and bought the drinks. When he returned, a few of the other kids from the dance floor – Star's friends, he guessed – were sitting at the table. There were no chairs left for him.

'Oh, yeah, pull up a chair,' Star said.

The Robert Smith kid jerked his head to the left. 'There's one over there.'

Elliott did as they said. He set Star's wine down on the table, then wedged in between her and a tall, bird-like boy with pockmarked cheeks and a wave of dark red hair falling over his eyes.

'This is...' Star pointed at Elliott and squinted.

'Elliott,' he said.

'Oh, right. Elliott. Sorry.' Star gestured around the table. 'This is Stevie, Zip, Blake, Gemma and Troy.'

Everyone nodded.

'Zip's real name is Bernard,' Gemma said, giggling.

'Fuck off,' said Zip, the boy with the red hair. 'Nobody calls me fucking Bernard any more.'

'Except your mum.'

'Fuck off. Give me a cigarette.'

'I'm all out.'

'I've got one,' Elliott said, offering his half-empty pack.

Zip slid his long fingers into the pack and pulled out two cigarettes. 'Cheers,' he said.

'No problem.' Elliott tossed the pack into the middle of the table, as if it were a poker chip, and took a sip of his beer. None of Star's friends looked older than eighteen. Their eyes flicked back and forth across the table at each other, and no one spoke for several minutes.

'Elliott's from America,' Star said.

'New York, actually,' Elliott said. 'Well, I grew up in Kansas, but I haven't been there in years.'

'Kansas? Like, Wizard of Oz?' Gemma was the only one who seemed interested.

'Yeah, only without the Munchkins.'

No one laughed.

'But New York's pretty cool, yeah?' Zip lit his second cigarette off the tip of the first one.

'Yeah, I like it,' Elliott said. He started picking at the label on his empty beer bottle. He could feel the bass-heavy music buzzing inside his chest. 'I'm going to get another beer. You guys want one?'

They looked at each other and shrugged. 'Sure,' Zip said.

Elliott brought the drinks to the table. Star's friends drank their beers in quick mouthfuls as they shouted to each other over the music and poked into Elliott's cigarette pack like carrion birds at a carcass. Elliott tried to listen and join in, but the music and background noise in the club – which had filled up as it approached midnight – combined with their accents, made them hard to understand. The group seemed to have come to an agreement on something. They nodded to each other and finished their drinks before getting up.

'We're going to go dance,' Star said.

'OK.'

'You can come if you like.'

'Nah, I don't dance.'

Star shrugged. 'Fair enough.'

The others waved and nodded at him before wandering off towards the dance floor. Star followed them, then turned around quickly and came back to the table.

'I forgot. Thanks for the drinks.'

'Sure,' Elliott said. He watched as Star disappeared into the music and the mass of flailing limbs. At midnight, the barman turned on a small television in the corner, and everyone shouted and kissed and hugged and clinked glasses while Elliott looked up at the footage of fireworks erupting soundlessly over London. He bought a shot of tequila and one last beer, finished them slowly, and then made his way up the stairs and outside.

It was late. His ears were ringing and his throat ached from all the ciga-rettes he'd smoked. He was sure he'd missed the last train back to Rebecca's, and would have to wait around for the first one of the morning. He started towards the station, cursing himself under his breath for not paying attention to the time. Every now and then, distant whoops and hollers of 'Happy New Year!' echoed in the street, followed by the occasional taxi stuffed with passengers. Elliott thought about getting a taxi himself, but the only place to go was the train station, and he saw no need to get there any faster; it would just mean more sitting and waiting. Walking, plus the heady warmth of a beer buzz, kept the cold away longer.

By the time Elliott reached the station, it was deserted. Ice crystals glittered on the dark concrete and a light wind blew through, whistling slightly as it swept debris across the platforms. Elliott shivered, rubbed his hands together and blew on them. He would kill for a cup of coffee. Or even tea. He started walking briskly towards one of the benches, and then he heard voices.

He looked down and around until he caught sight of a young man and woman huddled together. He thought they might be homeless – but they were clean and well-dressed – and Elliott supposed that, like him, they must be stranded. The woman leaned against the man's arm, eyes closed, her head resting on his shoulder, her hand slipped casually into his coat pocket. The man had a book spread out on his lap, which he read aloud to her. Elliott passed them, and they did not look up.

In the room the women come and go talking of Michelangelo.

Elliott knew the poem; he'd studied it in college but couldn't remember the whole thing. He stopped for a moment and listened, willing the man to look up and notice him standing there, to say hello, to introduce Elliott to his girlfriend. Maybe they would talk about poetry, or maybe the man would know of some all-night diner where they could go and have a cup of coffee. Were there such places in England? But the woman, smiling now, continued to lean against the man as he read and they didn't notice Elliott. It was as if he were a ghost.

'Maybe I am,' Elliott murmured to himself. 'A fucking ghost.' But he knew he was just drunk, acting melodramatic and irrational. It was the tequila – he never drank liquor. He walked as far away from the couple as he could and sat down on a bench. He closed his eyes and felt the spinning. It had been colder in Kansas. He remembered one winter, just before he'd left for college, when the temperature was well below zero and snow piled up in colossal drifts along the roads. They were stuck in the house for five days, their long driveway blocked by three feet of snow and ice.

On the second day, the chill caused some pipes running through their basement to freeze and then burst, throwing cold water and sewage over the floor. Elliott's father had made him go down and help clean up the mess. 'Ain't much good if you can't even clean up yer own shit,' he'd said, handing Elliott a pair of kitchen gloves and a garbage sack. Then he went out to shovel the driveway, leaving Elliott there to finish the job himself. He had told Rebecca this story once, when they'd first met, but she didn't believe him.

Elliott slowly opened his eyes again. The cold bench made his ass numb. He crossed and un-crossed his legs, thought about lying down, but didn't want to look like a vagrant. He rummaged around in his pockets and realised he was out of both matches and cigarettes. That was it then. A reason to get up and move around. Elliott stood and walked back across the station towards the exit. The couple was still there, huddled together, and the man had finished reading.

A group of black kids in puffer coats were standing outside the entrance to a twenty-four-hour shop. A couple of them moved aside as Elliott went in, and he thought he smelled weed. He bought two packs of Marlboro Lights and a book of matches. 'Happy New Year,' he said, and the cashier grunted. Elliott shoved the cigarettes into his coat pocket, turned and nearly walked into two young men queuing behind him. He looked up and noticed that one of the men had different coloured eyes – one brown, the other bright blue.

'Excuse me,' Elliott said.

The men said nothing as he went past. The black kids had gone and Elliott felt a little better. But it was a long way back to the station; barely anyone was out on the street and the slightest bit of fear began to build up in his stomach. He could hear people behind him, their footsteps falling hard on the pavement. He heard two voices. He walked faster, trying to remember which street he had turned down. They were all twisty and dark, spiraling out in different directions from each intersection, and it was hard to read the street names on the buildings. He was used to the bright, reflective green-and-white signs in America.

The voices and footsteps grew closer. Elliott clasped his hand around the pack of cigarettes in his pocket as if it were a weapon. He felt a tap on his shoulder. He jumped and turned around. A tall, wiry man in a white T-shirt and baggy pants was pointing at him. The man from the shop. The one with the eyes.

'Oi,' he said. 'The fuck you lookin' at?'

'Sorry?' Elliott said.

'What. The. Fuck.You. Lookin' at.'

'You got the wrong guy,' Elliott said, and he turned to walk away. The man grabbed him by the sleeve of his coat and jerked him back.

'Come on, Pete,' the other man said. 'Let's go home.'

Pete shook his head. 'Nah, mate,' he said. 'I wanna know what the fuck this guy was lookin' at.'

'Oi, Jamie,' Pete shouted to the short man. He tightened his grip on Elliott's arms and narrowed his mismatched eyes. 'You think he has anything to smile about?' Elliott could feel Pete's breath on his face, could smell whisky, and when he lowered his eyes, he saw Pete's small dark nipples showing through the thin fabric of his shirt. He hadn't noticed until now that Pete had no coat.

'Nah,' Jamie said. He was leaning against the adjacent building now, absent-mindedly playing with a cigarette lighter. Then he stopped suddenly and slid it back into his pocket. 'Go on then,' he said.

Elliott stared at Pete's nipples again. 'Look,' he said, 'I don't really know what the problem is, but I'm sure it can be resolved without violence.' He couldn't believe he'd just said something so asinine. That wasn't how these things worked.

Pete let out a short laugh. 'Check this guy out, yeah?' he said.

Jamie had gone back to playing with his lighter. He twirled it around in his fingers and tossed it from hand to hand like a hot potato. Then he reached into his pocket again and pulled out a pack of cigarettes. He tapped one out of the pack and placed it in his mouth. He took it out, as if he'd changed his mind, then quickly slipped it back in and lit it. He exhaled two furls of smoke through his nose and turned to look at the other two men. He had the air of an old sage about him. He took the cigarette from his mouth again and flicked it. Elliott could hear the tap of his fingernail as it brushed across the filter.

'Right then,' Jamie said, and he moved forward.

When Elliott was twelve, he saw a boy get beaten nearly to death. He had been out walking in his father's wheat fields – the nights were cool in the summer, the moon was out and he liked to listen for owls – when he heard shuffling noises. Frightened, Elliott dropped down on to the ground, still warm from the day's heat, and inched forwards on his stomach, following the sounds. He parted a curtain of wheat stalks and looked around, straining in the half dark, and then he saw them.

The two older boys, Bry and Sam, were brothers. They were tall and strong, with thick muscles and ruddy skin. The other boy looked younger than Elliott, maybe ten or so, with close-cropped, white-blonde hair covering his head like peach fuzz. Elliott thought he recognised him from school.

Bry held the boy up by the arms. 'Kick his ass,' he said, and the blonde boy folded into himself as Sam punched him in the stomach. The boy began to cough and retch. Bry let go of him and pushed him down on to the ground. The boy let out a weak, muffled cry, and then they began to kick him. Their boots made horrible, hollow thudding sounds as they hit the boy's ribs. He made no sound. They laughed and kicked him again.

Elliott began to feel sick. He knew that he shouldn't be watching. He knew he should go for help, but if Bry and Sam saw him, he might be next. He knew this and he was afraid, yet he couldn't stop looking, couldn't make himself get up and run. Elliott's hands dug into the earth; he held on as if he might fall. He held his breath. He could feel a hard lump rising in his throat. He kept watching. It seemed it would never end, and then, finally, they were finished. Bry and Sam left the boy there in a silent, trembling heap. Then they slipped away through the wheat, so close they could have stepped on Elliott where he lay.

ESKIMO, BUTTERFLY

from the novel by Rachael Bloom

One

Ella was born full term and there were no apparent medical problems. She has no known allergies and no history of seizures. She has never been hospitalised and has had no surgeries. Hearing and vision are within normal limits.

– Letter from Mrs P. Simms, Health Visitor,
   to Dr N. Stinger, SCMO, Developmental Paediatrics,
   re: Elena Rose, age twenty-five months.

It was Jessica who noticed it first. Angela found her kneeling on the kitchen counter, one leg dangling from her yellow dress on to a chair. Calamine lotion dotted the Formica in pink splodges. Plasters of every size and shape fluttered on to the black tiled floor.

'Ella got a boo-boo,' Jess said, by way of an explanation to her mother, who stood frowning in the doorway.

'I just finding a plaster, Mummy, 'kay?'

Angela followed her daughter up the narrow staircase and into the bedroom. Jess waved the plaster at her little sister, who sat in her wooden chair by the window holding a book open in both her hands.

'I got it, Ella,' she sang. 'Now we get you better.' She sifted through the green toy box, almost as big as she was, and re-emerged with a stethoscope, which she looped around her neck.

'Ella, baby, what happened?' Angela's finger was under Ella's chin. She raised her daughter's delicate face, inspecting it for damage. Sea-green eyes blinked and stared back from under a shock of downy chocolate-coloured hair.

Angela ran her fingers over Ella's knees. At three, Jess's idea of boo-boos ranged from peeling glue grazes to scratches which didn't even break the skin.

If she didn't look carefully, she'd miss it altogether.

'No Mummy, it's here.' Jess pulled at Ella's right arm. She took the plaster from her mother's hand and ripped the wrapper off with her sharp teeth.

Angela held Ella's arm in both her hands and stared. There, on Ella's fore-arm, was a bite the size and shape of a cherry.

'Jessica Rose,' Angela said. 'Why on earth would you do something like this to your sister?'

Jessica, still poised with the unpeeled plaster stuck to the end of a chubby finger, stared back at her mother with her round blue eyes.

'But I didn't.'

'Then who did, Jess?' Angela's face was flushed with irritation. 'There's no one else here.'

Jess shook her head, side to side to side.

'But it wasn't me, Mummy.'

Angela sighed. 'Jessica, you have to tell the truth. You were the only other person here.'

'But I didn't do it.' Jess burst into tears.

Angela sat down on the end of Jessica's bed.

'It's OK, Jess. I'm sure it was a mistake. I'm sure you didn't mean to hurt her.' She put her hand on Jessica's head, stroked her hair. 'But you have to admit it when you've done something wrong.'

Jess sat bolt upright. 'But I didn't.'

Angela stood up. She took the plaster from Jessica's finger and pulled Ella into her arms.

'Then you can stay here until you are ready to tell the truth.' She closed the door behind her.

'She must've done it.' Angela passed Jake his tea and sat beside him on the sofa. 'There's no one else. We haven't been anywhere today. We haven't even visited Susie next door. No one.'

'Could it have happened yesterday?' asked Jake.

Angela stopped and stirred her tea. 'No. It was fresh, Jake. Fresh like this morning fresh. And it's little. Who else do we know that's so little? It must have been her.'

Jake shook his head.

'I just can't see it Angela,' he said. 'A little whack or a kick maybe,' he said.

'But a bite? That's so mean. So out of character. I just couldn't imagine her doing that to her sister.'

Jake held Ella's limp wrist in his hand. He whispered to Angela by lamp light and glanced at both of his daughters. Jess slept close by, in a small wooden bed next to Ella's cot. Her blonde hair was spread out on the pillow next to her, eyes swollen shut and breath still shallow from lengthy crying spells. With her wide set eyes and fair skin, she was a miniature version of her mother. Only the china blue of her eyes belonged to Jake.

Jake inspected the wound and turned to Angela.

'See how the bigger marks are facing out?' he said. 'If Jess had done this, they'd be on the inside.' He pointed to the underside of the bite, in line with Ella's thumb, and dropped her hand down on to the pillow.

He straightened up. 'Come to think of it, it would probably be on the other side of her arm altogether.' He lifted Angela's forearm where it was folded in front of her and leant forward to demonstrate, his mouth open. He looked her in the eyes and kissed the bite spot.

'Of course, at two, it doesn't really come down to pass or fail, for this kind of assessment,' said Pam, the health visitor. 'And truly, she has a lot of strengths.' Pam smiled.

'And the biting?' asked Angela, 'You think it will just go away by itself?'

Pam nodded. 'All children go through these phases, Angela. It happens. At this stage, we just don't have any concrete reasons to be referring you on.'

Angela frowned. Kids bit each other, this was true. But biting themselves? She looked at Ella standing in front of her on the carpet. She'd tried to flatten her hair out this morning. Chased her round the living room with water spray and conditioner. It just didn't want to go flat.

Ella's hair wasn't course or wiry. It was soft and fine. Still, it stuck up and out, a sharp contrast to the porcelain skin of her cheeks. Wide eyes peered out beneath it, alert and inquisitive. Angela exhaled.

'She's just—'

'Different?' asked Pam. 'Children are different, Mrs Rose.' She nodded. 'Even siblings.' She tilted her head to the side and looked at Angela, who stared at her hands in her lap.

'Let me ask you this. Does Ella walk? Does she run?'

Angela nodded.

'Does she feed herself?'

Angela nodded again.

'Look at you when you talk to her?'

'Well, yes but—'

'She passed her hearing tests, right?'

'Ten fingers and toes?'

Angela smiled.

'Well there you go,' said Pam. 'Mrs Rose, she walks, she runs, she speaks. She even strings two or three words together. She plays. Admittedly she is a little unusual, but the bottom line is that she isn't delayed enough, in enough areas for us to be worried.'

'It's just that, well, she can be quite difficult,' Angela said. She wasn't the only one who thought so either. Even on the bus today, when Ella had refused to sit on the seat next to Jess, crawling instead on her hands and knees on the filthy ticket-strewn floor, she'd heard someone say again. 'That child needs a good smack.'

Last week when Tammy had been visiting, showing Angela her wedding photos. Ella ambled past and saw the yellow curls piled on top of Tammy's head. Her tiny fist clenched around them and glued shut.

'Ooh, Ella honey,' Tammy giggled. 'Let go sweetie.' Tammy's arms moved up behind her, wrestling with Ella's hand.

'Ella, no!' Tammy yelled as Ella began to walk away, with her fingers still wrapped around Tammy's hair.

Angela stood up and moved behind Ella to undo her fist. She wasn't quick enough. From under Ella's grasp, Tammy leant around and delivered a sharp slap to Ella's hand, releasing herself. Ella didn't cry. She just walked away, smiling, followed by a mumbling Jess.

Angela didn't say anything. Heat crept up her neck and spilled on to her face as she nodded through each of Tammy's peach bridesmaids, unseeing.

Angela looked down, rubbed her thumbs over each other. It was stuffy in here; a second-floor room with no windows. Sweat pooled in her armpits, at the sides of her hair. She reached for her water.

Pam sipped her coffee and leant forward, placed her hand on Angela's knee.

'Let me ask you this. Do you spend any time with Ella? Just the two of you?'

Angela looked at Ella, mouthing the blocks she had been asked to stack, and back at Jess wedged between an armless doll and a toy telephone. In Jess's hands was a cake made from big, brightly coloured Lego bricks, complete with candles. *Happy Birthday to You.*

Angela wet her lips.

'Probably not as much as I should.' She looked up.

Pam shrugged and opened her palms wide. 'Then she probably just wants some attention, Mum' she said. 'How about if we keep an eye on things and if we still have concerns in, say, six months, we'll revisit, maybe book you an appointment with the doctor?'

Ella rubbed her eyes and whimpered. Stumbled into the table and swept it clear of Legos until every piece was on the carpet. Jess picked up the red bucket and began collecting the spilled bricks. Added more candles to her cake.

A knot appeared on Angela's forehead, just between her eyes.

'Jessica is so contented and quick to learn,' said Pam. 'You were lucky. They can't all be like that.'

Angela looked at Pam and considered what she had said. Jess was good natured it was true. But it was more than personality with Ella. More than just her discontented nature. It was little things. The way she laughed at bare walls, but not when someone tickled her feet. How she read books to herself but refused to be read to. When they all waved at the low-flying airplanes, watching zigzag vapour trails or brightly coloured hot-air balloons floating across the sky, Ella never looked up. She never wanted to lick cake batter from the spoon when they baked. Never cuddled up and fell asleep in their arms. Of course these weren't the important things. They weren't the milestones in the book. Ella had reached all of those. Sort of.

Angela clasped her hands together and tried to think of something to say, some argument, something definitive, that would help Pam to understand, to see what she meant, but nothing came to her.

Maybe Ella was just different. Angela reached for her bag and was surprised to hear her own voice ring into the silence.

'You know, I would be happy to wait. It's just that we have orders to leave after Christmas. To move. To America.' She slung the bag over her shoulder and dusted herself off. 'It would be nice to go with a bit more information, you know?'

Pam sighed and removed her glasses. 'All right,' she said. 'I will write to the hospital and see if they can fit you in sooner. But really, I'm sure there's nothing to worry about. She has so many strengths, Angela. And such an interest in books can only be a good thing.' She nodded at Ella, now sitting square and dainty on top of Jessica's Lego cake, her fingers curled around the sides of the book she held in front of her face.

'See?' added Pam, with a knowing smile, eyes half closing with self-assurance.

The book was upside-down.

The consultant's waiting room was somewhat dark, especially considering the time of day, a late morning appointment, causing Jake significant difficulty in arranging time off work. First thing would be fine, last thing would be better; both would allow the semblance of dedication at least to one part of the day. But this appointment had to be smack bang in the middle of a work day, at a time when just about everybody would be wondering why Senior Airman Rose wasn't posted at the back gate of the base where he usually was at this time of day on Alpha shift.

It was a small waiting room lined with plastic chairs, dusty plants and a rectangular aquarium containing greenish water and a pair of unhappy, staring goldfish. There was a wooden rack loaded with children's picture books and a little blue table, which had been, on their arrival, laid out with coloured blocks, a ring stacker and a toy telephone.

Before they'd even sat down, Ella had crashed the toys on to the carpet with one outstretched arm, like one of those seaside slot machines, mechanically sweeping coins from shelf to shelf and out into freedom.

Angela sat cross-legged on the floor with Jessica's blonde curls draped across her knee. The story they were reading was punctuated only by her frequent pats on the hard brown carpet next to her and whispers of *Ella, Ella*.

Ella's eyes danced as she considered the pile of magazines laid out for waiting parents. Home style, gossip, *National Geographic*. Her hands darted for the *Reader's Digest* at the top of the pile.

'Ella, no,' Jake started.

Angela looked up at him and shook her head.

'Why can't we just pick them up when we leave?' She glanced at the reception window. No one was watching. 'Let's just keep her happy for now,' she said, attempting a smile, but her forehead wrinkled, just like Jake's did. Her hand moved to iron it out and dropped back over Jessica's yellow ringlets.

'Now. Where were we?' Angela asked.

Ella flicked through the magazines, discarding whatever didn't grab her interest. Nothing seemed to. She moved to the waste paper basket, dug through it, pulled out torn letters, sandwich wrappers, a styrofoam cup containing one residual sip of tea, as well as someone's lipstick loitering on the rim.

Angela looked back at Jake. He shrugged his shoulders. The styrofoam cup now dangled from Ella's lips, caught between her teeth. Angela tutted, pushed Jess's head from her lap in one movement and jumped up.

Angela snatched a half-eaten sandwich out of Ella's hands and picked her up. Ella thrashed, reddening, arms and legs akimbo while Angela wrestled her into the pushchair, pinning her down, one knee between her daughter's legs as she clicked the harness into place. She passed Ella a *Woman's Own* to flick through.

Angela blew her cheeks out to the side and straightened her ponytail. She stood for a moment and watched her tiny daughter. Her frame was small but soft. Her features were elfin. Downy brown hair stood in tufts. Her round cheeks smelt like banana rusk and baby bath, clean and warm and satisfied. But most noticeable were her green eyes which sparkled, sunlight on sea, as she glanced at the problem page of a woman's magazine as if it were *Alice in Wonderland*.

Angela sat back down on the carpet and stretched her legs out before her. She pointed and flexed her feet. Retied the loose grey laces of her trainers. She caught a glimpse of her reflection in the aquarium, her face floating next to the not quite gold fish, and sighed.

Angela knew she didn't appear twenty-one. Her face held a surprised expression. Raised eyebrows pulled her eyes wide open. Her lips parted as if she had something to say. Her body hung in a confused limbo, a small frame filled out by close consecutive pregnancies, dragging her into a shapeliness she wasn't yet comfortable with. She dressed in oversized and amorphous clothes, baggy pairs of jeans with large men's T-shirts, dark colours and long hair pulled back in a messy ponytail, safe from Ella's quick grasp.

'Now, according to the referral from your Health Visitor, you requested this appointment, Mummy, because of some...' the doctor paused, 'concerns you have about Elena?' She peered at Angela over her thin reading glasses and waited for a response. Angela shifted in her seat. Sat on one hand. Then the other. She nodded. Looked at Jake. He raised his eyebrows and looked away.

Angela cleared her throat. 'Er, yes,' she said.

Angela looked at Ella now, still sat in the pushchair. Her perfect curled fingers still flick, flick, flicking through *Woman's Own*. She exhaled her satisfaction and warbled to herself, finally pronouncing *cat* with a grin that glittered with her tiny pearly teeth.

Everyone smiled.

'Hmm. We do have speech then,' said Dr Stinger, 'and articulate speech too,' she added, turning to her medical student, eyebrows lifted.

'Perhaps then, as this is primarily an investigative appointment, I should examine Ella first, if it is all right with you, Mr Rose?'

Jake nodded his approval. Angela released Ella from the pushchair and stood her in front of the doctor. Ella's eyes flickered around the room, up at the crowded white shelves, out of the tall window rattling with rain and over at the two doctors.

Dr Stinger fumbled in her overcrowded drawer and pulled out a white drawstring bag. She wondered aloud what was inside. Jessica stood next to her sister, looking quite serious, while they waited to see what would appear.

The doctor's hand remained in the bag for some seconds. She gasped as she revealed a teaspoon, a miniature book and a small plastic Dalmatian; she placed them on the floor in front of her tiny patient. Ella sat down, put the spoon in her mouth and giggled.

'Which one is the dog?' the doctor asked.

Ella looked her straight in the eye and announced, *dog*. The spoon dropped from her mouth to the floor.

'Good. You said, "dog". But which one is the dog?' asked Dr Stinger. 'Give me the dog.'

Ella grinned at her, picked up the dog and placed it in the doctor's outstretched hands.

'Now give me the spoon,' said Dr Stinger, replacing the dog on the carpet.

Ella picked up the dog and the spoon. Looked at them both and passed the dog to the doctor again.

'That's the dog again. Can you give me the spoon?'

Ella regarded her cheerfully and kept the spoon.

'She likes spoons,' said Angela. 'It's the food connection.'

Dr Stinger's lips thinned. The corners of her mouth turned upwards as Ella put the spoon into her mouth once more.

That's when the questions started.

How many previous pregnancies had Angela had? Terminations? Still births? Was Jake the father of both children? Did she use drugs during pregnancy? Alcohol? Even the odd glass of wine? What about the birth? Did they use forceps to extract her baby from the womb? Was there much blood? What was the Apgar score? Cord around her neck? Was she breathing when she was born? And then—

'What does Ella like to play with?'

'Oh, lots of things,' Jake replied. 'Anything. You know kids. They have loads of toys, these two.'

'What kind of toys?'

Angela looked at Jake. 'Well, they have everything really. Garages with little cars. A kitchen with food and plates and things. The light-up kind of toys, phones, dolls, all kinds of things really.' She scratched her head.

'And which ones does Ella particularly like?' the doctor said.

Angela twisted her hair. It was hard to say. They'd given Ella a 'Baby Just Born' for her second birthday. Ella's eyes had twinkled as she pulled her baby out of the box, raising her up, pursing her cherry lips and kissing her newborn as if this was the happiest moment of her lately somewhat fraught existence. She had held her baby for the rest of that day and even put her to bed in the cardboard box she came in that very night. Angela couldn't remember where the doll was now.

'She's really interested in how things work, you know?' Jake's voice was shaky. 'She likes more mechanical things than toys actually.'

Ella was chattering her way through another magazine, a motorcycle magazine, pointing to the pictures and reading to herself. Expelling the hard consonant at the beginning of each word, with all her might.

Dog, cat, pig. Dog. Dog.

'Well, and books, obviously,' he added.

'Hmm,' said Doctor Stinger. She glanced back at Ella. The magazine was now upside-down, back to front. 'But does she like the books, actual stories and pictures, or just turning the pages?' They all looked back at Ella.

'What's that?' Ella said, holding her index finger authoritatively erect. 'That's pig,' she answered herself.

The doctor laced her twiglet fingers together and frowned. 'So, you say she likes to see how things work. What particularly? For example, in this field, we find that some children are especially interested in wheels? What exactly is Ella interested in?'

What field? thought Angela.

TWO STORIES
by Alexandra Bockfeldt

Firefly

The jungle started just twenty steps from the house. When he first came here, he could have sworn it was further away; now it seemed the shrubs and trees and moist earth crawling with insects were waiting for the right moment to advance even further and engulf the little blue house in its sonorous darkness. At night, Bruno would wake suddenly from the high-pitched scream of a monkey or the insistent hissing of a snake. Bruno remembered how the constant noise from the jungle had used to frighten her so; how she'd cling to him in the narrow bed, her sweaty breasts squashed against his chest, barely daring to breathe. *Did you hear that?* Or she'd sneak over to the glassless window and press her face to the screen, then come running back to the bed. *There's somebody out there – I saw their eyes looking straight at me, Bruno!*

Every other Thursday, Mbame arrived in the village from Bangui, usually having managed to find a battered paperback book in English or French for Bruno. On this particular Thursday, Bruno checked his watch, saw that it was almost three, hopped off the porch and walked down the dust track towards the village. It was so humid it was practically raining, and Bruno looked forward to the evening when the skies would just open, and he could sit on the porch listening to the drumming of the rain on the roof and watch the rising steam released by the earth.

Mbame was already at the crossroad leading into the village, leaning up against the side of his 1961 VW Caravelle, bartering loudly with the crowd of villagers gathered around him to see what treasures he'd brought back from the capital this time.

'Hey, hey, HEY, Mista Bruno,' he bellowed as he saw Bruno push his way through the crowd. 'Look wha' I gotcha this time, Mista!' Mbame passed him a small bundle of letters that he'd picked up for Bruno at the Central Post Office, and a French book with a picture of a cobweb on the cover. It was called

Arachnophobie – la Retour des Araignées.

Bruno returned to the house, poured himself a double gin and tonic and sat on the porch with the book and the letters. First he opened the book to the last page and read the page number: 378. He tapped three hundred and seventy eight into his pocket calculator, divided it by fourteen, and found that he could read twenty-seven pages a day until Mbame came back with a new book. Bruno picked a letter up from where he'd laid the pile down on the floor, and recognized the handwriting as his mother's. *Bruno Siguël, PB 1184, la Poste Centrale, Bangui, République Centrafricaine.* Bruno ran his finger over the stamp and the postmark: *Paris 16ème, 19 Octobre 1998.* This was the fourth letter she had written him begging him to come home for Christmas. For a brief moment, Bruno let himself consider the possibility; going to Bangui, catching a plane to Charles de Gaulle, stepping out of the terminal into the arms of his mother, so very old now. Wandering the concrete streets of Paris, breathing in cold air laced with pollution; sitting at small cafés in the Marais; searching the face of every woman rushing past for Aurèlie; always looking for Aurèlie.

The second letter was a long and sad one from Aurèlie's sister, Delphine, saying how she would like to come down to Africa again sometime in the new year to say a real and final goodbye to her sister. She asked politely if she could stay with him. Bruno knew he'd have no choice but to let her, but he remembered with dread the last time she'd come, around a month after Aurèlie's disappearance. Bruno could not stand the presence of the sister who looked so much like the woman he loved, who moved around his house slowly, heavily, occasionally picking up things that had belonged to Aurèlie and crying, her thin shoulders shaking pitifully. He'd driven her to the spot where the Land Rover had been found, and she'd stood quietly looking into the dense overhang of branches above, and staring into the jungle that was like a wall on both sides of the road. A couple of times she'd whispered 'Mais tu est òu, Aurèlie?'

Bruno poured himself a second drink as the rain began. For once, no sounds were heard from the jungle, or they were at least deafened by the torrential rain. Aurèlie had liked the rain, and it was she who had taught him to enjoy sitting out on the porch to listen to it as it came down. Every afternoon she'd sit on the very chair Bruno was sitting on now, and he'd sit on the other chair and watch her write long letters to her sister and friends in Paris. She'd whistle softly through her teeth as she concentrated, occasionally looking up and smiling widely at him, saying *What is it, Bruno, chèri?* to which he'd reply

Nothing. I'm just looking at you. Sometimes a stray drop of water would land on the letter Aurèlie was writing, and she'd move closer still to the wall, but she never went back inside until it was dark and it had stopped raining.

Bruno imagined that the daylight would last longer in the village than it did in the little clearing where the house was. Surely the advancing night was aided by the towering trees that surrounded the house on three sides. It was now almost completely dark, but when Bruno stepped off the porch and looked up at the sky he saw that it was still twilight, and too light for stars. Bruno looked over to the forest and saw hundreds of little points of lights twirling around between the trees like cigarettes pinched nonchalantly between two fingers and waved around by people trying to make an interesting point in a conversation. Sometimes the fireflies would all flash and blink in unison, and Bruno wondered how they arranged this phenomenon amongst themselves. He'd read once that it had to do with mating.

Bruno decided to go for a drive. It could be dangerous in these parts at night, especially for a white man in a nice car, but Bruno told himself he needed to see something other than the house and the clearing before the day was over. Sometimes on these evening drives Bruno played a game with himself, pretending he had no plans for where he'd go. *Shall I drive to the river and watch the last smudges of pink sunlight on the sky above its banks? Shall I take a left at Masa's hut and finally find out where that track leads? Perhaps I'll drop in on Pen and say hello...* But Bruno knew very well where he was going and after less than five minutes on the muddy roads, he was there.

Aurèlie's Land Rover had been found on a long stretch of dirt road leading to the main road to the capital. Her little bag was still secure in its trunk; there was no sign of a struggle. It was as though she had driven here, stopped the car, got out and simply wandered into the jungle. Bruno left the headlights on, got out of the car and walked around it twice; it was only then that he realised he'd had too much to drink to drive. He leaned against the car and lit a cigarette and waved it around to see if it would look like a firefly. It did. Tomorrow it would be eight months since Aurèlie disappeared.

Bruno and Aurèlie had come to Africa because he had been assigned the job as supervisor to aid workers from his organisation in France, stationed along the river Lombaye. He had a two-year contract but, eighteen months later, Aurèlie told him she could stand it no longer and wanted to return to Paris. He begged her to stay just another six months, but she insisted on leaving. They had a terrible fight. *My life is sliding past in this god-awful place! It's almost always dark in this house and the nights are terrifying! If you love me, take me home!* That evening when Bruno returned from his patrol he saw that the Land Rover was gone.

Bruno got back in the car and drove back to the house. He brought his things inside from the porch, but left the door unlocked. He took the book on arachnophobia with him to bed and slid the picture of Aurèlie that was his bookmark to page twenty-seven so he would know when to stop. He thought again about his mother's letter and decided that he would seriously consider returning to France around Christmas time. But in his heart, Bruno knew he would never leave Africa without her, dead or alive. That was why he was still here, months after his contract had run out, living off his savings. Sometimes he'd trek into the jungle on one or other side of the road near where the Land Rover was found and cut himself through the dense vegetation with his machete, looking for any sign of her. Hours later, bruised and cut and bitten, he'd give up and return to his car and pound the wheel in frustration before driving back to the house. He told the people in all the nearby villages that he would pay a very generous reward to anyone who could find out what had happened to Aurèlie, but nobody ever came forward.

And at nights in his bed, Bruno imagined his wife with a gun to her head, with some teenage soldier shouting at her, forcing her into the back of a truck where another ten or so soldiers were waiting, then the dust cloud rising as the truck sped away to an unknown destination. If she had waited, he would have driven her to the airport first thing in the morning, and by now, he'd be back in Paris with her, sipping coffee in a café on Rue Saint Antoine near their apartment. They'd eat dinner at restaurants with only two tables in Montmartre, and she'd look as beautiful to him as she did the first time he saw her. She'd sway in his arms as he'd dance her around their living room on their tenth anniversary, her white wine breath sharp in his nostrils. He'd pull her even closer, and burying his face in the nape of her neck he'd whisper, *Remember in Africa, how you'd cling to me at night in that little bed? Oh come on, chèrie, it was fun, too.* And she'd laugh softly and say *Yes, Bruno, it was fun, too.*

The bleak Siberian morning stares at me from outside the tiny barred window over the metal bunk that Adam and I share. I know it must be before six-thirty in the morning, because that is when the guards wake us. It is starting to get light outside but, from where I am lying, I can still see a small sliver of moon. I am not sure what month it is, or how long we have been here. Over a year.

It might be late August or early September. The last time I was allowed out in the dirty courtyard must have been about two weeks ago, and I had noticed a tinge of cold in the air that hadn't been there during the summer months. The thought of the coming winter fills me with dread as I remember the last: months and months without any real light at all; the dripping from the ceiling which had so annoyed me in the summer months ceased, but the floor in our tiny cell was covered in a thin layer of ice, and I only have to look at Adam's disfigured legs to see what real cold will do to you.

Adam and I are forbidden to speak to each other. We share a very small cell with one narrow metal bunk and one chair. During the day we take turns sitting on the bed and the chair. During the night we sleep close together, and only then do we bridge the gulf of silence between us. The only way we ever communicate is by tracing messages on each others' backs in the dark. Sometimes, he even traces pieces of poetry on my back, with what feels like little pictures to accompany them.

In Xanadu did Kubla Khan
A stately pleasure-dome decree;
Where Alph, the sacred river, ran
Through caverns measureless to man
Down to a sunless sea.

The last time we spoke was several months ago, and the punishment was so severe that I know we won't speak again for as long as we are here. It was February, I think, and back then we were still allowed outside to the courtyard together. We were walking around in circles, drawing frozen air into our lungs, taking every chance we could get to breathe fresh air, stretch out our sore limbs and use our withered muscles. Suddenly Adam stopped and said: 'We will get out of here. You know that, don't you?'

33

I was so startled by the fact that he had actually spoken and by the sound of his voice that I couldn't even reply. Suddenly someone grabbed me from behind, and I was half dragged, half lifted back to the cell by the guards, leaving Adam outside in the cold. The guards threw me back in the cell, shouted at me in Russian and laughed menacingly. They then did what they sometimes did to me, and afterwards they left. After about an hour they came back and threw Adam's boots at me without a word. I counted the hours. I listened for sounds, but couldn't hear any. I stood on the bunk and craned my neck in the hope of catching a glimpse of my husband in the courtyard, but I wasn't tall enough. All I could see was a slice of the cruel moon.

Adam was dumped back in the cell at the first break of daylight, barely conscious. He lost his left foot at the ankle, and all the toes on his right foot.

Adam stirs behind me. He traces H for hello on my back. I squeeze his hand. I get up, sit on the chair and look at the wall. I know that it is only a matter of time before we both lose our minds. I believe we have been forgotten here; all details of us were probably lost in the aftermath of the revolution. We must already be in the last quarter of 1918, and still we have not had any information about our status.

I miss music. I play Chopin in my mind. I close my eyes and imagine sitting in the plush sofa at home in London, surrounded by our friends, a glass of red wine on the table in front of me, Gustav at the piano, filling our drawing room with the achingly beautiful Fantaisie-Impromptu. It plays clearly in my mind now, its notes running through my brain like a river through valleys, through plains, through the world outside. Sometimes my reverie is interrupted by the constant *drip drip drip* from the leaking ceiling, and these interruptions fill me with an incredible anger. Other times, my concertos, sonatas and nocturnes are interrupted by a cockroach scuttling over my feet. I then squash it brutally, often stomping on it repeatedly, manically. Adam doesn't even look up any more. This also makes me angry. I want to scream 'Look at me! Yes, that's right, I'm finally going crazy! We are going to die here in this deepest abyss of hell, and it's all thanks to you, you goddamn fool!'

Drip, drip, drip.

My palms are bleeding, because I have embedded my nails in the flesh in anger. Blood drips on to the floor – its unapologetic red shocking in this landscape of grey. It bleeds a fair amount and I run my hands through my hair repeatedly, streaking it crimson.

Even more than music, I miss books. I think I would give ten years of my life to hold a book in my hands. I have asked for one many times, whispering one of the few words I know in Russian through the bars to whichever guard is sitting outside in the corridor.

'*Kniga.*' I say. 'Please. *Kniga.*' They never even answer.

I get under the blanket with Adam. I slip my hand under his tattered grey shirt, and trace 'book' on his back. He answers by tracing a question mark. 'B-O-O-K', I trace again, his skin soft under my fingertips. 'H-o-w?' he answers.

'Book. Book. Book. B-O-O-K!'

Adam takes my hand, which is still tracing those four letters in mid-air and holds it in his own.

I am taken out of the cell to the showers. Three guards are standing in the room as I wash myself clean of the blood. I think I am the only woman in this place, and after I am cleaned up, they take me off for their hour of amusement with me. I don't feel anything, nothing, because I am not there, not really. I am in a room bathed in candlelight, sitting on that plush sofa, my love's hand in mine, happy Mozart streaming from Gustav's hands at the piano as if by magic.

After, when I am being marched back to the cell, I turn to one of the guards – I think his name is Grishka. He is very young, with a plump, pink face and a downy mustache. His hair is mousy-coloured and carefully slicked back from his forehead. His eyes are small watery slits in his face. Overall, he looks remarkably like a pig.

'*Kniga.*' I plead. '*Kniga.*'

He doesn't answer, but I see a flicker of something in his eyes. Sympathy? Ridicule?

Then, after they have locked me in, I see Grishka turn and nod slightly at me. What does that mean?

It is almost morning, but I have not slept at all. Suddenly, I hear a sound; a soft, rustling sound, and I assume it's the cockroaches. I strain my eyes in the darkness and see a shadow on the wall. I sit up, my heart pounding wildly, but the shadow is already gone, and I hear footsteps retreating down the corridor.

And there, on the floor, pushed through the bars, is... something. It is a small parcel, wrapped in rough brown paper, which I tear off hysterically, because I can tell that it's a book. A book!

I am holding in my hands the most beautiful thing I have ever seen in my life. It is thick, bound in dark red leather, with slightly yellowed pages. I can tell that it has been loved, because the pages are worn thin in places by fingers surely not half as eager as my own. I notice that tears are flowing from my eyes, dripping off the tip of my nose and landing on the beautiful book.

I sit, for hours, leafing through it, although I obviously can't understand the labyrinthine Cyrillic letters. This does not bother me at all. I have a book. Just feeling it in my lap, just seeing the letters, is enough for me. The day has flown by; suddenly it is night again, and I don't want to tear myself away from the book to sleep. I feel Adam's eyes on me, but I don't pay him any attention. I finally crawl into the bunk, and wedge the book between Adam's body and my own.

Morning comes and I wake with the usual dread until I realise that everything has changed now. I have a book. *Kniga.* I sit like yesterday, leafing through it as if reading, and in a way I am – I imagine stories as I go along, stories of adventure, of love, of death, of life on the outside. Of life as it really is. I think of episodes from my own life, pretending to read them as stories in this beautiful *kniga.* Me as a child in Kent, playing with my sisters in a field. Me as a young girl at school, where I first discovered my love of books. Me as a newly-wed in 1908, looking into Adam's eyes and seeing myself.

I feel his eyes on me as I read, but I will not look at him. I have the book now. He touches my arm lightly, motions for me to let him look at the book. Of course, I don't let him. He tries to trace a message on my back as I read facing away from him, but his touch feels like that of the cockroaches, so I swat him away.

It has been many days, perhaps a week. I am still engrossed by the book. I have read so many interesting things in it, right now I am reading a chapter about a young woman called Virginia who accompanies her husband to Russia in January of 1917. He is there as a military advisor to Tsar Nicholas II, as the beginning of the end of his reign draws near. Virginia and her husband are caught up in the turmoil of the Tsar's abdication in March, and accused of working against the provisional government, and are sent as prisoners about sixty *versts* north of Tobol'sk. It's quite an unlikely story, really, but it makes for interesting reading. Suddenly I feel laughter boiling in my stomach, and have to fight the urge to let it erupt. Instead, I double over in near-hysteria, giggling quietly until I am practically out of breath.

It is night and I have woken from a sound in the room. I realise Adam's body is not next to mine, so I sit up, and then I see him in the chair, leafing through my book by the light of the moon. My book! The sound I heard was the turning of the pages. My pages! My body trembles with fury and I leap out of the bunk, grab the book out of Adam's hands and use it to batter him with. He lets out a muffled cry, but I don't stop, and beat him with strength I didn't know I possessed. Adam tries to grab me by the wrists, but he isn't very strong any more. I don't stop until blood shoots from his nose, staining the book. I get back in my bunk and, using my *kniga* as a pillow, drift back off to sleep.

It is morning now and the guards have just taken Adam's body away. I can now choose – bed or chair. Chair or bed. I decide to sit on the chair and listen to some nice music – a sonata perhaps, or maybe an etude, or even a waltz. I also bring out the book to accompany the nice music. It is bloodstained, and this fact naturally makes me very angry. I bring it to my mouth and slowly lick its puckered leather cover clean of the offending matter.

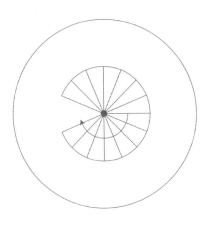

LOST PROPERTY

from the novel by Val Bridge

Blue Danube

Richard Strauss

As the full moon slips first through the shutters, then the herring-bone grille, then the muslin curtains, Mutti runs out, throws back her head and howls. The hens squawk, the goat meckers, and the rabbits bang their heels. Miri flinches: Mutti's howling might make witchy Baba Yaga ride out on her samovar. Judit squeaks. As Miri stuffs a corner of the featherbed into her mouth, Judit is already hiding beneath it.

'Pfui, Schmui,' she whispers.

When Vati-Daddy was last with them, he said in English Pfui-Schmui was pooey-pooey, and that Vati was a rude pooey noise, and they'd so fallen about laughing at these funny foreign words, that Mutti-Mummy had come in and told Vati off, and then Omi-Gran'ma had come in and said Pfui, Pfui to Mutti, and then Judit and Miri had giggled so much that they got the hiccups and Opi-Gran'pa came in and everyone stopped talking.

This isn't the first time Mutti's howled at the moon.

Since Vati has got lost on a beach somewhere, and has disappeared, whenever Mutti catches sight of Old Moonface, she's off outside.

One time even was when they weren't in Hadersfeld, but in their apartment on the Mollardgasse, in the 6th district of Vienna, where Opi always stayed during the week because he was Herr Ober at the Mozart Hotel. That time, after Mutti's first shriek, Miri and Judit thought Mutti must have fallen down all three flights of stairs into the inner courtyard, but then she emerged down there still howling enough to fetch the sky down.

'Pfui, Schmui, Dummkopf Mutti,' they'd whispered to each other.

Vati used to say Dummkopf was dumb-head in English and was a bit rude.

Omi said 'Verdammt,' rushing after Mutti in her nightgown.

The girls had to stay put.

Verdammt was a really bad word; it was damn in English and they were not to say it at all ever. Only grown-ups could say it.

'Verdammt,' Mutti shouted, when Omi dragged her back in through the flat door, locking it behind them and hiding the key in her knickers.

Maybe Mutti first started this *komische* charade when she was listening to scratchy voices and Vera Lynn's 'Homing' Waltz on the secret wireless kept behind the jam and Herr Pikorni brought a message. That night the howling woke them. Running to the window, they stared out between the criss-cross bars and saw a huge fat moon, and Mutti's head thrown back. Maybe this moon had turned Mutti into a Baba. They rushed back to bed, pulled the feather-bed up over their heads, and silently held each other's hands. Then Judit giggled, then they were both giggling, whispering 'Pfui, Schmui, Dummkopf,' until they nearly choked.

In the morning, Mutti didn't look any different. Omi went round with her mouth stitched up, but there was no sign of a samovar. The hens were cluck-ing under the verandah windows, and there was hard jam already set out on saucers on the verandah table.

Miri was six-and-a-half, and Judit five and a bit then. They'd watched the last of the snow in the yard turn grey as hen's porridge, and the leftover small heaps at the bottom end of the meadow, where it joined on to the forest, change into blue lace. They'd taken Blitzi, their sledge, back to the woodshed, and Omi had put away their thick navy stockings, and was hatching chicks in the range.

Was this before the telegram or after Mutti's nightmare?

Mutti was saying 'Verdammt' a lot after the thunderbolt storm, when the girls ran out, dropping their nightdresses under their walnut tree to get the electricity on their skin. Instead they'd got dragged in and smacked. 'Donner und Blitzen' they'd chanted, although the thunder and lightning had stopped.

They were up again, really late, stealing hard jam and Apfelkuchen from the leftover room, when Mutti'd started screaming. Old Moonface was shining.

Maybe that storm happened the same night, after Herr Pikorni came run-ning round with the message from the Gasthaus, which had the village tele-phone, and served Judit's favourite hot plum dumplings in white sugar with yellow cream.

The girls couldn't hear what the message was.

'Heilige Maria, Jesu und Josef,' Mutti said.

'Heilige Maria, Gottesmutter,' Omi said, falling on to her knees.

'Luftknodel und Papierschnitzel,' Miri said. She didn't like these prayers the grown-ups were always having to say; to chant air dumplings and paper cutlets was much funnier.

Then the girls hid under the verandah bench, not even whispering so dum!

Miri thought maybe it was the day after that when Omi packed them out of the smallholding up in the Vienna Woods, and took them back down the mountain on to the small train with the wooden slatted seats. They'd all had to bring rucksacks. Miri knew that was the time Mutti forgot to smack them for standing on the wobbly outside planks between the carriages, where there was no railing and where they'd eaten green walnuts and watched the railway lines snake and slide under their feet.

Back in the flat where Opi had died on his bed under the English tapestry, the smell of the Donau Kanal still came up through the plughole in the kitchen. They pretended to go in and kiss Opi goodbye, while the grown-ups knocked back tiny glasses of raspberry schnapps in the kitchen. No one wanted to go into Opi's Kabinet, even after the men removed his body. Nobody opened the piano. Everyone had to step over everyone else's toes and the girls had not to look in the cheval mirror that Opi had said was haunted.

Mutti kept having her nightmare about Opi on the Cross, and Uncle Fritzi wasn't allowed to bring his friend Andre to the flat again, even though they all loved him and he came three times on the tram, bringing white lilies, poetry books in crimson soft velvet jackets, and fresh ground coffee.

Uncle Fritzi and Andre had only been back three days when Opi fell over with his heart in the Hotel zum Oper. Miri listened in to find out that Uncle Fritzi had to meet Andre in a Stuberl or a Kaffee Haus. Judit heard that Uncle Fritzi had found Andre in France, and thought maybe he'd been helping with the Resistance too.

'O du lieber Augustin, alles ist hin,' they sang when Andre was kicked out; it was their favourite rhyming song, and was about everything being broken, or kaput.

At last the visas and tickets that Mutti kept wanting came through. Omi cried and Mutti laughed so hard the girls thought her glasses would end up smashed on the floor. They sat on the spiny edge of the day bed in the room next to the Kabinet.

'Dummkopf, Pfui,' they whispered to each other, hearing Mutti say, 'Aber nein. Ich will es nicht,' but she went and packed the tapestry after all.

Five days later, they walked through the night to the Westbahnhof, the biggest station they'd ever seen, each of them clutching a cardboard suitcase. Miri's had a plaited string handle that cut into her hand, right through her glove. The train was a monster, spitting and hissing into the blackness.

'Verdammt,' Mutti said, when she saw that it was already about to leave.

'*Kinder*,' Omi said, into her handkerchief. '*Gott sei Dank.*'

'Pfui,' Miri whispered, 'to such prayers!'

Judit was crying.

'Mirinka,' Omi said, her nose like pickled beetroot. 'Juditka, Auf Wiedersehen.'

'Adieu,' Mutti said, her tears dripping over Omi's face as she let down the window strap and leant out, 'Mama.'

On the three-day train journey to London, across borders where guards poked guns at them, Mutti didn't speak. When three soldiers got on and offered them pickled walnuts, Mutti kept looking back over her shoulder.

At the Channel Port of Calais, Mutti said '*ruhig*', and then said it in English, 'quiet!' She was too busy to talk to them. They started to giggle but stopped when she rapped their knees, but as far as they could see, she was just looking through the rain at the dark grey sea and the light grey beaches hemmed in by sagging barbed wire fences.

They had to carry their cases over wet railway lines, and haul them onto a big ship. The ship rode high waves and people were sick in the toilets. Judit was sick over the top rail before they got chased back down, Miri wasn't sick at all.

On the next train, in a closed compartment with people talking only in English, the girls muttered 'Pfui,' and giggled while they were unwrapping waxed paper sandwiches. Bits of gherkins, hardboiled eggs and black bread fell on to their laps.

Mutti said '*Kinder, Kinder*', and not to call her Mutti now, they had to call her 'Mama', and not talk anyway. '*Ruhig*,' she whispered, then remembered again: 'quiet!'

Homing Waltz
Vera Lynn (Decca, NME Charts 15/11/52)

When they got to Victoria, London, they had to sleep on a floor with other children in a house with high windows for three weeks, three-and-a-half days, while Mutti was put in a dormitory with other women. In the daytime they were allowed to meet up with Mutti, who made them laugh, telling them how horrid the English food and people were if you took any notice, but she didn't. She showed them how English people whispered behind their hands, unlike their soldier Daddy, who'd never whispered his English behind his hands,

Somehow they ended up in one room, and shared a kitchen and bathroom with five families. It was in Chelsea and was called a halfway house. Miri said, halfway to where? Ma said how should she know, maybe to Hell, and to stop asking questions.

They all had to live in that room for nine months, and it had too many mirrors in it. Mutti went out at night to work in a café. Sometimes she brought vanilla ice cream home.

At last they got moved to a terraced house in Bayswater, where they got to know a big family. Miri and Judit played hide and seek in the Square gardens and did hopscotch on the balconies with the younger Manalescus. Miri liked Alexis best, but he hardly ever played with them. Once he took her for a ride round all the Squares on the back of his new bike. When she got off, Miri was so proud she'd thought she'd burst.

One day, after Aunty Nora, Uncle Michael, big boy Alexis, little Kristina, and best friend Magdalena left, saying, 'forget us not, we forget you not,' nobody spoke to them. So they quickly learnt the English phrases Daddy had been trying to teach them before he got lost on that mined beach, plus some new ones.

Then they picked out phrases that Daddy'd never used, like 'bloody Germans', and 'Hitler only had one ball' and 'bloody foreigners'. They practised these in whispers under the nasty English tapestry that Mama had brought back with her. It had dogs hunting deer and one stag bleeding and dying. Other people said a lot of the new words when Mama had to queue for ID cards, ration books and rations. They weren't supposed to stare at other people, skip or talk except in English. They could do the new Cat's Cradle with strings. They still said 'Pfui, Schmui,' to each other, but not out loud in front of queues or the Englische Kinder, dumb English children.

At the English Junior School, Miri wrote compositions about witchy Baba Yaga and bears and wolves. Her teacher said she had a good imagination and she liked the way Miri decorated her pages with entwined flowers. Miri didn't tell her that the bears and wolves were real ones from Omi's stories, or that witchy Baba Yaga was real, or that the wolf might come round at the full moon to howl with Mutti.

Judit didn't like her teacher and refused to try. At playtime she ran with a pack of boys. In class, she fidgeted, blobbed ink on her books, and gulped her bottle of milk.

'*Endlich*', Mama said, 'at last, look', when she got the letter from the Council saying that they could move to the terraced house in Shepherd's Bush. '*Gott sei Dank.*' She still said prayers and swore mostly in German. Miri and Judit were called Miriam and Judy now at school, and didn't ever use German outside their home, where Ma made them wear crocheted slippers as soon as the front door was closed.

They moved all right, but Ma's moonlit shouting got very loud, and the railway vixen began to join in. Ma'd be out in the moonlight, banging the dustbin lid on the air raid shelter wall, throwing her head back and howling, and then the fox would start barking.

Miri and Judy learnt to keep to their beds, or get upstairs quickly on such nights, exchanging 'Pfui, Schmui' whispers, knowing what would come next.

The left hand side neighbours would open their top window and throw a bucket of cold water out. Usually it missed Ma, but if she happened to be shuffling back in, she'd get the full load, and she'd look up and holler '*Scheiss*' or '*Verdammt*' or '*Arschloch*', and get into the scullery fast, before Mrs Flanagan had had time to refill her bucket. Luckily Mrs Flanagan didn't know that the words meant shit and damnation and arsehole, but she knew enough to know that they weren't very polite.

'Does the moon shine into her bucket?' Judy asked.

'Silly thing, moonshine indeed,' Miri said.

Singing the Blues
Tommy Steele (Decca, NME Charts 15/12/56)

Years later, on this particular night in January, 1957, Miriam forgot that there was to be a full moon. She'd got to waving her hands about to show that at sixteen she knew it all. So she'd flushed when Ma's way of saying *mediterrinane* had slipped out into the dusty quiet of a geography lesson. Ma often had their Oxford atlas out on the deal table, covered with American cloth in case of disaster, so she could point out the countries mentioned in the wireless news, especially if they mentioned the Balkans or Hungary or Yugoslavia. Ma thought the English school system was *lauter Schmarrn*, which was her way of saying total rubbish, or shit. The girls weren't very interested.

Ma had been listening to news about the Hungarian Uprising on her precious Home Service. The girls heard the bit about how Stalin had been thrown off his column and only his boots were left. They heard that Russian tanks had driven over revolutionaries in a square where twenty thousand people had met up, and how some had waved flags, and planted them in Stalin's boots, and how a stream of blood had trickled down the street. Ma had kept on about blasted Reds, blasted Communists and *Verdammte* restrictions on broadcasts in a supposed blasted free country. The girls didn't know anything about Communism or an Iron Curtain.

This January night, when Miri forgot there'd be a full moon. Miri and Judy were in La Roche Coffee Bar, playing 'Green Door' and choosing 'Love Me Tender' to come on next. Her back to the jukebox, Jude was eyeing up a spotty blond soldier leaning against Rosa's shiny Gaggia espresso machine, when the plate glass door fell open and a gang of men with foreign accents surged in.

Miriam stopped tapping her foot and stared. Jude dropped her shilling and said, '*Scheiss.*' Rosa flicked a glance over the young men, mopped a dribble on the counter, and smiled. Three girls in shirt-waisters that Miri envied at a table by the door all put their cappuccinos down. One of them spilt some and traced her finger though foam. The blond soldier boy Judy was eying left, swinging the door shut behind him.

The way the arc of the door erased where he'd been suddenly reminded Miriam of... what? Now she could see him: the pimply blond soldier from ten years ago: he'd got on the train at a border to somewhere, shouldering his gun. He'd offered them sausages or maybe green walnuts or dried apples. When he'd got off, he'd swung the carriage door in the same arc, and created the same absence.

Miri couldn't imagine now how they'd not known that their dad had been erased one moonlit night by a mine on a beach. Had he been calling 'Now you see me, now you don't' to his soldier friend who had dared him to cross the fence?

Far above La Roche a full moon was gliding over chimney pots. Over near Shepherd's Bush Green, the girls' mother ran out in her crotcheted slippers, flannelette nightdress and tight curlers. Snatching the lid off the dustbin, she banged it on the shelter; the silver fox up by the rail-track barked.

Meanwhile, Miri again pressed the button for 'Green Door' as she watched the group of foreigners. One of them was saying something to another bloke behind him, then glancing towards her. Then he was walking over, clicking his fingers at the other chap to follow. Jude knocked her with her elbow.

In Shepherd's Bush darkness, the vixen called again. Someone putting out empty milk bottles almost dropped them; they chinked together in the quiet late night street. The moon sailed a snail line over an outline of chimney pots, and disappeared behind a fast-moving cloud. A tube train rattled through, almost hitting the vixen.

Now at La Roche the wheel of records in the jukebox spun, lights flashed, the arc fanned round to number five, the arm reached out, collected the record, turned it on its side, dropped it into position on the turntable, and the needle found the groove; the first 'Green Door' notes swung out.

The two strangers stopped directly in front of Jude and Miriam. The one with fire in his eyes said, '*Na! Mivan leany*?! Hallo girlz.' Whooping, they unhitched bags from their shoulders, grabbed at Miri and Jude, and whirled them into something like a jive.

Miriam tried to gaze into her partner's hooded eyes. He was not watching her, then he was. He clicked his tongue, lifting his shadowed jaw. The smell of rough tobacco slipped into her throat.

'I am Karlis,' he said. 'I am student of Hungary in the Revolution.'

Miriam couldn't lift her gaze from the way his full upper lip hid his thick tongue.

Jude whispered Pfui.

Suddenly over the Green's opaque and gauzy surface, the full moon was back in view, hanging in a hazy patch of spinning radiance. As their mother again raised her shovel, a cat screeched and the fox flashed past.

As 'I'm the Great Pretender' started to play, Miriam felt drunk on jukebox sounds, flashing lights and Karlis's Hungarian. He smelt of garlic and paprika. His hands were big and rough on her arm; now she couldn't keep her eyes off his Adam's apple.

Jude was flopping on to the nearest chair, when Rosa's apron appeared in front of the jukebox lights. 'This is not dance floor. I 'ave not got licence. Revolutionaries need understand. I spit on England but she now home. *Smerdt.*'

Karlis raised his arms, clicked his fingers just by Miri's ears, and smiled straight at her. Miriam blushed and saw black on white images of Marlon Brando, James Dean and Elvis entwined, and now in real life this real rebel was dancing with her in a West End coffee bar.

Over Shepherd's Bush, the moon was obscured again by cloud. A tube train stood at a siding; lit windows showed no passengers. In the forgotton long-overgrown bomb-site, where foxes had raised young, scurryings of rats shook brittle grass.

The girls' mother saw only blurred shapes. She lifted her head: the moon had disappeared. '*Dummkopf,*' she muttered She put the shovel down, and replaced the lid on her dustbin. Her feet were so cold. She climbed her steps, and turned the handle. No light from the *blode Englander* upstairs windows. Now she would make a cup of tea. As she went in, she thought she heard the fox again. '*Dummkopf,*' she repeated, switching her light on.

Standing by her Gaggia, Rosa called again, 'Time for closing down jukebox.'

Someone had put more coins in: 'Blue Moon' started up. Miriam started to sway, but Karlis moved away, exploding into talk; his mates lit fags, cheered, windmilled their arms. A map, boots, and a battered tin torch slid on to the table.

'Girls. You 'ave 'omes?' Rosa called. 'Time is midnight gone.'

'Blooming heck,' Miriam said. 'Jude, the trains will stop in a sec; come on.'

They ran to Oxford Circus tube station, getting a stitch, heels clacking, getting caught in cracks, shops dark, a taxi passing like a ghost of itself.

'We haven't even got a ticket,' Jude gasped. ' And all that crap, daddy-o.'

'Don't tell the whole world,' Miriam said, running on to the escalator as it stopped. 'Run!'

They reached the platform in time to see the train's rear lights dwindling.

VAL BRIDGE

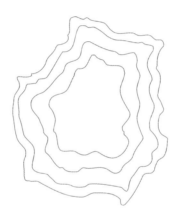

HOPE

fiction by Pj Buchanan

It was April. Before I stepped over the threshold of the little house, I felt that I could be happy here. Maybe for the first time – I was going to be happy. I was coming home to an empty house – blissfully, gloriously empty; of memories; of chattels. The house was polished by forgotten feet and fingers; warmed by an open fire; red roses clambered round the door; golden, brocade, silken sun flooded through the window of the biggest bedroom I'd ever slept in. My lover and I chose the house; we walked its empty rooms, smiling. There were no words – we did not need them.

There, like a Persian carpet spread before me, I was shown a new life; new colours undreamed of – no, not undreamt – dreamt, glimpsed – but so far off as to be unreachable – dreams forgotten as soon as they'd been dreamt; dreams of passion – red, rose-scented ruby; ivy emerald spiced with cumin; lustrous, fragrant, gilded cardamom; the musk of purple lilies; the ginger tang of burnt earth. All buried, suffocated under fetid air; under an existence filled with watching star-dust motes drifting down on to the dull surface that was my life, the dust rising until it choked me.

I am a twin. Before I was born my father refuted my presence – before our birth our separateness was denied. We were born in the cold, in November – Scorpio. Born far from the heat, from the jungle; far from tiger country, from hibiscus flowering in a garden – my mother's habitat is heat. We were born in Scotland, my twin sister and I. Ice formed on the inside of the windowpane. There was a fire in every room, the coal kept in its own little chamber by the back door, next to the pantry. So heat and sustenance, the two essentials of life, were conveniently to hand; conjoined; twins. We spent our first years in a double bed, my twin and I; the cord that once tied us to our mother now tied us to each other – invisibly it bound us. We spoke our own language – or didn't speak at all. Needing no words, why should we?

Father was older than my mother – by thirteen years. He was a clever man;

a doctor, but ignorant enough to deny my existence before I was born. His specialty was the mind; a psychiatrist; a trickcyclist; a trickster of the mind. *You'll end up in one of your father's hospitals* was my mother's future for me, as she guessed my unnatural dreams – dreams of women's thighs and women's kisses; velvet dreams; easeful dreams; demonic dreams. The demons rose up unbidden – there at every turn, they ripped my dreams away. What armour could I construct strong enough to hold them off? Jesu, help me. I ran the beads through my fingers and covered my head with hope and prayer.

The heat and the cold met in my mother and my father. They survived the war in different hemispheres – she in the jungle, he in the Atlantic – so heroic – the way ants are heroic, instinctively. The Japanese took her; she was confined, route-marched, browbeaten; eaten by insects; infected; neglected; disrespected; curiously grown up – curiously childlike. Teenage years were laid waste, stolen by the war; she was a privileged product of the Raj reduced to a walking skeleton; diamond rings changed hands for a pound of bacon. She was thirteen when they bombed Pearl Harbour. My father came back from the north Atlantic, from The Cruel Sea – young, dashing; a boy from the Gorbals with a degree in medicine; an oxymoron – tossed about; bossed about and hardened. He was a true man's man. It takes guts to climb out of the gutter – or an overwhelming urge to find out how the mind works – his mind, she said – tricks; trickcyclist.

The war was over. They met in Egypt, in Port Said, as she travelled west and north, and he travelled east and south; a collision of hot and cold – a hiss of steam resulted. She was naïve-nineteen when they got married – their love died of hypothermia, fifteen years after it had exploded into being on the deck of a ship; ninety degrees in the shade; a flare sent up in the monochrome glare; shades of white heat. Their love died on the granite slab of Scottish winters, under the weight of my father's fists. She starved on tatties and neeps in grey light. The white mosquito netting had been replaced by white freezing fog. He could not cope with her demands for mango and banana-scented warmth so he sought refuge in another woman's thighs – cold – dour – redheaded – alabaster-skinned; with fire between her legs. Mother escaped from his handy fists to the heat – we filed behind her, knotted together and bound to her – my sister and me; a melancholy caravanserai.

I remember the train – remember how the smell of coal billowed about us, rancid and dirty, smelling of rotten eggs. The steam rose from behind the engine, from the water that dripped from the hoses and connectors, like the hot blood of a dragon; I felt the power as the engine stood panting at the platform edge, the driver holding it back with his hand on the whistle chord – as though he could control the beast with just a whistle. It carried us from one life into another – from the cold of Scotland to the fragrant peach warmth of Italy.

In Italy she left us – semi orphans – abandoned to sundry relatives, friends, acquaintances, even. The deprivations of her teenage years came back to lay her low, ravages of malnutrition and malaria. The other deprivations came back too, and she found herself doing what teenagers do, but older, though not wiser – late night parties; one night stands – fitted in between long stays in hospital. She was freed from the tyranny of my father's fist, from my father's tricks of mind; she freed herself from us, my twin and me. And the cord that tied me to my twin split and frayed as time chewed through it – I crawled into that small, putrid space that lies between insanity and sanity; a mendicant – I became the beggar that pleads for ease – for a new twine to tie around my waist; female to female – to become conjoined; to become freakshow fare for others to recoil from; for demons to haunt – as I became caged, enchained by quilted satin, incense prayers.

Then it was October. The April dreams had faded into sepia; the rich, heavy carpet I had revelled in – had been wrapped up in – festered into a rank rug made of rags – tatters woven together with hope on a weft of dreams. The stench of broken reverie rose – I gagged on it. I wanted my lover to stay forever and save my soul – save my sanity. I wanted my twin to stay forever, to be my true mirror, my true reflection; I wanted my mother to be the Holy Mother. I wanted – I wanted; I hoped. I funnelled every dream of refuge and of joy into that moment when we – my lover and I – stepped across the torpid threshold into that sainted azure air.

Now the house is empty, except for demons fattened on hope, twirling in the dust, playing with frayed rope.

BRINGING BACK BORGES

narrative nonfiction by Stephanie Cage

I remember the day we decided to bring back Borges. We weren't even meant to be studying him that week, but something about his stories just wouldn't leave us alone. We were waiting for our tutor to come in and start the class on Pat Barker, but Catherine was still grumbling about the previous week's reading.

'Why don't you like Borges?'

I wanted to leap to his defence, but Andy got there first.

'He's so pretentious. All that Latin. And always showing off that he's read these obscure writers. Making the reader feel stupid.' Catherine leaned back in her chair, doodling a tree in the margin of her notepad, and watched the door. When the tutor came in, we'd have to drop the debate, but no doubt we'd get back to it when the class was over.

'I don't think that's fair.' This time I got in first. 'Latin was still a normal part of people's education when he was writing. At least, the sort of academic people he was writing for. The sort who read literary journals. It wouldn't have seemed like showing off.'

'And the words he uses,' she went on, as if I hadn't spoken. 'Dithyramb. What the hell is a dithyramb, for heaven's sake? Who on earth goes round using words like that?' Catherine persisted. The tree in the margin of her pad was rapidly becoming a forest. As she talked, she added birds and a sun.

'Borges, obviously,' said Andy, grinning.

'Borges' character,' I corrected, reminding them that 'Funes the Memorious' was supposed to be narrated by a pretentious would-be academic who expected his rambling account to be included in a volume of memoirs about the great man.

It amused me that even Andy, who enjoyed and understood Borges better than anyone I knew, still forgot sometimes to what extent Borges was a player of games and a wearer of masks, and how little you could equate author and narrator. Borges' stories masquerade as true accounts. (In fact, I first encountered the story of Funes in a book on memory and it was a long time before I realised it wasn't factual.) They pose as recovered histories of impossible events or studious reviews of non-existent fictions. Even when Borges emerges into the limelight, he undercuts the persona he has created. In 'Borges and I' he creates himself as a character in his own fiction, and by the end neither he nor the reader knows 'which of us has written this page'.

But before I could say a quarter of this, the door opened and our tutor came in, closely followed by the remaining few members of the class. I sat back and watched as the tutor encouraged us to present our opinions of *Union Street*, and Catherine perked up and began a panegyric on Pat Barker's talents.

Andy looked bored, and presently he began doodling something on the front of his notepad. A staircase. He added another step, then another. It turned a corner, then ascended further and turned again. Presently the top stair linked itself to the bottom one in an impossible circuit. He'd perfectly reproduced Escher's famous creation. It shouldn't have surprised me. He was such a good writer that I constantly found myself forgetting his background was technical. No wonder his doodles were mathematically formed and accurately drafted.

I wondered if that was what he liked about Borges. There was a certain mathematical quality to some of the stories, and the impossible architecture of the Immortals' city could have been taken directly from an Escher print.

At lunchtime I asked Andy about my theory.

'That's part of it,' he agreed. 'Borges just knows so much about so many things. Did you know there's an essay in *Labyrinths* that's about a mathematical paradox?'

'So he knew about maths?'

'Uh huh. Quite a bit, anyway.'

'Do you think he knew Escher? Or at least his work?'

'I don't know. I'd like to think so. There's so much of Escher in Borges – or the other way around – somehow I don't like to think of it as just chance.'

'Do you suppose we could find out?'

So there we were, surreptitiously eating our sandwiches under the 'No food and drink allowed' sign in the computer room as we ploughed through innumerable Internet biographies on Escher and Borges trying to work out whether they'd ever been in the same place at the same time. It turned out that Borges had been studying in Europe while Escher was beginning his career. It wouldn't have been impossible for them to meet. But there was nothing to confirm or deny it.

Two articles mentioned them in the same breath. One thought that Borges ought to have been the fourth member of the trio Dennet and Hofstadter wrote about in *Gödel, Escher, Bach: An Eternal Golden Braid.* Borges, the author argued, was the literary genius to complement Bach's musical brilliance, Escher's art and Gödel's mathematical prowess. Andy and I agreed. But Gödel, Escher and Bach hadn't known each other anyway, so that proved nothing.

Another paper was harder to figure out because it was in Spanish, but again it seemed to say that Borges and Escher shared a number of preoccupations, but stopped short of suggesting any causal connection.

'It's so frustrating,' Andy said. 'If they did meet, there ought to be some evidence of it somewhere.'

'If only we could go back in time and ask him,' I said.

'Maybe you could hold a séance.' Catherine turned from the next computer, where she was checking her e-mails, to join in.

'That's it!' Andy slammed his hands down on the desk with such force that the wheely chair he was sitting on shot backwards into the wall.

Catherine stared.

'OK, now I know you've finally lost it. Our rational friend here wants to hold a séance. Now I've seen it all.' She gave an exaggerated sigh and turned back to her keyboard.

I waited. I knew how Andy's mind worked. All would be explained just as soon as he'd worked it out, and I didn't for a moment suppose séances would be involved.

'No, no,' he snapped. 'Not a séance. But we can ask him.'

'Uh, yeah,' I said cautiously.

'There's this new technology my lab was working on when I left. A kind of expert system.'

I racked my brains for what I knew about expert systems.

'They collect information about a subject and you can ask them questions, right? Like, a computerised doctor would be an expert system, that sort of thing?'

'Uh huh. Only this system becomes an expert on a particular individual, their life experiences and knowledge and artistic style. It came out of an analysis of some of Shakespeare's disputed work, but I don't see why we couldn't apply it to Borges instead.'

So the next day Andy brought in a CD with a copy of the software on it, and fed it into one of the machines at the back of the computer room. You weren't meant to install stuff on the college computers, but a few clicks and key presses got us round that. I didn't ask him what he'd done. It's not as if I'd have understood the answer, and anyway I was more interested in seeing what this program would do.

What it did for quite a while was a whistle-stop tour of websites related to Borges.

'It's at the information gathering stage,' Andy explained. 'I already fed it a complete edition of his works, but now it's learning about his history.'

'Then what happens?'

'Then we talk to it.'

'Just talk?'

'Well, type. There aren't any microphones on the computer, otherwise we could talk to him instead. I did the natural language processing bit.'

He sounded proud of it.

I watched as a flashing cursor appeared on the screen, followed by a message: 'Greetings. Welcome.'

'Welcome to what?' I asked.

'I'm not sure,' Andy admitted. 'Apparently the individual appears in his or her normal context, so we might be visiting Borges in his house or at the library. It's probably best to keep it neutral until we know.' He gestured towards the keyboard.

'Hello,' I typed. 'We're very pleased to meet you. We'd love to talk to you about your work, if that's OK.'

'My work or Borges' work?' the machine asked. 'I am an ordinary librarian. You wish perhaps to ask about the work of Borges, creator of fictions? Or perhaps I am a creator of fictions, and you wish to ask about the library of Borges?'

We exchanged a glance. Clearly this was going to be hard work.

'I would like to talk to you about the book *Labyrinths*. May I ask you some questions?'

'A-maze-ing,' the machine punned. Andy rolled his eyes. 'It is so little understood. Fame is a form of incomprehension. Perhaps the worst.'

'He's quoting himself,' Andy observed, pointing out the relevant passage from 'Pierre Menard'. 'But does it mean something different in the context of Borges speaking to us, rather than the imaginary narrator writing about Menard?'

'Oh, don't,' I complained. 'You're messing with my head.'

'Yes, don't go all metaphysical on us,' Catherine joined in. 'Come on. Ask him about Escher before it gets any worse.'

So I pulled the keyboard closer and typed: 'Do you know of an artist named Escher?'

'I know of a mathematician named Escher. Is this the man of whom you speak?'

'Mathematician and artist,' Andy amended, and I typed in the words. 'You know his work?'

'People have compared us. But then, people make many comparisons. At times I am compared to Auster. I am sorry not to have been acquainted with him. He seems an interesting man. Perhaps now we will meet.'

'But Borges couldn't have known about Auster.' At the time, I had just finished reading Auster's Brooklyn trilogy, set in New York in the twentieth century. I could see why the comparison was made. The series is Borgesian in its labyrinthine complexities of author, character, watcher and watched.

'But now he can, because we've given him access to everything that's ever been written about him, including comparisons to modern authors.'

'So now anything he tells us is suspect, because we've given him the information we want to get from him. Great. He's not really Borges at all. He's just an Internet library.'

'He is Borges. He's Borges as he would be if he existed now.'

'That's ridiculous.'

We were beginning to get looks from people in the next row trying to work. Andy continued in a hushed whisper.

'Ask him, is he Borges?'

I typed, 'Are you Borges?' I didn't really expect to get a straight answer. We were, after all, talking to the creator of 'Borges and I'. He doesn't deal in easy answers.

Sure enough, his answer came back in the form of another quotation: 'The greatest magician (Novalis has memorably written) would be the one who would cast over himself a spell so complete that he would take his own phantasmagorias as autonomous appearances. Would not this be our case?'

'So... we created you. We can't trust anything you say.' I frowned as I typed. I wasn't liking this. I wanted answers, not more questions. I should have known better.

'Why would you not trust me?'

'Because you're talking about things you can't possibly have known. Borges wouldn't have read Auster. So how can I trust your answer about Escher?'

'But Borges would have read Auster, had the opportunity arisen. As you know, I am a great admirer of Menard, whose techniques of the deliberate anachronism and the erroneous attribution have infinite applications.'

'One of those applications being annoying students who are foolish enough to let Borges anywhere near the concept of "truth",' I muttered.

Andy grinned and reached for the keyboard, but I was still in full flow.

'Of course you admire Menard. You created him.'

'Is this a certainty?'

'There is no record of him outside your fictions.'

'There is no record of many things. There is no record that I ever met Escher, yet you consider the possibility that I did. Why not consider the possibility that Menard existed?'

'That's different. If Menard existed there would be records. Birth certificates. Death certificates. The papers he's supposed to have published. You could have met Escher without there being any evidence. That's why we wanted to ask you.'

'So if I told you that I met with Escher once, at a party in Switzerland, and that I admired his work, that the Immortals' city was taken from his sketches and his hands drawing each other inspired my parable about an author writing himself, this would be credible to you?'

'Yes. So is this what you are saying?'

'Perhaps. Or perhaps I am saying it is all a coincidence. Sometimes an idea's time comes and many people arrive simultaneously at a conclusion. If I told you Escher and I both came to our images through our reading of mathematics, this also would be credible, would it not? As Menard first came to the Quixote by steeping himself in Spanish tradition, history and language, we, steeped in the mathematical writings of the time, came by different routes to the same ideas.'

'Enough of the Menard!' I was becoming exasperated. 'Are you saying you met Escher, or you did not?'

'Do you believe I met him?'

'I think you knew his work, or he yours. Otherwise the similarity is simply too much of a coincidence.'

'Perhaps I did not meet him, or perhaps I met him and do not recall it. Unlike my creation, Funes, much of the past is lost to me, and so I tell myself stories about how it might have been. Put another way, we need fictions because our understanding of the world is imperfect. Only God would not need stories. To tell stories is to be human. It is to try to explain the world. To make a connection between my story and Escher's images is merely to create another kind of fiction.'

'An argument about ideas is just another kind of story,' I summarised. 'When Catherine says Borges is showing off, or I say he's playing a part, we're telling stories about the writing.'

'But we still don't know about Escher,' Andy frowned.

In the end, asking the author about his stories hadn't helped at all. We'd just ended up with another set of stories about the first set of stories. Interpretations of interpretations. An infinite hall of mirrors. An image worthy of Escher – or Borges.

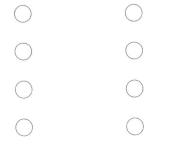

A SHOWER OF BASTARDS

from the novel by Neil Callender

Edinburgh, 17 November 2004
Morning

I have to get out of Edinburgh because the noise is killing me. Screaming cars, reversing trucks, construction, chip shop hip-hop, breaking glass, people shouting all kinds of shit that could be said quietly. I might have done something with my life by now if this city had given me a moment's peace to think.

I'm lying in my bed with an ache at the core of my head. Usually I down a litre of water after drinking but last night there was a girl and I forgot all the principles of hydration. Her scent and warmth are still in the bed next to me. She's in the bathroom. I'm waiting to see what she looks like, siren or monstrosity. I have an image of the women from *Sex and the City*, maybe from a DVD, but I hope the girl in the bathroom looks like the brunette.

Outside, men in luminous yellow waistcoats are reattaching a fifty-foot high sheet of decorative green metal which blew off the building two nights ago. I hear an elaborate wolf-whistle and see the lower half of a builder walk in front of my fifth-floor window. His stomach is escaping over the top of his tracksuit bottoms, he has a hard-on, and the two protrusions are almost touching.

A builder with an erection is a nasty sight, but I'm curious about the source. A woman who can give a guy one of those from five floors below, on a sub-zero morning, has got to be something special.

I throw back the covers and run to the window hoping to catch a glimpse of endless tanned legs before they disappear round the corner, but she's gone. She's gone, but thank God for women because without them I would never get out of bed.

The toilet flushes and my heart increases its beat. The part of my brain which handles recollection is groggy, but I try to shake it into operation. I remember being at a seventies-themed party and sharking three girls, but I don't know which one came home with me. One kept talking to me in a strange language; I think I told her that I knew Gaelic. Another was saying that she tried to kill herself by overdosing on antacids. The third kept going on about how *Rocky* is the best film ever made, and Sylvester Stallone would have been the next Marlon Brando if he hadn't chased the buck with shit action movies.

What do women do in the bathroom between flushing the toilet and coming out of there?

The handle turns.

The girl walks out and she's model-beautiful. She has blonde and pink hair. I like the blonde but not the pink. It reminds me of the plastic trolls all the girls had at primary school.

I notice that she's wearing my T-shirt and she gets marks off for this. It means I'll have to reek of perfume or pay a laundry bill. She looks good in it though. Her breasts fill it in a way my pecs don't.

I reckon this girl will be all right. Maybe we could have a relationship or something, because I'm twenty-three now and it's about time I had one of those.

I look down to check out her legs but this is impossible, she only has one. One real one anyway, the other is some kind of prosthetic job. How could I remember the *Rocky* conversation and not a plastic limb?

I scratch behind my ear and tell her, You should cover up, there's a builder on heat outside the window.

She looks down at herself and says, I am covered up, babes. Don't you like me in your T-shirt?

I tell her, I meant some trousers. You can have some of mine if you don't have any.

I don't care about the T-shirt any more, or it's at least fallen down my list of grievances.

The girl picks a pair of flares off the lampshade and shakes her head.

I can't believe we went to a seventies party, she says. The seventies are like, so 1998.

I sit down on the edge of the bed and she cuddles up next to me, resting her lips on the nape of my neck. This is problematic, it means she likes me. I try to keep my eyes on the whitewashed wall while I ponder the course of the next ten minutes.

The girl lifts her lips off my shoulder. Girls' lips getting lifted off my shoulder is usually one of my favourite sounds, but I can't hear it for the cement mixer on full throttle outside, and a chorus of 'Hit Me Baby One More Time' from the scaffolders.

The girl senses something is wrong. She stares at the side of my head and I'm afraid to turn and look at her.

You're going to dump me, aren't you? she whispers. I can feel her words blow against my bare arm.

What makes you say that? I ask with my eyes still on the wall.

My friend told me you would. She said it was one of the few certainties in life.

Who's your friend?

Abby.

I remember Abby. She's an American exchange student with the epitome of the apple-pie-grin. She studied dance and had a lot of male friends who wore make-up and made comments about my ass. We got it together one night and she wanted us to get serious. I told her all right, but only if she got rid of the homo friends and promised not to apple-pie-grin at me when I was in a foul mood. She walked out of my flat and came back five hours later to tell me she was, OFFICIALLY no longer a fag hag. By this time I had changed my mind and told her I didn't want a serious relationship after all.

The crazy woman attacked me with the yellow pages and I had to shut her in the bathroom and decide whether to call the police or the zoo. In the end, I let her scream herself out. Man that girl had some vocal chords on her.

Well? says the one-legged beauty, still five inches from my head, still looking at me, still expecting something from me. Why?

I close my eyes and scratch behind my ear and she seems to know what this means.

What is it? she shouts, pushing my arm with both of hers.

The violence in the shout blasts my eardrums and I almost topple off the bed.

Is it because I tried to kill myself or is it my false leg? she yells again.

I never know what to say when women ask me things like this, so I just rub the fake leg with my hand. Then, when she doesn't look appeased, I lean forward and kiss it. It tastes like a hospital.

The girl shakes her head, yells, Pathetic, and walks out of the room.

I get back into bed, pull the covers over myself and switch on the TV.

They're showing an episode of *Roadrunner*, my favourite cartoon. I like the desert setting and empathise with the coyote.

The front door slams and I stop concentrating on the cartoon. This kind of thing used to be so easy.

Around Midday

I sit in Ray's Ford Capri, which is parked half on the pavement outside his Georgian flat. He needs a lift to the airport. He won't take a taxi because the cabbies of Edinburgh are out to kill him after he hit one of them with a beer bottle.

Being only hungover, and not actually drunk, qualifies me as a designated driver in Ray's world. I pretend to move the gear stick around with my eyes closed while saying the gear number aloud. I'm only licensed to drive automatics.

Ray cracks open the door and climbs into the passenger seat; he reeks of breweries and cigars.

Ice is falling from the sky, mate, he says.

I lean forward and look up through the windscreen. He's right, it's not snow, rain or hail, it's liquid ice pissing down on a city which is every shade of brown and grey.

Ray takes a bottle of Grouse out of his bag and slugs it back. He's wearing khaki shorts and a now-soaked, short-sleeved shirt with three buttons undone and chest hair sticking everywhere.

I'm trying to inebriate the fear of flying out of my system, he says. If Osama and his mates want to blow us up mid-air, fair enough. If it's a big explosion and a quick death, I don't give two shites. But I don't want that bleeping, you know what I mean?

Ray imitates the bleeping in the highest pitch his gravel voice can manage. And the plane shaking about, he continues, and that breathing apparatus falling down, and all the self-important wankers screaming for their shitty wee lives. I can't take that mate. Right, come on, move this beast.

Ford Capris aren't beasts, I tell him.

I put the car into what I assume is first and we're away. The car half screams, half drones, to the end of the street, as Ray searches though his bag.

Have you got everything? I ask.

I've got a passport, two bottles of whisky and my books.

Ray has published three collections of poetry – *The Wandering Dickhead*, *Love is Like a Bag of Armed Monkeys*, and a new one which he'll début at Berkeley tomorrow night.

How about clothes? I ask.

Mate, America is the land of women, hamburgers and new clothes. I'm not packing a blonde, or a Big Mac, so why would I pack clothes?

Tell me what your new collection is called, I say. I promise I'll keep it under wraps.

All right, since you're my mate, and since nobody in this country who doesn't wear corduroy jackets or ankle-long skirts, gives a shit about poetry, I'll tell you. It's called *A Shower of Bastards*.

Why?

Because that's what I see when I look at the world. I've got itchy balls, what does that mean?

Could be eczema, crabs, perspiration, or diabetes, I reply.

I drive through the streets of Edinburgh, getting comfortable with the car. The ancient stone buildings are darkened by the rain but this makes the shop fronts glow brighter. Every third shop sells mobile phones, every second sells food or houses, the third is random. Neither of us knows where the airport is; we haven't left the city for years. I see a passenger plane in the grey sky and decide to follow it.

Ray pulls a note pad and pen from the glove/bottle/porn compartment.

Tell me about the gimp girl you met last night, he says. I need something to write about on the flight.

She wasn't a gimp man. She was a supermodel or something, but with one leg.

Yeah, yeah. Give me details.

His pen is poised above the note pad, his hand is shaking.

I don't want to talk about it.

We pass a housing estate and the Hearts football stadium, for the third time in twenty minutes.

Mate, where are you going? asks Ray.

I'm following that plane, I tell him.

I think it's circling. Look, go that way.

He points, I turn the car and head in the general direction of where Ray thinks the airport might be. Ten minutes later, we're on the motorway with big green signs telling us where to go. Hallelujah. I up the speed on the windscreen wipers and God ups the rain.

Ray, I want to ask you something, with you being a poet and that.

Yeah?

What is that feeling you get when a girl slams the front door behind her?

Ray drops the notepad and replaces it with a bottle which he cracks open with his pen hand.

That feeling, mate, is freedom.

It didn't feel good when the one-legged girl left. I don't know why.

Well not everyone likes freedom, Walt. If they did, nobody would ever get married. Nobody would have kids. Adolf Hitler would have died a painter. What position did you do it in with the peg-leg lady?

Do you know a girl called Camille?

Bloody hell mate. You're not going to give me anything, are you? No I don't know a girl of that name although that means nothing. Why do you ask?

A couple of weeks ago I got the name Camille tattooed on my arm. It was after Dean's party. I don't remember having it done, I don't remember the girl, I just woke up and it was there.

Heh heh heh.

I'm thinking she must have been something special for me to do that. You know, with my fear of needles, hepatitis and ink poisoning.

LEFT!

I drag the car left and nearly hit the barriers. There's an ugly clunk, and a deep rumble, and I look out of the side window down a forty-foot embankment, before dragging us back on to actual road. I feel sweat appear on my forehead. Ray doesn't seem to have noticed that we almost died and this calms me down.

I saw a sign for the airport, he says. Step on it. I'm going to be late.

For the rest of the way Ray drinks, I drive, the rain splatters, Ray does an impression of the windscreen wipers and ponders how to write the sound phonetically. We reach the airport and I park the car. I go into the terminal with Ray because he promises there will be an abundance of foreign ladies just waiting to be gawked at. I gawk at the foreign ladies while Ray checks in. We shake hands, say cheers and he heads for his plane via the duty free.

I leave the terminal and it's getting dark already. It's only 2 pm. I consider the fact that I am at the very edge of the city. I could drive for two minutes and be out of here, but I don't want to. I have a feeling that something has to be achieved here, or not achieved, before I can leave satisfactorily.

I look up and try to distinguish individual clouds but it's impossible; the sky itself is a single haunting cloud. I've forgotten where I parked the car and I don't have the capacity to deal with any dilemmas today, so I take a taxi back my flat.

Evening

I sit with my parents in a fancy restaurant somewhere in the New Town. It has chandeliers and a lady wearing a ball gown, playing a harp. I did my dissertation on Wagner and Nazism in Germany so I know a fair bit about classical music. I can't remember what I wrote exactly, mainly that he was a bit of a dick but wrote some good tunes.

My dad scans quickly down the menu. He looks like someone who has a desk job in the army. Straight back, square jaw, bulldog frame, buzz-cut grey hair, but wears glasses and is too old and short for the front line. I'm a foot taller than him and he hates me for it.

My dad sits to my right and my mum to my left. She's three years older than him, but looks ten years younger. Her hair is still fully golden and she wears a cardigan and a gypsy dress which she bought from Harvey Nicks.

Why have they got a harp player in a restaurant? asks my dad, looking genuinely disgusted. Stringed instruments and food? Pianos go with food, harps with drinks.

My dad is the manager of a five-star hotel off the Royal Mile; it's his job to know stuff like this.

My mum smiles sadly at him. The sad smile is what nice people do instead of roll their eyes. She works in an alternative health practice on Fredrick Street, catering for Edinburgh's Feng Shui and meditation needs. Their marriage seems to be based on a shared belief in good posture and the achievement of harmony through the strategic arrangement of furniture.

The waiter approaches and asks in a theatrical French accent if we want to order.

I quite fancy the quiche, says my mum. Do you know if they use eggs from caged hens?

No madam, he replies. The hens are not caged.

And it is vegetarian? she asks. There's no animal rennet in the cheese?

It is vegetarian madam, I can assure you.

And, so sorry, but just one more question, is it organic?

The eggs and cheese are organic, the wheat used to make the base isn't.

Then I'll have the hummus salad.

Sir? The waiter looks to my dad.

My dad doesn't look up, just hands him the menu. I'll take the Steak au Poivre.

How would sir like his steak?

Just file down the horns and wipe its arse.

The fake Frenchman pretends not to understand.

Blue-rare, says my dad, glancing up with a smug grin.

The waiter looks at me. I'm still studying the menu for the vegetarian dish containing the most omega 3 oils. None of the dishes scream out, HEALTHY HEART, or DELAYED ARTHRITIS, so I decide to order off the menu.

Could I have an avocado and roast aubergine sandwich please? I ask.

Certainly sir, says the waiter jotting it down and turning on his heels.

My mum looks admiringly at me. She's always afraid that I'm going to slip into being a carnivore.

My dad stares at me too, but not with admiration, love, or even reluctant tolerance. I've seen him look at his ingrowing toenails with more affection.

My dad believes in meat, the redder the better. His philosophy on life is that if you get up at six, eat steak, wear a tie at all times, and work your arse to the bare bone, then you'll be healthy, wealthy, well-liked, well-adjusted and well-respected. Nothing has shaken him from this, be it the black bags under his eyes, the excessive perspiration, the dangerously high blood-pressure, or the stomach ulcers.

My mum believes the same goals are better achieved through t'ai chi, an awareness of karma, breathing from the diaphragm, a largely vegan diet, and devoting an hour of each day to staring at the end of your nose. The big problems of life can be solved with an Indian head massage and the small ones with a strong-brewed chamomile tea.

So, another job down the skank, says my dad as if he were announcing it.

Your gran's funeral will be in two days time, says my mum.

Yes and OK, I reply to both statements.

She looks at me solemnly.

So how are you, spiritually, these days? she asks.

I'm broke, I tell her. A waitress floats past me in the tightest of skirts. My dad looks too, although he could be glaring at the harp lady.

Well, she says, Jesus said blessed are the poor in spirit.

My mum is more of a Buddhist than a Christian, but she'll quote any religious figure if he's got something worth saying.

What did he mean by that? I ask.

The waitress swings her ass with too much class to be British. She must be French, or French-Swiss.

What you need is a career... says my dad.

Or maybe French-Canadian.

...You need a career, and a good pension scheme. This lifestyle of yours...

My mum twirls her hair and interrupts with her ethereal smile. Oh come on now, Robert, she says. There's nothing wrong with Walter's lifestyle.

He smells like malt.

Do I?

He's young. He's experimenting with life.

He doesn't have a job – again!

He's still trying to find himself.

Elaine, you know what that phrase does to my diastolic readings.

I hang my head and play with a bread roll, tearing it open with my hand. My dad reaches over, picks up my knife, puts it on my side plate and points to it. I pick up the knife and cut open the rest of the roll.

My dad says, It would have been a nice tribute to your gran if you were employed by the time of her funeral.

Robert!

Elaine.

If it's a problem, I could just not go, I suggest.

That's not an option, Walter. You've missed the last three family occasions and it offends people on a personal and collective level. There's nothing worse than someone who continually misses family occasions.

Twenty minutes later, the food arrives. I watch my dad stick his fork into one piece of meat, one piece of potato, and one piece of veg, then chew each mouthful exactly forty times. When my brother Blair is around he chews exactly in time. It's quite a sight.

My mum picks delicately at her salad, which looks like the leftovers of a pruned hedge. She's is a very sophisticated eater and always knows when she has a piece of foliage between her teeth.

I try to keep an eye out for the waitress. I want her to come back so I can try and find a fault in her. She looked too perfect. Long legs, wavy hair, dark eyes, wide hips, firm ass, flat stomach, tight shirt, tanned skin. If a woman that perfect fell in love with me, I'd probably feel ill.

The harp lady moves her fingers from string to string, brushing each one with precise pressure. She has her eyes half closed and I'm pretty sure she spends the morning licking her own reflection on the bathroom mirror. Then I notice she's got a huge birthmark on the back of her neck. It looks like she's had a hicky from a Doberman and I spend the rest of the evening gazing at her instead.

FAMILY AFFAIRS

from the novel by Judith Cameron

She had expected the phone call but not the news. Her knees melted. She sank to the bed beside the unopened suitcase. The fiesta sounding through the open window faded. Dry eyes and a haggard face stared at her from the wall-length mirror: a head hung between slouched shoulders, lips cracked open between jowled cheeks, dull hair straggling at the neckline of a creased, beige shirt. Her head swivelled, her gaze roaming the monochrome room until it rested on Dali's depiction of the Minotaur. For moments that could have been minutes, she felt herself drawn into its darkness. She became the monster with crimson tongue and claws spilling the contents of its womb.

Monday, 7 February 2000

Sarah was not a morning person and never had been. But looking through the kitchen window at the clear blue sky, she felt wonderful. It was one of those dazzling winter days when the sun bounces out of the sky to create the illusion that green shoots are about to appear on grey branches.

She held a mug of coffee between her hands, feeling its warmth as she watched the bare trees bow to the wind in obedience. It blew down the chimney rattling the windows, but she still enjoyed the relative silence of the house.

Leisurely, she skimmed the newspaper and drank her coffee. Drawn by a photo of an elderly woman, she read the accompanying story of a mother's prosecution for murdering her brain-damaged son. She claimed to have killed him out of love because he no longer had a life, merely an existence. There was a deep sadness in the woman's eyes that made Sarah shudder before folding the newspaper.

Gathering the detritus from the children's breakfast, she turned her mind to the next family meal. After taking onions and chuck steak from the bottom of the fridge, she rummaged in the pantry for garlic and a bottle of red wine.

With a few stale rashers of bacon, a beef bourguignon was quickly assembled and tucked into the bottom oven of the Aga for that night's dinner. After a cursory wipe down of work surfaces, she made her way upstairs for a shower. The phone rang. She continued to the landing where she picked up the reproduction bakelite receiver to the delay of a callbox.

'Mum,' said Miles. 'Really sorry; I forgot my games kit. Can you drop it off?'

'All the way to the sports field?' Sarah calculated the extra twenty minutes this would add to her journey. At least when he moves school, she thought, it'll be just up the road. The letter had only recently arrived confirming that Miles had won a scholarship to prestigious King's, and its recollection still made Sarah feel warm inside. She liked to think the children were having opportunities she and Owen had been denied.

Fifteen minutes later, in tailored beige trousers and a dark green cashmere jumper, she headed back down the stairs, Miles's sports bag in hand. She checked herself in the large hallway mirror. Sarah had never been a beauty but she was reasonably attractive. She maintained a trim figure, good skin tone and large blue eyes. Her bobbed hair was expertly cut and shiny; her face was lightly made up and she wore discreet diamond studs in her ears. Smoothing a few stray hairs, she knew that her outward appearance conveyed more confidence than she usually felt.

She was in the cloakroom, collecting jacket and briefcase, mentally listing the day ahead when she heard the front door open.

'It's a gale out there!' A gust of wind blew Ellie through the inner glass doors. 'And I might as well have stayed home: Mrs P's off sick.' She dropped her school bag on the flagstone floor, and shrugged off her fitted black suede coat, brushing past Sarah to hang it up. At seventeen, Ellie still had a gamine shape, her poise and manner of dress defining her age rather than her figure. She looked elegant in a short grey skirt and jersey, tights and high heels. Her thick dark hair, almost frizzy by nature, had been tamed into luscious curls that framed her face. With almond-shaped blue eyes, high cheek bones and a full mouth arranged on a clear complexion, people frequently commented to Sarah on the striking looks of her elder daughter.

'You've not forgotten tonight?' Ellie walked back into the hallway. 'Make sure Dad's not late.'

'We'll be fine; I've already put supper on.' Sarah buttoned up her jacket and felt for the car keys in the pocket. 'I'm off; are you going back to school later?'

'I've got a chemistry module to hand in before the end of the week.' Ellie picked her bag up and walked into the kitchen. 'And Caron said she'd be here in a bit so we can do a run through together; I had to put a new reed in my clarinet.' She turned round, hugging the bag to her slim body and grinned. 'Just think, Mum, this time next week, I'll be in New York!'

'I do wish you were coming with us instead.' Although Ellie was grown up and sensible, it was so difficult learning to let go of her beautiful girl. Especially when she was going to be meeting up with a man old enough to be her father. Sarah walked across and quickly hugged her. 'I just love you too much. I'll be worried. See you later.'

With keys in one hand, briefcase and holdall in the other, Sarah opened the front door to the violent wind. Despite the radiant sky, it felt like a freezing tornado was trying to rip open her jacket and cut into her face. She clicked her car keys and ran down the steps to the blue Audi.

By the time she had reached the main road, the car was comfortably warm. With the familiar voice of Jeremy Paxman on *Start the Week*, Sarah began to feel ready to start her own. It was going to be busy.

She drew into her parking space on the southern outskirts of the city where the surrounding concrete buildings offered little visual contrast in colour or texture to the smooth surface of the treeless car park. Sarah sighed as she reached for her briefcase, wondering again how permission was ever obtained for such monotonous structures on the slopes of a beautifully unspoilt valley.

She was buffeted by the wind for only a few paces before pushing open the plate glass door to Jameson Partners, Designers and Manufacturers of Fine Upholstered Furniture. The entrance foyer was an exhibition space as well as the company reception area. It was as impersonal and lacklustre as an airport passenger lounge. Simply laid out with a few chairs and sofas carefully positioned so their occupants could gaze on wall displays of other Jameson creations, it was boring and devoid of character. Owen assured her that the streamlined, minimalist design conveyed the perfect message to prospective clients. Given the continuing growth of the business, she concluded he was probably right. She glanced around to check everything was in its place before walking through an open door into the office behind.

Jane was on the phone, fiddling with her half-moon glasses; she and Sarah smiled a hello to each other. The glasses were a recent acquisition that Jane seemed incapable of leaving alone. If she wasn't shifting them up and down the bridge of her nose, she was chewing one of the arms, or hooking them into her heavily back-combed hair. Jane had worked with Sarah and Owen since the early eighties and was almost part of the fixtures. Interior design had changed a lot since then, but Jane remained firmly Laura Ashley with her matronly figure and flowery prints that stood rather incongruously beside the clean lines of the black modular work stations, steel-framed furniture and vertical blinds of the Jameson offices.

Sarah turned on her computer and started to tackle the morning's post as Jane put the phone down.

'That was Munich confirming the additional lighting for the exhibition. You can have access for setting up on the Tuesday afternoon.' She resettled her glasses and wrinkled her nose. 'Good weekend?'

'Mmm, s'pose so. I left Ellie at home practising for a school concert to-night. She's getting excited about her trip to New York. How about you?' Sarah continued to work through the pile of paperwork, refusing to be sidelined by the glasses or the idea of Richard Newland waiting in New York.

'It seems strange her going away without Alex,' Jane said. 'Being twins, they must find it hard.' She sighed before turning to her own computer screen. 'Right. Not much on today but the ALC buyer's here tomorrow. Woods for lunch?'

'Make it for 12.30.' With an invoice in her hand, Sarah stood up. 'If you need me, I'll either be with Owen or in the workshop.'

Going back through reception, she walked straight across to an opposite door and entered a broad corridor. With light streaming through windows set into the pitched roof, it was immediately a more interesting space than the reception. Photographs of furniture production were hung along the length of the windowless walls, like square portholes in a rectangular ship.

The first room on the left was Owen's office. She found him on a high stool at his drawing board, back to the door. Despite being leant forward, Owen sat with his shoulders still broad and square; he never hunched or slouched. A few dark curls touched with grey licked the collar of a pale blue cotton shirt. He never wore jeans to work but rarely wore a suit either. Today he had on navy moleskin trousers that Sarah had chosen; blue suited his lean, solid build.

Miles Davis played softly in the background. Owen looked up as she got closer. He still did preliminary sketches by hand and the drawing board was adjacent to a large window. It offered far-reaching views towards the Mendips; whatever the season, the fields, woods and hedges of the rolling hills always provided a wonderful landscape. Owen claimed it was his muse. Putting his pencil down, he softly placed his arm around Sarah's hips and drew their heads together.

'What do you think?' he asked. In front of him was a large sheet of white paper with a sketch of a sofa frame that Owen had been working on for some time. 'By adding this piece here,' he continued, pointing to a shaded oblong, 'it will give much more stability along the whole of the back.'

'Right.' She kissed his temple. 'But I'm more concerned about the here and now.' Placing the invoice on his drawing she asked, 'I thought this fabric was snagged; didn't we return it?'

He quickly scanned the sheet of paper. 'I reckon that's for the stuff that arrived on Friday. Check with Martin. And we'll probably need more – it'll only take a couple of exhibition orders.' Swinging his chair around, he stepped down towards a large oval desk and reached across for a file, handing it to Sarah. 'The show pieces were collected this morning. I was thinking that if we leave here on Friday, we can have some skiing with the kids and still get to the trade fair first thing on Monday.'

'Apparently, setting up's on Tuesday.' She leaned against the desk and flicked through the file before handing it back. 'I do wish Ellie was coming too.'

'It'll be fine.' Owen put the file down and took Sarah's face in his hands. 'It will.' He looked into her eyes. 'Alex and Miles can help out – Leah will find the whole thing an adventure. It'll be a good week.'

'Yeah, but knackering... ' Sarah kissed him briefly on the lips before making her way to the door. 'We've got ALC here tomorrow. And this evening, it's Ellie's concert. I promised we wouldn't be late.'

'No problem.' Owen returned to the drawing board. 'I even remembered to phone Simon and cancel squash.'

She continued along the corridor to the workshop. The sound of Kylie Minogue could easily be heard above the din of cutters, staplers and sewing machines. It was a large barn-like room buzzing with energy that reminded Sarah of a Lowry painting, busy with people on the move. Her experienced eye immediately took in the breadth of activity. She found Martin effortlessly shifting an enormous wooden frame.

'How's it going?' she asked, approaching the khaki-overalled foreman.

'These should be ready by the time you get back from Germany.' He indicated to the skeletons of several sofas and armchairs. 'And we've been promised the frames for the ALC order later today.'

'Good timing,' Sarah said. 'Their buyer's here tomorrow. Is this for the fabric in on Friday?' She gave him the invoice.

'I'll check.' Martin glided his bulk effortlessly through a maze of half built sofas rather like a teddy bear on skates and came to a gentle halt next to several plastic-covered giant rolls of fabric.

Sarah followed. 'We're not leaving till the end of the week, but I won't be in after Wednesday. Can you check it's OK before then?'

Looking at large labels pasted on to each roll of fabric, Martin passed the paper back to Sarah. 'No problem – yes, that's the right invoice.'

'Thanks.' Sarah hummed to the Kylie number, 'I Should be so Lucky', still playing as she left the workshop, and she laughed to herself at being able to enjoy such a song.

Seeing every window in the house lit and the twins' little red car in the driveway, Sarah guessed all the children were home as she turned into the drive. Although it was only five-thirty, the sky was dark and the wind still whistled through the bare trees. Letting herself in, she felt the welcome of the house envelop her and wished there was time for a glass of wine before dinner.

She opened the living room door to the four children watching TV, sprawled across sofas and the floor.

'Hi.' There were a couple of empty crisp packets and glasses on the carpet that she chose to ignore. 'Sorry, but we've got to eat early. Leah, can you come and lay the table please?' Grunting a response, the nine-year-old slowly rose to her feet and grudgingly made her way to the door and out into the hallway.

'Can I have an apple?' She followed Sarah into the kitchen.

'Have one after supper.' Sarah rinsed her hands at the sink.

'Why is it always me who has to lay the table?' Leah leaned her body over the table.

'Don't whinge.' Sarah deftly reached for a pack of half-baked baguettes from the freezer and placed them in the top oven of the Aga. In the fridge, she searched for the contents of a salad before looking up to see Leah doodling over a photo on the newspaper. She took a deep breath. 'I want the table laid now.'

Leah put the newspaper on the dresser before fumbling in a drawer for napkins.

'Mum, I'll make the salad if you like, though I couldn't eat before the concert.' Sarah hadn't heard Ellie walk into the room, but was grateful for the offer. 'We'll leave you some for later,' she replied.

'Is Dad back yet?' Ellie opened a bag of lettuce leaves.

'He shouldn't be long – I left him checking some despatch stuff.' Sarah checked the time before walking across to a cork wall board. In one corner was a large black and white photo of the family in skiwear on top of some mountain the previous winter. Sarah liked the feeling of unity the picture conveyed and had never got round to putting it away. Other photos, postcards, lists and reminders were randomly pinned up, along with the two concert tickets. Sarah heard the front door close and, a moment later, Owen walked into the kitchen.

'Daddy!' Leah left a handful of cutlery on the table and, pushing her arms under the flaps of his jacket and around his waist, cuddled into his chest. He returned the hug and her pigtailed head almost disappeared into the folds of dark brown corduroy. All that could be seen of her was the navy skirt and tights of her school uniform with outsized animal slippers on her feet – two grey hippos.

'That smells good,' he said as he released Leah. 'And I'm famished.' After a brief kiss to Sarah, he came up behind Ellie, leaning his chin on her shoulder. She was snipping spring onions into the salad bowl.

'I'm looking forward to a virtuoso performance this evening.' He hesitated for a moment. 'Courtney Pine's 'Children of the Ghetto', OK?'

'In your dreams,' she replied half laughing. 'More on the classical side, me thinks.'

'Why can't I come?' Leah was walking round the table, placing cutlery with imprecision beside the plates. 'I don't see why it's only for adults.'

'We've only got two tickets.' Sarah turned to Owen.

'Can you call Miles and Alex? It's time we ate.' Basket in hand, she bent to retrieve the bread from the oven.

'There's loads of people in the orchestra, Leah,' Ellie explained. 'So it was only two tickets each. I'm sorry.'

'Can I wait up till you get home?' Leah hugged Ellie, who looked across to

Sarah for an answer.

'It's school tomorrow, Leah. Bed by nine.' Sarah carried the casserole to the table.

Owen laid his hand on Sarah's arm as they jostled their way through the entrance of the school chapel. She was hoping to sit far enough forward to get a good view of Ellie, but not so close as to make her more nervous. There were many other parents she knew, by sight if not by name, and she felt she was nodding like a clockwork dog by the time they sat down. It wasn't warm and she kept her jacket on as she craned her neck to find Ellie in the mêlée. The girls all wore white blouses and black skirts, seemingly impervious to the cold, and it took a moment before spying Ellie's distinctive hair.

The concert got under way. Sarah glanced around the chapel with its ornate candlesticks and carved wooden pews, thinking of the countless school performances she and Owen had attended there over the years. She tried to ignore the inadvertent squeals, screeches and missed beats of the various ensembles as they plodded through the programme. She knew that, as it advanced, the compositions would become more recognisable and that Ellie's solo with Caron accompanying on piano was the finale. But instead of enjoying the evening as the music improved, she felt progressively anxious for her daughter. Despite the lack of heating, and the freezing weather outside, by the time Ellie stood up, Sarah had taken off her jacket; she felt hot and sticky.

Ellie gracefully carried her music stand to a suitable distance from Caron and the grand piano. She stood up straight and lifted her hair over her shoulders and out of the way of the clarinet, which she brought up to her pursed lips. Sarah thought she could see Ellie's legs tremble below the short black skirt as she looked towards the pianist. Sarah closed her eyes to Mozart's concerto.

She had heard the long low notes and vibrant trills played over and over during the hours of practice. She knew which parts could make Ellie stumble and felt her heart race as they approached. But to Sarah's ears, the playing was exquisite, faultless.

Ellie had no plans for a musical career – her dream had always been to become a doctor. Early on, she had discovered she needed to work hard to achieve her ambitions. As a result, she was well organised and diligent. Sarah remembered Ellie explaining to Alex that 'the more you put into something, the more you get out of it'. She and Alex were about fifteen at the time and Sarah had been impressed by the sagacity of the remark. Ellie's offer for medicine had been hard won. Even so, she was an accomplished musician and her careful interpretation had not let her down.

As the concerto finished, Ellie bowed, grinning radiantly, and acknowledged Caron. The audience was rapturous in its applause. This was from gratitude that the long evening was finally over as much for her daughter's performance, but Sarah was still immensely proud. Looking across at Owen who was pumping his hands, she knew he felt the same.

When the clapping died and people started to leave, Ellie pushed through the crowd, instrument still in hand.

'Well?' she gasped. 'Was I all right?'

'All right?' Owen rubbed his chin, as if considering the question seriously. 'I suppose it was all right.'

'He means you were fantastic.' Sarah touched Ellie's face and held it close to her own. She could feel the huge wave of love and pride pass through to her daughter like an electric current. Both sets of eyes were shining as the two heads separated. No words were needed.

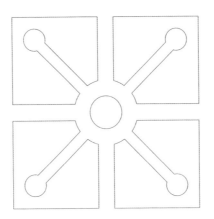

INTAGLIO

from the novel by Vincent Cassar

Vignette

Intaglio is a way of printing. It is derived from a Latin word meaning 'to cut into'. When you take a blank plate and make marks upon it, the deeper the marks the blacker the lines produced. I have found it is similar to how I learn to love. The lines that cut me deepest are those that were made earliest.

As children, we are taught about love by our parents. The family environment we are brought up in, the examples they give us of how to express love, what love means, and how we receive it, are all lessons firmly embedded in our psyche. We can add to the once blank slate of ourselves as we get older. Our first lovers, our children, and subsequent emotional experiences that carve out our emotional map, are all part of the eventual picture of who we become.

This story is about my journey from the emotionally bleak landscape of my childhood, through my troubled adult relationships, to the peace I have found in latter life. This is my story of how I became an artist and how I learnt to love.

Impressions

The whole day was in darkness. We were on our way to the asylum to see my dad. We had taken a bus and left the pushchair behind. Mum and I were walking down the busy main road. I was tired and irritable. She let go of my hand and I felt panicky. I wanted to wail. Her head was high above me and she seemed hard and distant as she walked by my side. It started to rain again. My head was exposed and all the raindrops felt like tiny cuts. Lorries thundered by and caught us with their spray.

She let my hand slip into hers as we went up some steps into a big grey building. As we went through the wooden doors, I touched the polished brass handles and listened to the echoing sound of our footsteps on the chequered tile floor. I heard the stiff rustle of the nurse's uniform as she approached.

'Salvu Camilleri?' she asked. 'This way.'

We followed her down the hall and passed through a door. I gazed up at my mum for reassurance, but she looked concentrated, as though her whole self were being distilled, down to the last drop. A feeble foreign man was there to greet us, sitting in a chair, large and distinct. His face showed a mixture of tears and joy.

Words passed between them on the state of my health and size. He held me tightly in his arms and all I could think of was suffocation. The odour of another world clung to my nostrils, his red jumper smelt musty, his black hair greased and pungent.

He let me go and I leapt into my mum's lap, as though on a spring. I stared at this man as he spoke. He was older than anyone I had ever seen before. He had rough olive skin and black hair. I saw flashes of gold in his mouth as he talked. His brown eyes were watery and weak and his chin had a small indent.

He said he had made me a rocking horse and pointed to the corner of the room. He had a thick foreign accent and it was difficult to work out what he was saying. Perhaps the horse was in the room already and he wanted me to ride it. It was incongruous, a shiny wooden monstrosity whose appearance and motion seemed to ridicule me. It was a *mocking* horse. Mum asked me if I wanted to sit on it. I did not want to leave her and I couldn't even shake my head to refuse. I just stared back at this man's expectant eyes. The gravity of his disappointment told in his face and I felt I had let him down. He suddenly went somewhere else and it was as though an internal darkness had escaped.

They started talking again while I looked around. Strange men wandered about in their pyjamas, or sat on chairs like dead souls. One man was staring out of the window and running his finger along the pane. Someone else was singing loudly and I heard the noise of a vague protest. They radiated a crazy chaos, which made their madness seem exotic. It felt as though I was watching them in another reality. I glanced back at my dad and wondered if he was the same as them.

When we came to leave, he kissed me with his fleshy mouth and I smelt the smoky sour breath against my cheek. He made my face itch with his rough beard and scratchy clothes. When he looked at me, his eyes suggested a hidden knowledge I could not deny. I squirmed, attempting to resist him. He stood up to kiss mum goodbye and I noticed he was smaller than her. It didn't seem right, somehow.

As we walked out, I peeked back into the room. He had sat back down in his chair and he looked like an invalid, lost and discordant. My mum grasped my hand and we left. It was still raining.

'I need to go to the shop, Sammy,' Mum said. 'Will you be all right on your own?'

I said nothing. She picked me up and pointed to Dipino's, the corner shop across the road. 'I am just going to Dip's. I won't be long. OK?' I nodded, with wide-open eyes and clenched mouth. 'That's it; be a brave boy for Mummy. I'll get you some sweeties.'

She put me down on the floor and walked out the front door. The flat was suddenly huge. The furniture towered above me, the air empty and vast. I peered into the darkened hallway; shadows were cast, big enough to hide anything. The distance between the front door and me seemed enormous. My mum was gone, the clocks ticked on, yet silence filled the air.

Something terrible could happen to her on the way to the shops. She could fall down the stairs, get eaten by a monster or simply slip out of the universe and cease to exist. I needed to see her on her way across the road. I pushed a dining chair nearer the window and climbed on to it. I was too small to see out and the windowsill was too slim for me to get on to. All I could see was sky. A blanket of grey like a lid shut fast on my world. I looked around. I hadn't seen the room from this angle before. It worried me. Everything appeared different, as though the colours were diluting. I sank back to the floor.

The shiny plastic of the lino flooring felt cold beneath my bare legs. I reached out my hand and picked up Edward, my teddy. He had light, golden, slightly threadbare fur and a look of permanent surprise. I hugged him tight. The sideboard creaked, its wood cracking and splintering, about to break into life. My heart beat hard inside my chest; my head started feeling fuzzy. I could feel the blood coursing through my body as though it were about to overflow. I tried to stand up, but gravity held me down. The air was solid and impenetrable. I felt I didn't have the right to exist without my mum's presence. Tears were pushing at my eyelids; balls of muscle were forcing themselves down my throat.

Eventually I managed to get to my feet. I stood there shaking, ready and waiting for the moment I could run to her, but it was like standing in water. I held on to the thought of her return. Her smile, her kiss, the warm hug of her arms. Nuzzling into her snug body, like trying to climb back into the womb. My heart was beating even harder now, wondering just how much longer she would be.

I heard a noise outside the front door. It was her. I tossed Edward aside and went running toward it. But it wasn't her. It was the loud clack clack of someone else's shoes on the stone landing outside. It was so close I could probably open up the letterbox and see them as they passed. The thought of the outside world being within touching distance frightened me. I didn't want anyone else. I wanted my mum. But now I was in the hallway, far too close to the danger. I ran back to the front room and jumped to the floor. I picked up Edward again, and started pounding his hollow stomach. Repeatedly whispering, 'Mummy, come back'.

I heard the click of a key in the door and almost exploded with relief. Still I stayed motionless. She walked in and I lifted up my arms. She patted my head and pressed some sweets into my hand. She set up the ironing board and went to work on a pile of washing.

'Were you OK, Sammy?' she asked.

I said nothing, not wanting to let her down.

Jimmy Greaves was my dad, for a while. Until I knew better. While he was away in the asylum, I slept in a cot by the window in my parents' bedroom. There were two pictures next to me. The first was a black furry cat made of felt, which I used to rub my finger on for comfort. I could just get to it through the thickly painted, white, wooden bars, which had turned yellow with cigarette smoke and age. The other was of a footballer with a white jersey and Mediterranean appearance.

We had no photographs of my real dad, so my mum told me he looked like Jimmy Greaves and hung this picture by my cot. I thought this meant my dad was a footballer too, and the longer he stayed away the more the two became enmeshed in my mind. I would stare at it just before sleeping and conjure up glories I couldn't properly imagine. Initially, when Dad came out of the asylum a part of me still thought he was a footballer, so I was disappointed he was just going out to work in a factory all day. Wouldn't he have preferred to be playing for England?

When my dad returned I was displaced. Unexpectedly arriving like a doubtful guest, he was not just in the family home; he was in my bedroom too. He returned to sleep in my mum's bed and I was moved out of the comfort zone and into the hostile den of my elder brother, Frank. Now I became separate from my mum and just another one of her children. She would never kiss me goodnight again. She would say, 'Good night. God bless,' to the pair of us from the doorway. She might as well have been shouting through the letterbox. I missed the warm touch of her breath, the smell of her soft cheeks, and my arms around her neck. I hugged Edward tighter instead, but it wasn't the same.

From then on, everything became different. There was heaviness in the air, there were whispered conversations, there were things to be done that hadn't been done before. It became the time to be serious. My mum had less time for me, and all our meals were sullen events. Dad would sit in judgement and misery in the corner of the room or at the head of the table. His grim face scowling, his dark mood glowering through his olive skin. It seemed every time my mum reached out to do something there was the harsh bark of his voice like a whip cracking down on fun, love, spontaneity or care. She spoke to him with a solemn face. Where once my world was down around the floor, it all now took place miles above me.

My name changed as well. My dad called me Salvu, like him, which was Maltese for Sam. But, while he was away, my mum had been calling me her 'little Sammy'. I liked that.

When my dad was angry, he would push his knuckle into his mouth as though trying to bite away the fury. One time he caught me putting my finger into the electrical socket. We had a two-way plug; the live pins came out from the brown casing plugged into the wall. Frank dared me to stick my fingers in. So I did. The current ran through me sharp and fast like an express train. My mum appeared in the doorway and screamed at the sight of my supine body. I jumped up to show her I was all right. My dad responded to all this commotion with a thud and a grunt, and before I could blame Frank I knew I had to run.

He removed his belt as I backed off. Standing, cowering in the hallway, I was rapidly running out of room. I felt my back against the front door. Maybe I could run away, go back to the time when my dad wasn't around. Fear coursed through my body. He was shouting in that odd language of his and biting his hairy knuckles. He came down the hallway at me, a beast of rage. I was too scared to cry, too uncertain to know what to do. My mum was standing to one side holding on to my brother for protection. I cried out, 'Mummy!' But she stayed still, as terrified as I felt.

'We are going to hide the Christmas things in here,' my mum said as she put a brightly coloured box in the sideboard, behind some blankets. I watched her. Christmas wasn't for months, yet she was already buying extra provisions. That was exciting. 'Don't tell your father,' she added.

'OK,' I said, feeling heavy with the responsibility. I was confused as to why I could be trusted with such a secret but my dad couldn't. I knew that I mustn't let her down, though. She looked serious.

As I watched her take out another colourful box of sweets from her bag and put them away, I felt the need for something, so I asked for a biscuit.

She sighed. 'You won't be able to have biscuits when you go to school,' she said.

I stood, anxiously wondering how I was going to cope. I didn't want to go to school if I couldn't eat biscuits whenever I wanted. I followed her into the kitchen. It was a dark room. There was a small window to the left, but it didn't appear to let in much light. A coal cupboard was in one corner and there was a bath across the back wall. A hinged board came down over it like a door. Frank and I joked about having a bath while we were eating our tea.

Mum got down a familiar dull red tin and brought out a Jammie Dodger. She came down to my height and held it out. Just as I was about to take it she said, 'Biscuit or kiss?'

I wanted both. I didn't want to have to choose. To be so close to a biscuit and yet not have it was unbearable. I could already taste its sticky red sweetness and sugary butter.

'Biscuit or kiss?' she said again and pursed her lips, while holding back the biscuit.

Of course, I wanted a kiss, as well. That's all I ever wanted. It was an impossible choice and so unfair. I couldn't think of the right answer as the blood rushed around my head. I could feel myself blushing.

'I... I...' I managed to stutter, my lips trembling. I hoped mum would take pity on me and issue me with both.

Finally, she laughed and said, 'I know what you want.' And as I went to open my arms for a hug, she placed the biscuit in my hand and stood up.

Because mum had no willpower, I knew that if I were not able to get what I wanted, she would always give me something to eat. She used to feed me a lot. Every stressful situation was met with an edible treat. It started with Carnation milk, when I was still a baby. She would give me the sickly, creamy, liquid straight from the tin whenever I got irritable. It progressed to biscuits or cake whenever she could not give me her attention. She worked in a cake factory so she was always bringing home cakes, practically on a daily basis.

Frank was small-framed while I was large, and even though he was five years older and taller it seemed as though I ate all his food as well as my own. He used to call me 'Fat Sam' and I hated it. But whenever I told mum she would just give me a biscuit. I decided if I couldn't have kisses or kind words, Granny cake would do, or a Garibaldi or a marshmallow. The next treat became the only thing to look forward to.

When the parcel arrived from Malta, even my dad looked excited. I marvelled at the fact that it had come all the way across the seas. Malta meant nothing to me; it was just a strange place where dad belonged. When he spoke his foreign words, they sounded odd. He would make a throaty noise like a choking camel or say phoney phrases that weren't real talk. It made me hate him more.

He had started teaching me a few expressions, but I was reluctant. It was only fear that made me learn how to greet him with *bon_u* every morning, or say a garbled, *jekk jog_bok* at the end of each request. *Grazzi* was required constantly, as was *sku_i*, whenever we passed wind or wanted to pass by. I also learnt other words, but that was only because I heard them so often. Words such as *Ieqaf*, which meant 'stop'; *Le* – 'no'; and *Haqq Madonna*, which was something too rude to mention.

Because of his Maltese accent, it was sometimes difficult to work out what he was saying. There were certain English words he couldn't say properly. Birthday, for instance. He would say *Bird-day* instead, like a Sicilian hood. I think Mum was embarrassed by his inability to pronounce English correctly and she didn't like being singled out.

We rarely got post from anyone, so the arrival of a parcel was a very special occasion. We all gathered round my dad, as the package was unwrapped. It was covered in lots of brown paper and was so big it could have contained a football. When the paper was off, a bright red tin was revealed with scenes of a port with lots of ships and palm trees all around. Mum remarked how nice it

VINCENT CASSAR

was, but we were all more interested in knowing what was inside.

It was from my dad's sister, Annette; she had stayed with us at some point and she was now sending him some of the things he missed from home. Mum tried to cook the food he liked, but he always said it didn't taste the same, as though her English ways tainted the Maltese ingredients. And, of course, no one could make *pastizzis* like his mother. That was the first time I tried *kaghak tal-Ghasel*, which were rings of treacle in dough that tasted sad and dusty. There was some *biskuttini tal-lewz* (macaroons) and *pizzulati tal-Qastan* (chestnut fingers) too. I didn't think that any of them had survived the journey well. They had been sent weeks before and tasted stale. Our joy turned to dis-appointment, but even more so for my dad, as he read the letter from Auntie Annette.

He had tears down his cheeks as he said, 'My mother has died and these are the cakes they had at her funeral.' I watched, shocked, as the crumbly, tired dough fell from his mouth to the plate.

WALK ON WATER

from the novel by Kristin-Marie Combs

One

Daniel and Marta O'Shea's most generous contribution to society was keeping the neighbourhood property taxes low.

They graduated from the same high school, on the outskirts of Los Angeles, in 1946. A year later they ran into one another at a minor city official's re-election party and began dating. Eventually, the two were wed at St Dominic's, the city's flashiest Polish Catholic Church. The wedding was thrown by Marta's elderly parents, who could not have been happier than to see their only child wrapped in ruffles and wed to a nice Irish Catholic boy.

Mrs O'Shea, Daniel's mother, smiled all evening, enjoyed the free fancy beer, and remained completely oblivious to the eyebrow raises she received from the other guests.The wedding was one of the few successful days of the O'Shea's relationship.

Within a year of Marta and Daniel's marriage, when the newly weds had not yet used up the superficial amount of love they had for one another, their first and only child, Cindy, was conceived. However, by the time the time the baby arrived, all the china, tools, and kitchen appliances that were received as wedding gifts had lost their novelty, and so had the bride and groom in the eyes of each other.

Two

Marta O'Shea was a beautiful woman – tall, thin, and naturally blonde with sharp, petite features that announced her Polish descent. She was a member of every women's league in the area and made sure she had a gathering to attend each evening, even if she had to organise it herself. Marta would put little Cindy to bed with air-kisses and palm pats that would spare her fresh make-up and manicure, say goodbye to her husband, then go out cheerfully into the night.

Soft, feminine compact clicks would often lead Cindy to the small bathroom. She would sit crossed-legged in her pajamas on the white, wicker hamper and watch Marta prepare for her nightly engagements. Her mother was always in a good mood before she went out. She had more to say to her daughter and never got irritated by the four-year-old's questions. Department store perfume and puffs of Avon powder would cloud Marta's image and fill Cindy's senses as she sat on the hamper and spoke to her mother's reflection.

'What's this?' Cindy asked from the top of the laundry hamper. Marta's costume jewellery bag was open on Cindy's lap. She had been told to find something red.

'What's what, honey?' her mother responded. Marta stared at the mirror while surrounding her head in multiple halos of hairspray.

'This,' Cindy coughed, holding up a ceramic pastel pin.

'That is one of Momma's brooches, honey, you know that.'

'But what is it?' Cindy said. 'What's it supposed to be?'

Her mother looked confused for a second, and then laughed. 'It's not supposed to be anything, honey, it's just a design. It's just supposed to look pretty.'

'Oh,' Cindy said looking at the abstract shape. She still didn't understand.

'So have you found Momma anything red yet?' Marta asked, putting on a final coat of lipstick and smiling broadly in the mirror. 'I need the prettiest red thing you can find.' Marta clipped the plastic tube back together and began clearing the cosmetics that were spread across the counter. 'Julia is always so fashionably dressed. Momma does not want to get lost in the crowd of ladies at dinner tonight, now, does she?' Marta turned from the mirror to see what Cindy had chosen.

Cindy held two pins out to her mother, one in each palm.

Marta looked at the first pin and grimaced, 'Oh no, honey, that one's orange, not red.' She took the offending pin from Cindy's hand and laughed. 'What a faux pas that would have been! We are lucky Momma's better at her colours than you are, aren't we dear?' Marta threw the pin back in the bag. 'But this one will be perfect,' she said as she took the other brooch, a bunch of red wire and rhinestone forget-me-nots, from Cindy's palm and held it up to her dress in the mirror. 'Perfect, perfect, perfect,' Marta said as she gave her hair a gentle shake to test the hairspray application. 'You found one that matches Momma's lipstick as well, Cindy. What a good little girl you are.'

The four-year-old smiled at the praise as Marta fastened the brooch to the front of her full-skirted shirt-dress.

'Yeah, the other one was orange,' Cindy said.

Marta straightened her collar, smoothed her outfit and grabbed the white cotton gloves she had left on the counter. 'All right, honey, off the hamper and out we go. It's time for bed.' Marta shooed her daughter from the bathroom and went to find her handbag. 'In bed, Cindy,' she called from the front room. Cindy could hear her mother checking her purse for keys as she climbed under the covers.

'I'll come say goodnight in a second, honey,' Marta called. More rumbling. 'Daniel, do you know where my house keys are?' Cindy's father had just returned from work. 'Ope, never mind. I found them. I always place them in that little pocket so I won't lose them, but I forget they're there every night!' The gathering and organising continued. 'Lord-a mercy,' Marta suddenly burst out, 'Look at the time! It's almost seven-thirty. I'm going to be late!' The clicking of her mother's heels on the tile got faster. 'Cindy's in bed and your dinner is warming in the oven. I have to run.' A jingle, a snap and the side door slammed.

'Momma?' Cindy called from her bedroom. 'Momma, I'm in bed.'

Daniel begrudgingly lifted his green eyes from the evening paper and looked towards the calls of his daughter. He got up and checked the progress of his dinner in the oven. It would just be a minute. He ran his hand through his dark hair and leaned back against the oven. He'd wait until it was ready.

Cindy stared at the textured white ceiling of her bedroom for as long as she could keep her eyes open, but within fifteen minutes they slid closed.

When Daniel remembered his daughter he was halfway through his reheated, pan-fried steak. 'Shoot,' he said and putting down his silverware. He walked down the hall to the child's bedroom. A few blonde curls stuck out between the white pillowcase and a thick pink comforter. Cindy was already asleep. Daniel pulled the nursery door closed and went back to his dinner.

Three

As the months went on, the soft evening compact clicks became a chaotic fury. Perfume filled not only the bathroom, but the rest of the house as well. Cindy stopped perching herself on the hamper because her mother was no longer in a good mood before she went out. Marta never wanted Cindy to help clasp a bracelet or hold a mirror so she could see the back of her hair. And she definitely did not want anyone to talk to, so Cindy had lost her role in the evening routine.

Marta began visiting different doctors every week. Cindy spent hours playing in waiting rooms, but she liked the time she would be left there. Every office had different toys and the receptionists were always nice. They gave her peppermints and talked with her much more than anyone else did. Sometimes other children would come into the waiting area with their parents and Cindy would have a friend to play with for a bit. She didn't have friends to play with at home. All the other kids on her block were at least six years older than her and she wouldn't start school for another year. Cindy always wished she could stay a little longer with the friendly receptionists and other children. But when Marta came out of the doctor's examination room, Cindy knew it was time to leave.

Marta woke up and went to bed in a bad mood. Her eyes always looked tired. She snapped at both her husband and child with little or no provocation. Over the months Marta's shoulders slid forward and her back began to arch. She cursed her doctors and looked through the phone book for new ones – screeching at her husband when he mentioned money. She no longer sat tall on the edge of the chair while she ate, but leaned heavily on her right forearm. The medicine cabinet was cleared of cosmetics and filled with pill bottles the doctors had given her.

For a while Marta would simply gather her handbag and leave. Then slowly a new routine emerged. She would dress then sit alone in the kitchen, hunched over a martini or glass of wine, and stare at the wall. When she had finished a drink or two she would fill a small purse flask and walk out the door.

Once the new routine was established, Cindy was tempted to climb up on an empty kitchen chair and try to talk with her mother like they had done in the bathroom. But with a five-year-old's intuition, Cindy could sense it was not a good idea.

By the time Cindy turned seven Marta avoided everyone, including herself, and her husband didn't care to challenge her behaviour. The teetering towers of liquor bottles were rivalled only by growing stacks of pizza boxes.

As Marta's 'Goodnight's turned into 'Go to bed's, Cindy's father began working much later into the evening. Daniel worked as a field manager at the local aggregate yard, so working late wasn't difficult to do. He made sure to return home after Marta had left for the night.

Cindy sat in the living room watching *I Love Lucy* on the small black and white television. She was hungry. Marta had stopped preparing dinner for the family on the nights she was gone. Cindy stood in front of the pantry looking for something to eat. Crackers didn't seem appealing so she decided she would wait for pizza. Cindy heard Daniel's car pull into the driveway and skittered off to her bedroom. She lay awake in her bed, playing with her stuffed animals and listening to her dad rustle around the house. Then she heard Toni, the neighbourhood pizza man's son, come to the door. Cindy liked Toni. In her nightgown, she ran on tiptoe out of her bedroom to the front door.

'I'll get it!' she called to her father who was a few feet behind her. Cindy flipped the latch and opened the door. 'Hi Toni,' she said, pulling the door open wide.

'Ah, Bella, good evening to you!' Toni said, taking off his cap. 'I didn't expect to see you this evening. You're up late.'

Cindy shrugged, smiling.

'Is this pizza for you?' Toni asked, his left eyebrow arched high over a dark blue eye.

Cindy shook her head. 'It's for my dad.'

'I thought this was a large pizza for a small girl,' he said.

'Hello Toni,' Daniel said from behind Cindy. 'I'll take that from you.' The pizza exchanged hands over Cindy's head. 'Thank you for bringing it out, again.'

'Of course, Mr O'Shea. You're my dad's best customer,' Toni responded. 'And you, Cindy, may be our cutest customer.'

Cindy nodded.

'See you tomorrow, Toni,' Daniel said.

'Sure thing, Mr O'Shea, I'll see you then.' Toni pulled his cap back on his head. 'Ciao, Bella.' He waved to Cindy, 'Goodnight.'

''Night,' Cindy responded, pushing the door closed.

Daniel set the latch and took the pizza into the living room. Cindy followed behind him. He turned the television so it faced his armchair and opened the pizza box.

'The fight starts in fifteen minutes. It's Sugar and Young, tonight. Who are you going to put your money on, Cindy?' Daniel asked, settling into his chair and starting on his first piece of pizza.

Cindy's eyebrows drew together. 'I don't have any money,' she said, through a mouthful of cheese.

Daniel sighed. 'You've got to work on your sense of humour, Cin,' he said. He turned back to the television.

'OK,' she responded. Cindy finished her slice of pizza, and slid off the couch. She walked silently past her father and off to her bedroom.

Four

'Where am I supposed to sleep?' Daniel yelled at a ten-year-old Cindy who was protesting about the aerial dislocation of the few possessions she owned from her bedroom into the hallway. 'I can't sleep in my own damn bedroom and I sure as hell ain't sleeping on the couch in my house. I pay for it. I'll be where I want.' A stuffed animal given by a long-deceased grandparent bounced off the wall and knocked over the collection of bottles that were stacked outside her mother's bedroom door. Cindy covered her ears to block out the crash.

'God damn her!' Daniel cursed as a few of the bottles shattered into the car- pet. He pounded on the door with the side of his fist. 'Take care of these damn bottles,' he shouted. 'If you're going to drink yourself to death like a lazy cow – hurry up! I'm not walking over glass shards in my own hallway,' he pounded. 'You hear me!' Daniel gave the door one final swing before turning his atten- tion back to Cindy. She was trying to reach her bear without falling into the broken glass. 'You're just going to have to sleep somewhere else in the house, Cin. It's not my fault your mother's a bitch. I've got to go to work every day so she'll have a place to stack her goddamn bottles,' he said. Daniel walked into Cindy's bedroom and slammed the door. The pink 'C' which had been nailed to the wood since her birth finally popped its loose nail and slid sideways.

Cindy gathered her things from the hallway and dragged them into the dining room. The family hadn't used the room in years, so she decided she would sleep there for the night. She went to the linen closet and took out a bunch of extra sheets, blankets and pillows, then pushed some old couch cushions the far into the far corner of the dining room and wrapped a sheet over the top. Cindy lined up her stuffed animals on the edge of the cushions against the wall and then piled on the rest of the bedding. She buried herself in between the layers and fell asleep.

Cindy spent the next weekend setting up her new 'room'. It was apparent Daniel's move into her childhood nursery was not temporary. She pushed the china cabinet and table into the half of the room next to the entrance and then nailed a sheet from one wall to the other. Neither parent complained. She took a few more things from her bedroom – a picture from the wall, her clock, a few books – and stacked them in her new room. She also took the radio from the living room that no one ever listened to.

Cindy liked her new spot in the house. Her old bedroom was too pink. She mastered the tuning knob on the AM/FM radio and would lie on her bed and listen to music while running her fingers back and forth over the metal radio grille, pretending to be somewhere else.

Five

'Miss O'Shea,' Mrs Madison, the long-nosed dean of Cindy's middle school began, 'if you think this sort of truancy will be tolerated at Sunny Brook, you are sadly mistaken.' Mrs Madison exhaled loudly and leaned over her folded arms on the desk. 'A third letter was sent to your parents on Wednesday, due to your unexplained absences last week, and now you have earned yourself a two-day suspension.' She paused, eyes averted, as if waiting for Cindy to break down in tears.

Cindy remained stoic in her metal armed chair. She was staring at the wood panelling behind Mrs Madison's desk and counting the months left until her sixteenth birthday.

For the past three years Cindy had been hanging out with the caravan tours that camped at the trailer park a couple of miles from her home. Occasionally, she missed a few days of school. Cindy suddenly became visible when she disappeared.

'Ms Button will be phoning your home this afternoon, personally, to discuss this matter with your parents,' Mrs Madison continued.

Cindy could imagine nervous Ms Button spending the day working herself into a state, preparing to make the pointless call.

'We hate to exclude any student, Cindy,' Mrs Madison continued, 'but your behaviour has left us no choice. You may not be on school grounds or make up any homework assignments you will miss during your absence. And you can save your breath with me, Cindy,' she said, head tilted and palm raised. 'I am sure you will need it when you arrive home this afternoon.'

The palm was Cindy's cue to leave. The charade had been perfected over the last three years. Cindy was sick of being pestered, but Mrs Madison never tired of hearing herself speak.

When Cindy graduated from middle school, she still had seven months until her sixteenth birthday. However, she realised that no one at the high school knew her so she could easily slip out of the school system by not registering in the first place. She would turn sixteen four months into her freshman year anyway. Even if someone noticed, they wouldn't waste their energy.

Six

It was time. Summer was fading and Cindy wasn't going back to school. She stuffed her clothes into a duffel bag, yelled goodbye, and left her home.

When she turned into the camp, she saw the group up ahead and smiled. She was sick of having to watch the place she liked most drive away.

'Welcome aboard, Cin-der-ella,' Smokey said, flopping into a deep bow in the RV doorway. 'Your fairytale awaits.' He turned his lanky body sideways, joint hand extended, and let Cindy pass. 'And this story will be far better than any of the others you have starred in, my dear, for the clock is stuck forever at the eleventh hour.'

Cindy grabbed a freshly rolled joint from a pile on the fold-away kitchen table.

'This coach,' Smokey continued, 'shall never become a pumpkin. Unless,' he waved a bony finger in Cindy's face, 'you smoke the psychedelic shit Greggy just got.'

Cindy pushed Smokey's hand away.

'You don't have to worry about lost shoes, for we rarely even wear them. Fairy godmothers, and their dust,' he grinned and made a wide sweeping gesture to the drugs and paraphernalia covering the kitchen table, 'are everywhere...'

Cindy threw her small duffel bag on to the carpeted seats that lined the wall and sat down beside it.

'And we are always, always, having a ball.' Smokey finally finished his soliloquy and attended to his joint.

'Just light it, Smokey,' Cindy said, before he could begin again. Cindy handed Smokey the joint she had just picked up. 'God, I want to get moving.'

'Restless, Princess?' Smokey said with mock surprise. 'On the train there is no restless.' He lit the joint and handed it back to Cindy. 'Oh, did I leave out the part about the prince?' he asked, sticking out his bottom lip and sliding himself on to the seat next to her.

'Get off me,' she said with casual disgust, elbowing him away and standing up. She started walking toward the door. Smokey grabbed her joint-free wrist, twisting her arm behind her back and jerking her against him.

'Smokey,' she yelled, 'you're gunna make me drop my joint!'

'Just remember, my dear,' he hissed in her ear, 'the ride is all about togetherness.' Smokey's thigh was pressed against the back of her own, and his long, scraggily hair scratched at her neck. 'Cin and smoke – one almost always leads to the other,' he said and he began to laugh at his own line. Cindy pulled her wrist from his grasp and turned. Smokey's deep laughter was turning into a giggling fit. She took another drag of her expertly-rolled joint and pushed him back into the sofa. He bounced, limbs splayed, and continued his giggling. She rolled her eyes and walked out the RV door to go talk to the others.

So she lived as a hippy; a hard core, rockstar-style hippy. But her daisies always had leaves of razor blades – the accidental edge of her childhood.

Cindy now went by Cin, the nickname her father had started, and it was fitting.

Cin followed the bands, drank, popped, partied, and exercised her right to free love. Her eyes were rimmed in coal black, lips corpse white. She wore large jewellery, tight jeans, and was always braless. Her leather was embroidered, and chiffon sheer. She was the epitome of a smudged late-Sixties dream.

Johnny was born when she was eighteen. She considered his father to be the scene.

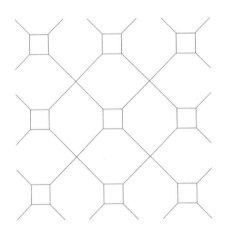

ARGENTINA

from the novel by David Craik

Brothers Rob and John and their childhood friend Mark are travelling to the Scotland-England game at Hampden Park in 1978 – the last game before the Scottish team leave for the World Cup in Argentina. (They will lose 1-0.) Despite the reality of a team which is struggling to live up to manager Ally MacLeod's claims of greatness, plus a battered Glasgow landscape and hard lives, a magical optimism shines through.

Rob and John were standing on the red stools in the King William. Their blue and white knitted scarves were knotted thickly and high on their throats but their songs still came out loud and passionate. Their friend Mark had started the singing, climbing on to the bar, stamping his left Doc Martin'd foot and clapping his hands together over his head. His blue and green kilt swayed as his large red cheeks puffed out the words. As soon as he had begun, all the men in the pub had risen like they were in church, some on stools, others on tables and still more on the shoulders of their friends. Tammies were tossed into the air and scarves, held tightly in the fingers, whirled like helicopter blades above the heads of the crowd. This whipped the air around rattling the windows and the unused glasses hanging at the back of the bar. The yellow and red Lion Rampant flags that every day were hung from the top of the bar were stretched up to and handed down to Mark. He held each one out in front of the crowd. Every one carried the names of cities around Europe and the world like battle flags – *Munich 1974, Eindhoven 1958, Paris 1973*. These flags had travelled with the men and their fathers and grandfathers before them, and had returned to the bar with a new rip here, when that goal was lost in the last minute, or a new stain there, caused by that tear or a beer stain when that penalty was saved. Some of the flags were covered in black markings: names of men who had carried them who had now passed away. *Duncan Grey 1907–1957. John McManus 1920–1975.* They had drunk in the pub, maybe worked in the docks, perhaps fought in the subs, and their names were engraved in memorials elsewhere. But with the fans, with this Tartan Army, their names on the flags were held in the hands of hundreds, sung to, held high in foreign stadiums and kissed by hundreds of lips. The men had always believed in the flags and the spirits within them. But never as much as they did now with Ally McLeod in charge.

The flags were passed over the heads of the men.

'Time to get to the buses, boys. Drink up and let's get going!'

The pints were downed and the glasses were left standing, upright or up-turned, on radiators, on jukeboxes, on some unfortunate person's head and on the snooker tables, as well as on stools and the long, curved bar. As the men shuffled out of the pub, the glasses stood packed together, alone and as silent as rocks.

Outside the pub the songs kept coming as the men walked to and got on the coaches. Each one had a white sign in the dashboard – *Hampden Park, Glasgow, Scotland V England May 1978*.

'We're on the march with Ally's Army!
We're on the way to the Argentine!
And we'll really shake them up when we win the World Cup! Cos Scotland are the greatest football team!'

Mark walked up to Rob and John on their coach. He crouched down by the brothers' seats and shouted to make himself heard above the din.

'I went up to the Campsie Fells last week,' he said looking beyond the men and out of the window. 'Right to the top of one of the hills. Windy as fuck like, almost off my feet. A big man like me. At the top it's all exposed, eh? Look behind though, there's trees and from those trees there must have been birds singing. But because of the wind like, the noise must have carried and the birdsong almost seemed to come down at you from the clouds.'

Mark stopped and turned his eyes to John and Rob. 'Reminded me of my first ever time at Hampden. All those voices, all those songs drifting into the air and coming at you from every direction. I want that today boys. I want our songs to drift with the wind and for the English to look up and have the heavens singing to them in Scottish.'

The brothers smiled as Mark's eyes began to water. They had known him since playschool and often liked to remind him that on the first day they had met he had burst into tears in front of all the kids from the scheme.

'Just because one of the adults had offered you a plain digestive biscuit eh Mark and no a chocolate one?' one or both of the brothers would chide him with from time to time. Mark would laugh with embarrassment when the story resurfaced. He would always reply:

'Aye lads and who could blame me? That woman was a witch I tell ye. I swear. I ran home to tell my mother and she agreed with me. No more play-school for me. Only for wee fools like you.'

Mark had been very close to his mother. He was an only child and had never known the father who had left him when he was still only big enough for a cot. Mark had always had a red mark on his right cheek as long as the brothers had known him. It was oval-shaped and the size of a postage stamp, and as the years passed by it grew as he grew. It never diminished from his face. His mother had told him that that was the spot where his dad had kissed him as he stood over his cot and whispered goodbye. Whenever Mark cried the mark would shine and cling to the tears like water on raspberries after a downpour.

Mark would cry with thanks after his mother insisted on taking him to the cake shop after a trip to the dentist.

'But Ma. The dentist said no sweets for a couple of weeks.'

'Ach, what does he know son? A wee cake never harmed anyone.'

He would cry when going too fast on the roundabouts or on the swings in the park with the concrete floor which had scraped and bumped and bruised children for years. He cried when, in the middle of a bike race, leading other and bigger boys from the estate, he had turned a corner and saw a whippet staring straight at him. He had turned the bike round in one quick instant and rode past his bemused competitors balling his eyes out, his red mark pulsing in his cheek.

Last summer Mark had buried his mother, and as he helped to carry her coffin his tears were so plentiful that they had turned the hard dried earth to slippery mud. Some of the coffin bearers behind him had slipped and lost their grip. Mark powered on alone. Half carrying, half dragging the coffin. Unable to see what was going on behind him because his eyes were filled with water. Rob remembered his dad, Jack, leaping up to help Mark with the weight as the other bearers picked themselves up and rushed back to the coffin to do their duty.

'You heard about Alex and Tommy Souter?' Mark continued.

'Na,' the brothers replied in unison.

'Fuckin' crazy like. They took a plane to New York last week. Going to stay there for a couple of days, and then guess what?'

'What?'

'Going fuckin' cycle it doon to Buenos Aires on a tandem. Like the fuckin' Goodies they say. Can ye imagine it? These mad jocks with long tartan scarves, kilts going through Central America. Fucking nae chance of making it.'

The brothers laughed. Jack had told them at tea last night that a group of five supporters, all no more than eighteen years of age, had asked how much it would cost to hire a submarine to take them to Argentina. Jack and his workmates at the shipyard had gone along with the joke, giving the fans a tour of the yard and a glimpse of a couple of the submarines. Jack had gone through some prices with them as the fans looked on excitedly, nudging each other in the chest and saying, 'I told ye we could dae it. No one ever believes me.' But then Jack had shown them the room where they kept the jars of insects that they scooped up from the subs or the workfloors or the grounds around the dock. Huge spiders as big as a man's fist, ants the size of telephones. All affected by the radiation from the dockyards. The lads had taken one look, confirmed that these 'things' lived on the subs and had ran out of the door.

'I was talking to one guy in the hairdressers the other day,' said Rob slowly shaking his head. 'Giving him a buzz cut. One all over eh? Says he wanted it for aerodynamic reasons. I kind of stood back from him with the razor in ma hand shouting at him AERODYNAMIC REASONS? I said. Ye'll never guess what he says to us.'

'Nah. What like?' Mark said giggling.

'Told me that he's gone and made himself this massive wicker basket. Says he's worked out how to fly a hot air balloon to land slap bang in the middle of the Argentine.'

Mark and John laughed loudly.

'Thing was, though,' Rob continued. 'The guy had no fuckin idea where Argentina was. Thought it was south of Italy. Can ye believe it? I don't think half these guys know where the hell we're going. They plan to just go on a plane, a bike, a submarine, a balloon, land somewhere vaguely near, get pissed and watch some fitba. Crazy.'

Mark patted Rob on the shoulder and then placed his hands straight out in front of him as if he was about to dive into the sea. He rocked his legs and hips back and forth, and with a mighty heave he raised his bulk from the seat and walked away to the front of the coach.

'I've never seen him carrying so much beef,' John whispered to Rob.

'Aye, it's bad like. Just getting bigger and bigger the lad. Too much booze. Too many chips. Nobody around any more to tell him to stop.'

'De ye think they'll allow him on the plane like? Ahm no being funny but I wouldnae fancy getting up into the air with him on board! I can never understand how the bloody things stay up anyway, never mind having twenty stones of Scottish pork pie to deal with an all,' said John, pretending to make his body shake with nerves.

'You and your flying, man. How can anybody prepared to go down into the sea, down hundreds of feet in only a steel sausage with a bunch of neds from the West of Scotland be scared of going up into the sky? It's ridiculous, man. Safest form of travel, that's what they say.'

'How the hell would you know? Or any of you guys. Not one of you have been fucking anywhere. You said it yerself just a minute ago. Look at the smiles on these guys' faces! They're ecstatic just to be travelling on a bus. On a fuckin bus! Can ye imagine them on a plane? They'd be jiggin' about like Pan's People. All because of what Mad Ally is telling youse. WE'RE NO GOING TO WIN! WE'RE SCOTTISH. WE NEVER WIN FUCKING ANYTHING!'

Rob smiled and closed his eyes. His older brother was wrong about the football. Ally was right to say Scotland could win it. That was the problem with Scottish people. One half of them dreamers, guys who wanted to fight and believe they could do anything with a little bit of charm and passion. Then the other half the dour merchants. Blaming the English and our small size and our bad weather for all our problems. Mostly both these characteristics were bound up in the same person. Usually the dour merchant side of the Scots won. But occasionally eh? Occasionally the Scots dreamed and believed and they did things. They did great things. Great inventions. The television, the telephone, the bicycle, the steam engine, the computer. Fuck knows maybe even the toaster, sandwich maker, hedge trimmer and hat stand an all.

That's what the Scottish team and Scotland had always lacked, he thought. Just a bit of belief. We've got the players – Dalglish, Jordan, Gemmell, Robertson. Why can't we win? Ally knew we were special. Wanted to bring that charisma, that magic, out of us. Whae's like us? Now it wouldn't just be talk, the magic would walk the walk.

But his brother was right about the travelling. He had never been any-where. Holidays with the family were spent by the grey beach and the dark sea of Arbroath, or visiting the relatives in Kirrie or Forfar. Arbroath wasnae too bad. The smokies were tasty but they made the town smell. And the hiring of the caravan for a couple of weeks had its moments. Being sent off by his ma to get the morning rolls and sometimes a new jar of jam from the campsite shop every day at 9 am. Cheering whenever the sun came out from behind the clouds. Hurting badly when the burn arrived as night fell, being soothed by the cotton wool and the Camomile lotion and his ma's hands, then going to sleep with the cool, sweetly smelling lotion hitting the strange and crisp bedsheets.

No. He had never been anywhere.

'I could live to a hundred and never see every part of Scotland that I wanted to,' his dad told him often as they made their way up the same motorway and through the same A roads to Arbroath as they always did every year. But any-way where could you go on his wages? Where could you fly to? He wasnae Alan Whicker, he could never go on Concorde. He couldn't afford to follow the sun just for a holiday. But now Ally McLeod had given him a reason to explore. It was his duty to go and support his team. To go to Argentina and to come home with the World Cup.

Rob opened his eyes and quickly patted John's knee. He turned and saw Rob pointing to an area of rough grass surrounded by a high barbed wire fence and festooned with square yellow signs. Beyond the fence lay a large red-bricked building with tiny holes in it that weeds clung to. Pieces of ripped wall-paper would occasionally protrude through the holes when the wind caught them just so.

From the top of the building three white tall chimneys rose like upturned table legs.

'Talking of flying, John,' said Rob looking at the building.

'What's being done to it?' asked John.

'It's going at last. Well that's what the paper says, anyroad. Going to be demolished in a couple of weeks.'

'Really? Christ. It's been there for ever like, eh? What they going to do with it?'

'No sure. Sports centre, library maybe. No idea. Was talk of making it into offices again but I don't think that's happening after all.'

The bus slowed down and its engines rumbled heavily, as if made angry by its sudden idleness. Rob thought of the book he had just finished reading – a conspiracy special about James Dean's death car – the Porsche Spider. How after the actor's death the tangled, burst and broken vehicle had been resurrected and rebuilt. How the next owner had also died in a car crash. How the car was rebuilt again and then sold to another owner. How he died when the car went up in flames. How the car was then destroyed for good and buried where nobody could ever find it. People thought the car contained an evil spirit, a conscience, had feelings and emotions, wanted to cause catastrophe.

Just like this building.

It wasn't unusual in the city though. The gaps in the streets and the landscapes caused by the bombs of the Second World War still existed over thirty years later. Most of the buildings had been left forgotten. Only remembered by the children who played between the gap tooth bricks and long-ago burnt and mangled metal.

No one had found a use for this or any of the buildings. Jack had told his sons that this wasn't just due to the lack of imagination of councillors or politicians. It was because people wanted the buildings to be left alone. That not enough time had passed to forget what had happened there and why.

When they were young boys Jack had walked his sons past this building and told them the story of the fourth chimney that had fallen.

'I went to school just there,' he said pointing round his shoulder to a small white building surrounded by a concrete playground. 'A wee library now I think. But during the war we played on that playground every break time and every lunchtime. One day I remember sitting on a step just eating a jammy piece when one of the boys shouted at everyone to look at the sky. Every head went up as far as I can remember. We had heard quite a few planes over the previous few weeks but we had never seen one in the flesh as it were. Certainly not in daylight. One of the laddies shouted out that it was a German plane. That made some of the girls scream and run inside the school. But we looked and looked at this sight. This bird-like thing in the sky, but so much bigger than any bird and so much noisier. We saw that it was one of ours. Another laddie shouted out that it was a Spitfire. And by jeez it was. Everything about it was just like it was in the comics I used to read. The green and blue colouring, the beautiful elegant, angular shape and the blue red and white circle. The RAF. We all started cheering. I imagined the hero that was sat in the cockpit. Imagined him returning back from a battle with a German plane over Scapa

Flow. Trying to protect our Navy. We started waving at the pilot and you know what? He waved back at us. With one hand and then with two hands. When he did that we all gasped as the plane began to dip to the right. He managed to get it back again, and then I don't know he must have seen the chimneys. He started to circle one of them. He kept going round and round it. By now some of us were still cheering and jumping up and down excited like. But others, me included, just stood there with our mouths opening. I could feel the blood rushing from me. I felt myself getting paler and paler and, as I did so, as I continued to watch this plane going round and round, I fell over. I was so dizzy watching it. And I remember lots of other boys and girls falling over as well. Because this plane just kept going round and round and we were mesmerised. Hypnotised they say today eh? Anyway as I lay on the ground I heard this massive explosion. It was so loud that all the people who had fallen sat up immediately. I saw this orange and black cloud and I saw bricks and dust falling to the ground. And then I saw the wing of the Spitfire fall. I saw the red, white and blue sign spinning away to the ground and then I saw the shape of a man with red flames illuminating him against all this smoke and blackness and dirt also falling. He fell the slowest. The chimney landed first and smashed into little pieces, the wing landed next and we saw it shake and buckle and break in two and then we saw the man land with a simple thud. No smashing or buckling with him. Just a simple thud. We found out later that the pilot had fought in London, had come up here for rest and relaxation. But he had had too much of the bottle one lunchtime and had taken to the skies. So drunk he smashed into a chimney trying to show off to some kids who only wanted to see him fly and be heroic and be magical. After that this building, which was council offices I remember, were hardly ever used again. People didn't like working here. Didn't feel comfortable. Didn't feel right. Everyone who worked here said they felt scared.'

NOMAD

from the novel by Tara Diamond

Charlotte and Zuzu pressed their noses against the cool glass, their breath forming little pillows of mist as they watched the great storm billow down from the mountains towards them. Neither of them had seen anything like it before. On the adjacent farm, Oom Kobus's beasts brayed and bleated in panic as nervous herd-boys whipped their sticks to the ground and the sheepdogs weaved between the skittish legs. Oom Kobus could be heard barking orders as he slapped the rumps of his cattle, keeping count as he herded them into the barn. The radio had been warning for days of an enormous storm predicted to blow down from the Sahara Desert; a storm that had gathered speed as it rampaged towards the Drakensburg Mountains. Even the Sangomas, Africa's witch doctors, had precognitions of something terrible: a creature with jaws of razored teeth flying down from the centre of Africa; they could smell it, it was on its way. Only the night before, Mom's horses had become skittish, their ears pulled back, they tottered forwards and backwards in their stables so that even she had been unable to calm them. The cats, which had spent the morning chasing the wild circling leaves, had now retreated indoors where they sought out nooks and crannies to curl themselves into.

Immaculate had been the first in the household to spot the oncoming storm. Bounding first upstairs to alert her boss, she came back down to warn the girls, with threats of smacked legs, not to venture from the house. Charlotte and Zuzu knelt up on the sofa, noses to the glass, transfixed by the sight of the encroaching bulbous clouds rising and falling over every mountain, like an evil wave that had broken free and clambered onshore. A cracked fork of lightning spat out green and white and green as the mass pulsated forwards.

Bruce, Charlotte's dad, threw himself from his bed and rushed out to the driveway, shouting orders to the stable boys to help him drive the three cars, the tractor and the caravan into the garages and under the carport. There was no room left for the boat. Behind the girls, Immaculate wrung her hands, trilled, and crossed herself. This put the girls on edge – what had been an exciting spectacle had suddenly turned sinister by the nervous movements of their usually unflappable mama.

Charlotte knew she was not meant to think of Immaculate as mama any more, not since her dad had that chat, 'It is not reg,[1] to call your maid *Mama*,' he explained, and the way he said it with his lips squeezed into a purse and his chin falling into his square neck, made it clear to Charlotte that it was a very bad thing, so she had nodded her head, learned to say Immaculate while still thinking of her as Mama.

What would become of her hut? Immaculate was wailing. What about their television that the baas[2] had recently given them? Her hut would not withstand a storm like this, she told Mom, Charlotte's real mother, who had wandered, bleary eyed, downstairs.

'Find Thulani,' Leyla instructed, 'and if he's finished securing the horses then you can both go and retrieve your stuff. You may store it in our games-room.'

Immaculate thanked her madam and dashed outside. Her maid's kappie whipped from her head and flung to the branch of a tree but she did not stop to claim it. Instead she pushed against the wind, down the hill towards the stables. Charlotte and Zuzu clambered over to the French doors and watched Immaculate's head disappear from view.

'Do you think the wind will blow Mama away?' Zuzu asked, chewing her lip nervously.

'Ag, no,' Charlotte reassured her friend, 'she's too fat, the wind is not strong enough for her.'

Zuzu nodded thoughtfully. 'I suppose you are right. But my pa is not fat, what if he blows away?'

'No, man, your pa is too tough for this wind, his muscles are too big.' Charlotte hoped she was right. 'Anyway if the wind blew him, he would just hold on to a tree.'

Zuzu nodded in agreement, her pa was as strong as a lion.

Minutes later, the girls spotted Thulani running up the hill with Immaculate puffing behind him. They did not come straight into the house. Skirting

---

[1] Right, correct

[2] Boss

108

it, they made for the servants' quarters just as the clouds gobbled up the last of the sun and the rain began to fall; huge drops drumming deafeningly down on the corrugated-iron roof. Then the door burst open and the workers rushed in, all carrying their precious items. Last in was Gogo Bongani, helped by Immaculate, his walking stick thick with the mud that had already formed in the square of the servants' quarters. Dad followed behind – a plastic bag tied to his head in an attempt to keep the rain off his Brylcreemed head – and stopped dead at seeing the ragged group of workers that stood, dripping, in his kitchen, each clutching some bulky item: a television set, a cards table, picnic chairs.

'Jislaaik man, what's going on?' He shouted over the thrum of rain, turning to Immaculate as head maid of the house.

'Baas,' Immaculate began, standing her ground. 'What could I do? The kayas[3] are going to drown, the mud is turning to soup, we have babies and ou-mense[4] here.'

Bruce looked round and all eyes stared back. From the group a baby began to cry.

'Ag, well, I suppose so, hey.' Bruce shrugged, aware that Immaculate had won.

Charlotte and Zuzu listened as Charlotte's mom told her husband that she had allowed the workers to store their belongings in the games room. Charlotte guessed that her dad's irritation was due to a hope that he would ride out the storm in the games room by drinking vodka and playing darts.

'Ag, ja doll, you are probably right' Bruce relented. 'That would be the safest place.'

The bedraggled group then trudged off in the direction of the games room, Leyla and Immaculate in front, Leyla giving orders for Immaculate to bring down all the swimming towels and old blankets in case of flood.

After the rain came hail the size of golf balls. Clattering on to the roof, they bounced and shattered on the patio below. Charlotte was scared that if the wind changed direction the hail could come crashing through the French doors, and kept turning round to keep an eye on it.

In the corner of the games room, the babies whimpered, their mothers unable to soothe them while Gogo Bongani mumbled monotonously about

---

[3] Huts
[4] Old people

angered spirits until the baas told him to shut up, threatening to throw him to the storm. Gogo Bongani waved his wrinkled arm at him and turned his back to talk to the wall, continuing his mumbling when Charlotte cried out; the pool outside the French doors was flooding, water had begun to lap over the sides. Everyone rushed round picking up the blankets and towels, and stuffing them against the glass doors. In the kitchen, Charlotte's dad was on the walkie-talkie to Oom Kobus: the news was that Oom Scheepers over on the other side had a tree crash down on his house, destroying the sitting room, and Mr McNeale from over the road had lost some cows from heart attacks.

'Jussis doll,' Bruce shouted over the clatter of hailstones, 'I'm telling you what, this is a hele[5] catastrophe man.'

Having become bored with the ongoing chaos, Charlotte and Zuzu tiptoed upstairs to Charlotte's bedroom to play. Taking the dolls out of the cardboard box, Zuzu dutifully picked up the doll with the chewed fingers; this one was always hers. But today Charlotte felt like being kind and so she also passed her the one with the pretty pink dress. Charlotte would have the Queen doll.

'Hey Zu,' Charlotte said, after playing Cinderella for a while, 'if the storm ruins your kaya maybe you can come and live with me.'

'Don't be stupid, Lotty,' Zuzu scolded her. 'If my kaya breaks, then the baas will just build us a new one.'

Charlotte was quiet for a moment as she struggled to hitch the Queen to her white steed.

'Ja, but it would be good though? Then maybe we could share a bedroom and you could sleep here with me. I'd like that.'

Zuzu pursed her lips, concentrating on getting the man-doll's hair flat and into place.

'Ja-nee, but it would be great, wouldn't it?' Charlotte pursued, 'then we could share my toys.'

'But Charlotte, you would only give me the rubbish ones, like this one,' Zuzu answered, dangling the chewed doll by her hair, her brows knitting in anger. 'And where would I sleep? On the floor like a dog? And where would Mama sleep, also like a dog on the floor?'

Charlotte felt a rush of heat tingle her cheeks.

'I was just saying, stupid, that's all. Anyway, maybe Dad would decide that you guys could be the same as us—'

---

[5] Entire

Zuzu stood up and walked towards the window, chewing on one of her beads that decorated her hair. 'No, Lotty, even if the rain takes all the kayas in the whole land I wouldn't want to live here with you.'

Charlotte sat amongst her dolls, wanting to say she was sorry. Wanting to explain to her friend how sometimes she felt confused. That she loved Zuzu and Immaculate and Thulani more than everyone else in the world. That it wasn't her fault that Zuzu couldn't live with her. But she couldn't find the words; they were just emotions, washing nameless and directionless through her. She felt angry then that Zuzu had this power to make her feel so bad.

Thunder rolled from the hills behind them and the lightning crashed, causing the sky outside to swell in neon green. Then came an explosion so loud that Charlotte jumped up, running to the window to stand beside Zuzu. There was a buzzing sound, like a plague of locusts that Charlotte had once seen on a nature programme, but louder; it buzzed and screamed and hissed. The girls opened the window and leant out just in time to see the power cable, that straddled both theirs and Oom Scheepers' farm, snap from its metal frame and crash down to the floor, the fat wire snaking and slithering as it spat out electricity from its exposed, live wires.

The girls raced downstairs, their argument forgotten for now, where they found Charlotte's father crouched by the French doors, his hands over his face, his mouth hanging wide.

'Daddy, what happened?' Charlotte screamed, imagining the horrors that could lie outside.

Grabbing at her, Bruce pulled her writhing body into his.

'Shh, now my kindjie.⁶ Shh, man, it's OK, it's fine. It was only the boat.'

Charlotte followed her dad's finger as he pointed out towards the driveway. The boat was lying, cut in half. Its metal black and jagged, it steamed in the hissing rain. Around it the power cable still danced, slapping its wires on to the scattered pieces of shrapnel.

The next morning when the rain and the hail and the wind had finally ceased, the troop of workers headed up to inspect the damage to their homes. Charlotte struggled to keep up with Dad's wide strides as he walked on ahead of the group, holding his clipboard in the crook of his arm in readiness to note the damage. Zuzu lagged way behind; she was still not talking to Charlotte, not

---

⁷ Traditional round huts

after what had been said.

The square in the centre of the servants' quarters was now a mud pool in which bits of cutlery and crockery lay half immersed in gunk. A tree had toppled over, squashing a couple of old bicycles, but apart from that and the insects and the smell, the rondavals[7] were fairly undamaged. Bruce noted down the repairs that were needed on some of the thatched roofs, also putting down pots of white paint for the mud-streaked walls and some red for the floors, which were covered by two inches of sludge.

Later on that day Charlotte drove into the dorp[8] with her father to buy the brooms and buckets and other supplies. This had always been one of her favourite things, to sit up next to Dad in his bakkie[9] as they whizzed down the narrow roads, when, if she was really good, he would allow her to change the gears for him as he drove at reckless speeds. But this time their trip was slow and cautious, Dad having to manoeuvre the truck around the trees and debris that had fallen on to the road. Here and there a dead cow or sheep lay, their eyes open and glassy. Whenever they passed one, Dad slowed down to check the brands on their rumps, in case they were his farming neighbours' animals.

On the side of the road small groups of people huddled together, the man of the family clutching the few possessions they had managed to salvage, the women carrying babies on their backs and heavy baskets on their heads. Charlotte's dad eased slowly past so as not to splash them with the river of water that cascaded down the road.

'Jussis, sunshine, I tell you, it's these blacks I feel sorry for,' Dad said, shaking his head as they passed the groups.

Charlotte turned and stared out the back of the bakkie at a toddler with green candles of mucus hanging from his nose, whose nappy was brown with mud and bulging down to his knees. The little boy's eyes caught Charlotte's and he lifted his small hand to wave.

'Ja, man, poor people,' her father muttered. 'Looks like they don't have a good baas like me and Oom Kobus, us okes[10] who look after their folk.' He clicked his tongue, 'Poor people, man; just left to rot, I don't know.'

Charlotte turned and opened her hand to wave, but the boy and his family had disappeared behind the hill.

---

[8] Town

[9] Truck

[10] Groups of men

England, 1998

For as long as Charlotte could remember, her father had had trouble sleeping. In the early hours of the morning she would find him pattering around downstairs in the semi-dark, his dressing gown pulled over his expanding belly, his slippers slap-slapping on the kitchen tiles as he paced up and down in-between scavenging for food. Charlotte believed that it was because of their shared insomnia that her and her dad's relationship had grown closer since coming to England, as both were plagued by private nightmares. And it was in the dimness of this kitchen that they had found each other and become secret midnight buddies, keeping their pact of silence when, the next morning, Mom would question the whereabouts of the biscuits or the strange disappearance of her cheesecake. During these illicit snacking sessions, Charlotte and her dad would shelve the arguments of the previous day, and for those few stolen hours, he would shift his cloak of parentage from his shoulders and treat her like an adult. They never discussed the night fears that kept them both awake; their talk of South Africa being silently, yet carefully, regulated to snapshots of simple nostalgia. For instance, when Ouma accidentally crunched on a cockroach that had found its way into her potjiekos stew, or when the storm brought the electric cable crashing down on Dad's new boat slicing it almost in half, or when they found a family of dassies huddled in the rockery by the pond. Not once did they discuss the night they fled their home.

Charlotte found Dad at the breakfast nook when she tiptoed in, still out of breath from her dash across the green. He sat with his back to her, a glass of whisky in his hand.

'Hi Dad.'

He turned, and in the dull light of the kitchen lamp, Charlotte noticed how old he looked. It must have happened slowly and imperceptibly; only the shadows caught the changes, the deepening of lines, the sagging of skin around his jowls. Taking them in, Charlotte felt a sudden rush of affection for him.

'Hey pikinini, how was the party?'

'OK,' Charlotte sat down opposite him. 'What's for snacks?'

'Don't know, I haven't checked.'

That was odd; she had never known him to miss out on a rummage through the fridge.

'Do you think there's a cheesecake lurking in there?'

'Could be; help yourself,' he said, taking a swig of whisky and pursing his lips as it went down.

They sat in silence together, half listening to the hum of the fridge and the click-tick of the wall clock. Both jumped when the clock doors sprang open and the cow burst out, mooing the fourth hour of the day.

With the spell broken, Dad looked up. 'So how was the talent tonight? Anything you wished you could bring home?'

'For your information, Dad, actually there wasn't. And even if there was, I wouldn't tell you.'

Bruce's eyebrows danced teasingly above his bifocals, Charlotte ignored him, stood up and rifled through the ready-made dinners until she found the cheesecake. Chocolate, her favourite. She took out a carton of double cream and poured it thickly over both their slices.

'Just like old times hey?' Dad mumbled, smiling at her through a forkful of gooey cake.

Then, shaking his head, he sighed. 'Ag, I miss you man. I know I'm just being an old fool, but it's true. It's been a long year without you.' He laughed grudgingly. 'Ja, man, you spend all your life waiting for your kids to grow up and leave and then they do and—' he sighed again and dropped the spoon into his bowl.

'Ah well.'

'How's Mom?' Charlotte asked, changing the subject, embarrassed by her father's sentimentality.

'She's well. Enjoying herself. She's on all sorts of committees these days. Funny isn't it, how she's changed? I remember when all she did was sit around the pool sunning herself in her tiny bikini, or—'

'Riding her horses?' Charlotte cut in.

Bruce clapped his hands. 'That's it, my sunshine, lazing by the pool and riding. What a little madam she was. I tell you something,' he was slurring now, having washed down his cheesecake with another glug of whisky, 'when we first came here, that mother of yours fell so high off her pedestal, jislaaik, it was the end of the world as far as she was concerned.'

His eyes milked over and he stared into the distance. 'Ag, but she was a beautiful woman once, your Mom.'

Charlotte shifted uncomfortably on her stool. They never discussed Mom, as she was before they moved. She knew next to nothing of her history; all she had were fragments, pieces picked up from overheard conversations. She knew that Mom had grown up wealthy and that her father, Charlotte's oupa, had once owned a successful car dealership in Bulawayo, that she had been the hockey captain at school and a Rhodesian swimming champion. Once she had overheard Mom telling friends that she could have followed a modelling career, but that Oupa had forbade it. Then she had married Dad. Charlotte did not know when or why; there were no wedding photos. In fact almost none of the family snaps had been brought over with them when they had moved.

'Ja, we had the life back then, my chick,' Dad continued, his words thick with nostalgia, 'like kings and queens we were.' Leaning precariously forward on his stool he reached for the whisky bottle and refilled his tumbler. Picking out the little lumps of ice that floated on top of the gold liquid, he threw them in the direction of the bin.

Charlotte watched him uneasily. 'Dad, are you drinking more since I've been away?'

He snorted, ignoring the question. 'Ag, but those were the days. Of course you were too young to remember much, just a little shrimp you were. Shame, man.' He leaned across and squeezed her cheeks. It hurt.

'I remember a lot, Dad.' Charlotte twisted round and flicked the kettle on, unable to look him in the eye.

'Ja? What about our house, do you remember that?'

'Yeah, it was bright pink and just enormous.'

Dad burst with laughter, slapping the counter. 'You know, your mother never forgave me for buying that house. She hated it, said it looked common.'

'I thought it was beautiful, it was like a castle, with its own hill—'

'And the maids, the pool, the stables, all we needed was a moat,' her father sighed and shook his head, 'I want to go home, my chickie.'

'Dad?'

Charlotte held her breath till she though she might pop, feeling pinpricks of blood dot her cheeks. 'What happened that night?'

For a long time her father said nothing. He stared into his tumbler, swirling the gold liquid against its sides. Then he stood up and refilled his glass.

'We've never spoken about it, have we, Dad? Do you remember when we first came here, I used to get nightmares?'

He nodded.

Charlotte watched his jaw pulsate; a barely perceptible movement behind his grey-brown beard.

'The nightmares I used to have, they were about it, that night, I mean. I couldn't sleep because in my dreams I would forget I was here, I thought I was back there.'

She waited. Tic, tic, of the clock. Hum of the fridge. Nothing more.

'Dad?'

'What do you want me to say?' He peered over his bifocals at her, his jowls now slack.

'I thought we should talk about that night. Now that I'm older, now that I can understand.'

'No, Charlotte, you can't understand,' he said sadly. 'You've been living here too long, you've grown too soft. You'll never be able to know what it was like back then in the eighties.'

'Please, can I try?'

Dad shook his head. He looked so utterly defeated standing there in the lamplight, his scraggy gown pulled round his belly, his silly golf slippers on his feet, that she couldn't bring herself to pursue it. Not tonight, she told herself. Soon, when she had some evidence: something more concrete than childhood nightmares, and a letter from a continent so far away she almost couldn't believe it still existed.

ALL THAT REMAINS IS

from the novel by Lindsay Flynn

It's 1968. Vanessa's second child is due. Her first, Cordelia, was born in 1964 exactly nine months after Vanessa married Gerald, one of her tutors at art school. He is an acclaimed sculptor, but domesticity has swamped Vanessa's love of fashion and design.

It was two o'clock before he came home and slipped into bed, smelling heavily of whisky and cigars.

'Where have you been?' she asked, when his breathing deepened and it was clear he was going straight to sleep without saying anything.

She heard him sigh. He turned over and lay on his back. In the half darkness she could see him staring at the ceiling.

'At college,' he said. 'Why?'

'Until this time?' She hated herself for the question.

'There's all hell breaking loose.'

'You said you'd be home by ten.'

'I just told you, Nessa. There's trouble brewing. The students are going to take over the college buildings.'

'Why do you have to be involved?'

'Christ, Nessa, what's happened to you? This is about what colleges teach, the role of the artist in society, the future of art... things you used to think were important.'

'What about our future, Gerald?'

'What are you talking about?'

'Us. You're hardly here any more. You're either at college, or your studio.'

'You knew the score when we got together. I thought part of my appeal was that I was a sculptor.' His voice had that mocking edge she'd heard him use so often to others, but only towards her in the last few months. 'Together we'd set the art world alight, you said.'

She shifted uncomfortably, her hands on her belly as if she could contain its massiveness. The baby always seemed to choose night time to kick.

'That's not fair,' she said, although the thought that she'd said those words made her go hot. Set the world alight. Had she really been so naïve?

'It's true, though, isn't it? You were going to be a famous artist too, but you became a mother instead.'

'How can you be so cruel? It's all right for you; your career's going from strength to strength.'

Earlier on in the year, Gerald had an exhibition in New York and the critics heaped praise on his bronze statues – *Provocative depictions of the human form.* Left at home, Vanessa tried not to be jealous, but it was hard not to wonder what she'd be doing now if it weren't for Cordelia.

'I didn't plan to have a child so soon,' she reminded Gerald. 'It's not your life Cordelia's changed; it's mine.'

She listened to his breathing quicken and waited for him to throw back the bedclothes and storm off to the spare room. It wouldn't be the first time in recent weeks it had happened. Instead she felt his arm slip round her. He cupped her breast in his palm. 'I'm sorry, Nessa.' His voice was gruff, the words muffled in the material of her nightdress. 'I'm a selfish bastard. I don't know how you put up with me.'

Her anger dissolved. He so rarely said sorry that the word on his lips had the magic of a rainbow. She lifted her bottom from the bed and shuffled closer to him.

'Once this little beggar's out,' he said, his breath warm against her back, 'you'll feel a million dollars. We'll get someone to help in the house and you can start working again.'

'Do you mean it?' She caught hold of his hand with both of hers and followed the path of his stroking movements.

'Definitely. We should have done something before. Carla asked me the other day what you were working on at the moment.'

'Carla? I thought she'd left college.' Vanessa's voice was sharp. She'd always suspected Gerald and Carla had had an affair, but he'd laughed when she asked him.

'She has. But I see her for lunch or a drink sometimes.'

'You didn't say.'

'I don't tell you every time I breathe, my darling.'

The baby was born on the twentieth of June. It was a short labour and four hours after Vanessa arrived at the hospital, she was sitting up in bed, her dark haired daughter in a cot beside her. There was no sign of Gerald. He hadn't been home the night before, and when the pains started in the early hours of the morning, Vanessa woke Sabina who was staying with them.

'I look after Cordelia,' she said, going to the telephone and counting out 'Nine... nine... nine'.

The dial seemed to take an eternity, clockwise to the nine, clacking anti-clockwise to its resting place.

'A taxi. Get a taxi.' Vanessa sat on the stairs as another contraction took her breath away.

'Darling, don't be silly. You're having a babee. Of course, you have an ambulance.'

Vanessa clutched at her head. 'Where's Gerald? He must have had an accident. He would have phoned.'

'Give me telephone numbers.' Sabina said. 'I find him for you.'

'There's only the college. He hasn't got a phone at the studio. He doesn't like to be disturbed.'

'Don't get upset. It's no good for babee.'

'What would you know? You've never had one.'

'Main thing is to get to hospital.'

'If you can't reach him on that number, try Carla, Carla Scott. Her number's in the phone book on the desk.'

Vanessa walked up and down the hall, gasping at the pain of each new contraction. They were coming every ten minutes now.

'Here's the ambulance,' Sabina said at last from her post at the window. 'You go. I find Gerald for you.'

The nurse put the baby to her breast, but it wouldn't suck. 'You're too agitated, Mrs Blackstone. The baby senses it.'

Vanessa kept her eyes fixed on the doors of the ward. 'I want to see my husband. Something must have happened to him.'

'He'll be here soon. You know what these men are like.'

It wasn't the first time Gerald hadn't come back. Sometimes when he was in the middle of a major piece of work he'd carry on for days, surviving on fruit and biscuits, snatching just a few hours' sleep on a camp bed in the empty room above the studio. But he'd never stayed away without phoning before.

In the afternoon Sabina brought Cordelia in to see her and the new baby who still didn't have a name.

'Where's Gerald?' Vanessa asked as soon as they arrived beside her bed. 'Is Gerald coming?'

'We don't know where Daddy is,' Cordelia told her. She pulled at the baby's shawl. 'Is this my sister?'

'He's not at studio,' Sabina said, pale despite her olive complexion. 'I try number you give me for college many times, but either engaged or it just ring, ring.'

'And Carla? Did you speak to Carla Scott?'

'There was no answer.'

At ten o'clock that evening, the main ward lights were switched off. The babies were taken to the nursery and the nurses were settling the mothers down for the night, when there was a noise in the corridor outside the ward. A nurse approached Vanessa's bed.

'Mrs Blackstone,' she whispered.

Vanessa turned her head. What did the stupid woman want now? Probably the baby was crying and she'd make her try feeding again.

'Your husband's here.'

'What?' Vanessa sat up. The movement pulled at her stitches, and she screwed up her face. 'Where is he? I want to see him.' She couldn't believe he was here at last.

'The thing is, visiting time is over.'

'If you don't let him come in, I'll never be able to feed my baby.'

'All right, but just for a few minutes, and tell him to keep his voice down.'

Gerald burst into the ward with a bunch of red roses in one hand and a bottle of champagne in the other. 'Darling, I'm so proud of you! I've seen the baby and she's gorgeous.' He dumped the flowers and bottle on the bed and put his arms round her, almost lifting her off the mattress. 'What do you say to calling her Esme? I had an Aunt Esme and I always thought it was a fine name.' His eyes shone and his black hair was even wilder than usual.

Vanessa buried her face in his jumper. It was a thick woolly one she'd knitted to keep him warm, as he would never have any heaters on while he was working. It smelt strongly of cigar smoke and was covered in bits of fluff. She could feel his heart beating against her cheek.

He put his hand to her chin and lifted her face to his. 'Nessa, darling. Are you all right? Was it very bad?'

'Where were you, Gerald?'

'There was a big meeting at the Royal College. Just about everyone was there. The students are really fired up about the future of art education. I tell you, this is going to shake up the Establishment.'

'Why didn't you phone? I thought something terrible had happened.'

'My darling one.' He cupped her face in his hands. His rough skin grazed her cheeks. 'There was so much going on, I just didn't think. I told you I'm a selfish bastard. Now, what do you say to the name Esme?'

121

Vanessa came home from hospital when Esme was four days old. She was a good baby, soon sleeping through the night and contented during the day. Vanessa gave up her attempts to breastfeed and her body became her own again. Cordelia too seemed happier now her sister was here, sitting drawing at the kitchen table while Vanessa fed Esme, or rocking the cradle and singing nursery rhymes when Esme cried.

Almost straight away Vanessa felt the desire to feel some knitting needles and wool between her fingers again. She went to the spare bedroom and began sorting through the bags of yarn. She found what she was looking for – a soft white wool with some angora in it. It would drape beautifully and be perfect for the long dress she wanted to crochet for Esme.

When Cordelia saw what she was doing, she asked, 'Can I do knitting, Mummy?'

'Of course. You could make a scarf for your dolly.'

Vanessa found some short needles that she used for knitting belts and Cordelia chose a ball of bright red wool.

'I'll cast on for you and then I'll show you what to do.' Vanessa put a few stitches on the needle and placed it in Cordelia's chubby hand. 'Hold the second needle like this and put it into the front of the wool.' Vanessa leant forward and took both Cordelia's hands in hers. Cordelia's face was fierce with concentration, her tongue sticking out above her top lip. Together they completed the first stitch. 'Yes, you've done it! Now let's do another one in the same way.'

By the time Gerald came home, they'd finished, and Cordelia thrust the doll wearing only its red scarf at him. 'Daddy, look what Mummy helped me make.'

'Wow! That's wonderful, Cordy.' Gerald lifted Cordelia into his arms and hugged her. She clung to him, her arms tight round his neck and her legs circling his waist.

Watching them, Vanessa felt shut out. She began to tidy the balls of wool into a bag, but then over Cordelia's head Gerald smiled at her, and love for him caught at her throat. It was going to be all right, she thought. It was all going to be all right.

One morning at the beginning of October, Vanessa was in the garden hanging out washing. A row of nappies hung heavy and sodden from the line. Further along, Esme's nightdresses gave way to Cordelia's skirts and T-shirts.

Cordelia came to the top of the steps that led down to the garden. 'There's someone at the door, Mummy.'

Vanessa finished pegging Gerald's shirt to the line. She didn't get many visitors, apart from Sabina, and she wasn't up to a dose of her sister-in-law. But at the front door, she was surprised to find not Sabina but a young woman she'd never met before.

She looked about nineteen or twenty and was dressed in a bright orange mini skirt, knee-high black boots and a white ruffled shirt. She had waist-length straight hair and wore enormously long false eyelashes, which merged with her fringe.

'You must be Vanessa,' she said.

'Yes. Who are you?' Vanessa was on the defensive. She'd hardly had a chance to look in the mirror today and she was wearing some baggy blue corduroys and a checked shirt of Gerald's.

'I'm Frankie.' The young woman waited expectantly.

'Oh.' Vanessa waited too, and just when it seemed the impasse could go on indefinitely, Frankie said, 'Gerald sent me.'

'What for?'

'I'm one of his students and he asked me to look after the children for a couple of hours, so you could have some time to yourself.' She must have seen Vanessa's scowl, because she quickly added, 'He said he'd arranged it with you.'

'Yes, yes, he did. I'd forgotten.' Vanessa was blowed if she was going to let this young girl know how angry she was with Gerald for springing this on her. 'I've been busy with the children.'

'Yeah, I can imagine. I've got five little brothers and sisters.'

Vanessa opened the door wider. At least Gerald hadn't asked someone completely inappropriate.

Vanessa set out at a swift pace for the park. The bag with her drawing pad and pencils banged against her hip. She'd left Frankie and Cordelia sitting cross-legged on the floor of Cordelia's bedroom with all the dolls and teddies in a circle round them, while Cordelia handed out pretend cups of tea. Esme was fast asleep in her cot. They should be all right for at least two hours. She couldn't believe Gerald hadn't told her about Frankie, but she seemed nice enough and Cordelia had clearly taken an instant liking to her.

She wandered through the park looking for a subject. It was so long since she'd tried any serious drawing that she was frightened she wouldn't know where to start. She stopped and looked up into the ash tree above her. Thin October sunlight filtered through its cobwebs of leaves, and against it, the branches stood out, bony and dark. The intricate leaf pattern suggested an attractive design, but she moved on restlessly. A gardener was clearing the last of the summer plants from one of the beds. He worked his way along the begonias and dahlias, lifting the flowers on his fork and throwing them into the back of his truck. Vanessa looked in at the tangle of reds and yellows and oranges and imagined the different shades she could get from mixing those colours, but again walked on without taking the drawing pad out of her bag.

She sat on a bench by the lake and watched the mothers with small children throwing bread to the ducks. It was such a long time since she'd been out without Cordelia and Esme, she'd almost forgotten how to be on her own. Her mind drifted.

'Do you mind if I sit here?'

Startled out of her daydream, Vanessa looked up. The voice belonged to a very tall, very thin, woman who was looking down at her.

'No, please do.'

The woman sat next to her on the bench and took a book from her bag. She was soon immersed in it. Vanessa cast sideways glances at her. She looked about thirty and was dressed entirely in black: trousers, black polo-neck jumper under a black jacket. In contrast, her hair was a pale straw colour and her skin was as delicate as porcelain.

Vanessa took her pad from the bag. She kept her gaze in the direction of the lake as if she was drawing something down there, but managed surreptitious looks at the woman at the same time. She didn't usually draw profiles, but this one was interesting – a strong aquiline nose, an upward curve to her mouth as if what she was reading pleased and excited her.

Vanessa glanced again and this time the woman was looking back. Vanessa turned away quickly, embarrassed at being caught out and startled by the vividness of the eyes. She searched for words to describe their colour: emerald... aquamarine... turquoise? They were like all the greens she could think of and yet none of them.

'Can I see?' the woman said.

Vanessa clasped the drawing pad to her chest. 'It's not finished.'

'Oh well, perhaps another time. I'm Lizzie, by the way.'

'Vanessa.'

'Are you an artist?'

Vanessa shrugged. 'I haven't done much for ages. I dropped out of art college when I was pregnant.'

'You don't have to tell me. I've got three under five. Wednesday afternoons are my bit of sanity.' Lizzie waved the book. 'Chance to catch up on my reading.'

'Do you paint?' Vanessa asked. Perhaps she'd found someone she could talk to about work.

'I'm a writer.' Lizzie laughed. 'Well, I try to write. That's my goal – to get a novel published.'

'Wow! I'm impressed.' Vanessa considered what *her* goal was. To get through the next day. To keep Gerald in a good mood. If she spent more time thinking about her designs instead of feeling sorry for herself, she could be –

'I don't suppose I'll ever manage to write anything as good as this.' Lizzie indicated the book she was reading.

'What is it?' Vanessa asked.

'*Madame Bovary*. Have you read it?'

Vanessa shook her head.

'Emma Bovary's a trivial woman who has affairs to relieve the monotony of her life and her dull marriage. It's set in provincial France in the nineteenth century.' Lizzie sounded angry. 'Just think, that's a hundred years ago and it still applies to women in England now.'

Vanessa felt out of her depth. She hadn't had an opinion about anything other than what to have for dinner since Cordelia was born.

Lizzie was looking at her watch. 'My time's up for another week.'

Vanessa pushed her sketch pad back in her bag. 'I'd better get going too.'

They stood up. Lizzie towered over Vanessa; she must have been nearly six foot.

'Would you like to meet up again?' she asked.

'Yes, will you be here next week?'

'Same time, same place.'

Vanessa slammed the front door shut.

'I'm back, Frankie!'

'We're down here,' Frankie's voice called from the kitchen.

Vanessa ran downstairs, desperate to hold Esme in her arms, and listen to what Cordelia had been doing; it seemed as if she'd been away for days instead of hours.

'Gerald!' To her surprise, Gerald was sitting at the kitchen table, a glass of whisky and the bottle in front of him. His eyes were bloodshot and unfocused.

'What's wrong?' she asked. 'Has something happened?' Her gaze went to Frankie who was standing over by the sink, Esme cradled in one arm, while the other circled Cordelia's shoulder. She raised her eyebrows.

Frankie shrugged. 'He got home about half an hour ago. I'll take the children upstairs.'

As soon as they'd gone, Vanessa drew out a chair and sat next to Gerald. He twisted round and grabbed her head. He pulled her towards him and fastened his mouth on hers. His tongue forced open her lips, and she recoiled. His breath reeked as if he'd been drinking for days.

'See,' he sneered. 'Even you don't want me.'

'Tell me, Gerald. What happened?'

'I've been sacked.' The words were slurred and she had to lean forward to catch them.

'From college?'

'Where the fuck else?'

'But why? I don't understand.' It must have been a student. He must have had sex with a student. That was the only reason they'd sack him.

He reached for the bottle and sloshed some more whisky into the glass.

'They locked me out. Me. Gerald Blackstone.' He gesticulated wildly, stabbing his finger in the direction of his chest. 'The best fucking tutor they've got. Called the police to remove me from the premises.' He got to his feet and staggered across the kitchen, waving the bottle in one hand, the glass in the other. Whisky splashed on to the floor. Vanessa grew scared. He was going to fall. He was a big man and she'd never get him upstairs on her own. She had to calm him down.

She moved towards him and put her hands under his arms to support him. 'But why? What have you done?'

'Supported the sit-in... believed in students instead of the authorities. What the fuck do those pygmies know about art?' He began to sway. She got a chair underneath him just in time as he crashed forward on to the table.

THE STAYMAKER

from the novel by Sally Gander

Jude lay in bed, her mouth dry with a yearning thirst and sickness tumbling in her stomach. The taste of vomit was thick on her tongue. Her limbs ached and she knew they would be bruised, especially her arm. Her ears were ringing from the loud music in the club the night before, still pulsing to a rhythmic beat. Kes had been there, with a woman she didn't recognise, and so was Eddie. She couldn't remember who'd turned up first, but Eddie had stood beside her as she watched Kes dance, close and slow with his new woman.

'It was good to see you the other day,' Eddie had shouted into her ear. 'Made me realise how much I missed you.'

He slid his hand from her hip down to her thigh. She instinctively recoiled from his touch, but when she glanced over to Kes he raised his hand to her, so she leaned towards Eddie and kissed him. Eddie grinned at her then and she turned to see Kes coming towards her, leaving the woman alone on the dance floor.

'Let's go,' she said to Eddie. 'I can't hear you in here.'

She heard Kes call her name, and she turned briefly to see his eyes narrow in disappointment. The sound of his voice made her limbs ache for him, her mouth eager for his taste.

Eddie talked all the way back to the flat, about their friends, the people they'd hung out with together. Jude had distanced herself from all of them since Gabriel had taken her in, lifting herself out of a life that was getting dangerous. She wouldn't sink that low again; living on the streets, begging, pickpocketing, doing whatever she needed to do for money to fund Eddie's habit. She had a life now.

'Frank's got himself a sentence,' Eddie said. 'GBH. And Mary and Dave buggered off to London. Richer pickings, they reckon, but I reckon there's just more competition, you know? Fucking hundreds of us up there. Jake's still around, he's got a new girl, Daisy. She ain't no daisy though, can fight like a bloke when she's bladdered.'

Jude walked and let him talk. She knew he probably just wanted money or a fuck; she wouldn't give him either, but she didn't have the strength to tell him to go back to whatever doorway he was sleeping in that night. She remembered too well what that felt like. The sound of Kes's voice stayed with her. He'd wanted to talk to her. Maybe he wanted to get together again, maybe...

'Well, thanks for walking me back,' Jude said as they approached the flat. 'Good to see you again.'

'Hey, I thought we were having a drink or something.' He took her hand and smiled, a lopsided grin that made deep grooves around his mouth. That smile had hooked her to him years ago, and still it seemed to snag her even though she could smell the dirt and poison of his life on his breath. 'Just one drink, Jude. For old times.'

The image of Kes dancing close with someone else flashed through her mind, someone else breathing in the scent of his skin, feeling the touch of his lips.

Just one drink, she thought. Just one.

In her room she'd poured vodka into tumblers and he stopped talking then, making the most of the free drink. He sat on her bed, watching as she moved around the room clearing clothes from the floor, taking off her boots, switching the radio on and turning the dial to find some music. She didn't want to sit and look at him, she didn't trust what he would do if she were still.

He rolled a cigarette. 'Want one?' he said.

'You can't smoke in here.'

He shrugged and lit the cigarette anyway, inhaling deeply and letting smoke rings drift up to the ceiling.

'Come here,' he said. 'Let me look at you.'

'I just need to... I—'

'Come here,' he said, pulling her on to the bed beside him.

He lifted his hand to her face, pressing his thumb gently across her eyebrow, then let his hand fall to her arm.

'New tat?' he said, his finger brushing the dressing on her wrist. 'You were always good with pain.'

'A starfish.'

'I've been thinking about you,' he said, running his hand up her arm. 'About what a team we made. We were good together.'

'We had some fun times.' Jude pulled away from him, but he reached out and curled his hand around the back of her neck.

'I was pissed off when you left, but I've got over that now. I can see you've got something going here.'

Jude was silent, waiting to hear what it was he wanted. His dark pupils twitched and flickered, making her think he'd been looking for her a long time, probably since she'd left.

He moved his hand to her face, smiling, tilting his head to one side and touching her cheek as though stroking a puppy he was about to drown. 'Got any money?'

That was all he wanted, just money. She relaxed then and stood up, ready for him to leave.

'I bet you've got some hidden away – a little nest egg.'

'Fuck off, Eddie. I don't have any money and I wouldn't throw it away on you just so you can shoot it up your arm.

In a moment he'd jumped up and pushed her back on the bed.

'Fuck it, Eddie...'

With his hand at her throat he straddled her, pinning her hands beneath his knees. She tried bringing her legs up to throw him off balance but he barely moved, just glared down at her as he dug around in his coat pocket.

He leaned over and whispered in her ear, 'I've always liked it when you struggle.'

There was a sharp pain in her arm that made her cry out. She looked down to see he'd pushed a hypodermic needle into the crease of her arm, his thumb ready on the pump. The barrel was cloudy with brown liquid. She stopped struggling.

'It would be easy,' he whispered, 'to make you an addict too. A couple of visits, that's all it would take, then you'd know how it feels. I need money, Jude. You're going to get it for me.'

His thumb was pressing on the pump and in his eyes she could see he was still deciding. His hand taut – fingers white with the pressure – it would only take one slow, steady movement. He'd had the needle ready in his pocket so he must have planned this, knowing she wouldn't just hand the money over.

'You know I'll do it... I'll fucking do it.'

She could feel the needle moving in her arm as his hand shook, but his other hand was still tight around her throat, steady and sure. Sweat broke out across his face and there was a familiar desperate quality to his voice.

'Do you really need to think about it?'

'I've got... I think I've maybe got... a tenner. Take it.'

Eddie's face was only an inch from hers. His breath was on her lips and for a moment she was sure she felt the pressure of liquid, cold in her veins, but then he jumped off, ripping the needle from her arm. A tear of blood emerged and spread across her skin in a narrow line. She pressed her hand to the pin-prick hole and curled into a ball.

'In my coat pocket,' she said.

She didn't watch as he searched her coat, just kept her head down, feeling the softness of the blanket against her cheek, only moving her head slightly to feel it brush against her skin. He made a small satisfied grunt when he found the note and then his breath was against her face again.

'Meet me tomorrow,' he said. 'Usual place, usual time. I want fifty.'

She heard his footsteps on the floorboards move to the door. As he opened it he said, 'I know where you live now. Thanks for that, darlin'.'

When he was gone she'd reached for the vodka bottle, pulling the blankets around her until the alcohol did its job and enabled her to sleep, dreaming of dark shadows pursuing her, the thud of music, a tight rope pulling at her throat. When she'd woken she was cradling the half empty bottle. Pain throbbed in her arm and she put the bottle to her lips again, drinking until it was empty. Sometime after she vaguely remembered getting up and seeing Marissa in the kitchen. Gabriel was there too. There was something wrong, Gabriel was angry with her. Of course – she was drunk. He hated that.

Jude stumbled out of bed and was sick in the sink, then held her mouth under the tap. She wiped her lips with the back of her hand and held up her arm. There was a deep purple bruise and the blood had dried to a speckled stain.

'Fucking cunt.'

She went back to bed and pulled the covers over her head but the darkness made her sweat and it felt as if Eddie was still above her, pinning her arms to her side. She pushed back the covers and took deep gulps of cold air.

There was a knock at the door. 'Are you awake?'

It was Gabriel.

'Yeah.' Her voice came husky and raw, her throat burning with bile.

Gabriel came in and winced, either at the sight of her or the smell of the room.

'Jude,' he said, sitting on the bed beside her. 'Are you sober?'

'More or less,' she said, pushing her bruised arm underneath the blanket. 'Whatever I did, I'm sorry.'

'You were very aggressive, Jude. You know I can't tolerate that kind of behaviour. You can't stay here if—'

'I know, Gabriel. I'm sorry, really... I'm sorry.'

'You need to apologise to Marissa.'

Jude groaned, feeling like a child again after an argument with Lucy, when their father made them shake hands and give each other a kiss.

'OK, OK.'

'It won't happen again, right?'

Jude felt the ache and sting of her arm, Eddie's breath against her face, the cold needle moving in her vein.

'No,' she said. 'It won't happen again.'

Stays are usually cut in four parts, all of which are generally upon the cross, as this assists materially in making them set better to the figure.

– *The Workwoman's Guide*, by a Lady, 1839

Marissa stood looking at the calico corset dressed on a mannequin in the cutting room. She touched the fabric, then walked around it to run her fingers down the laces at the back.

'I was reading in the newspaper,' Gabriel said, as he came through from the shop, 'about the rise in plastic surgery. As though it's something new. Body enhancement. Hair extensions. Piercings. These things have followed us down the centuries.'

He pulled the curtain around to contain them, then loosened the laces, freeing the corset from its bindings.

As he talked, Marissa relaxed, infused by a calm stillness that would welcome the corset's embrace. Scarlett's fittings had been the same; still, like a meditation, the vanilla scent of her skin, her dark eyes in the mirror.

He left the loose corset on the mannequin and said, 'Let me know when you're ready.' She nodded and he slipped through the curtains. He stood for a moment and took a slow, deep breath. There was no sound except for the movement of Marissa as she took off her clothes, so he talked again to fill the silence, an empty space that opened out now, more than at any other time since Scarlett had died. He talked of primitive man painting their bodies, kneading the heads of newborn babies to a point, stretching necks and lower lips, Chinese foot binding, how the ancient Egyptians pulled clothes tight around their bodies and wore wide wigs to emphasis their line.

'It was often more than just image,' he said. 'The Crow Indians pierced their bodies with skewers. It gave them supernatural visions. The Mandan Indians cut off their little fingers; a sacrifice to the Great Spirit. The Bafian tribe of Cameroon. They scar their bodies. Believing it's what makes us different from the apes.'

'You know so many interesting things,' Marissa said. 'I love people who have a passion for what they do.'

Silence fell between them then, so deep and encompassing it made Gabriel's hands tremble, a knot of nervousness tying up in his chest. Scarlett had once said the same thing to him during a fitting of her first dress, before they were lovers. Now, years later and with only a curtain between him and Marissa, a crackle of connection repeated itself.

'In the eighteenth century,' he said quickly, 'men used to wear false calves in their stockings if they weren't blessed with the required muscle.' He tried to laugh but it sounded hollow, like an echo.

'I'm ready,' Marissa said.

Gabriel pulled back the curtain an inch and went through, avoiding her eyes in the mirror. She had pulled her hair over one shoulder so he could tie her laces, and her bare skin glowed with the scent of spices; cardamom and cloves.

He pulled the laces, loosely at first but gradually tightening until her body changed; her torso exaggerated to a powerful V-shape, her waist moulded to a circle, the laces like a ladder of perception climbing her spine. With the final tug a small gasp escaped from her lungs. He stopped, his throat tight, his fingers pulsing with the laces wrapped around them.

'I know this is the rough version,' she said, her voice coming low and narrow, 'but it's still beautiful.' She let her hands run down the fabric, from her breasts to her stomach.

He concentrated on tying the laces at the base of her spine, and took a blue biro from his jacket pocket, marking the calico where it needed alteration, where the fabric didn't sit perfectly against her skin.

'Do you think it's possible,' she said, 'to change yourself? Not just your body or your hair, but inside. Change the person you are?'

'True change,' he said, still moving around her, focused on marking the fabric, 'can only come from inside.' He stood back then, adding, 'Where do you come from?'

Her hand went to her forehead and she tipped her head slightly, biting on her lower lip.

'I don't know,' she said. 'I was adopted.'

'I'm sorry. I didn't want to...'

'No, it's OK,' she said, holding up her hand. 'It's not something I... I trust you.'

'Do you want to find your birth parents?'

She shook her head.

Gabriel nodded, the stillness of her body like the silence of gathering thoughts.

'I was abandoned, so there's no paperwork.'

Marissa's hand dropped to her stomach, firmly sculpted by the corset. Their eyes caught in the mirror then, and she gave him a smile so small and fragile that he had to step back through the gap in the curtains; to breathe, to place a barrier between them, to prevent that connection crystallising into permanence.

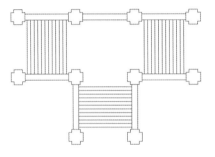

STAR BORN

a short story by Lorien Hallama

'We have to talk,' she said.

I knew by the tone of her voice that this was big, that I would not be able to leave tonight. I would try anyway, I decided, and so straightened my back and cleared my throat. 'Me too,' I said. My voice came out low and uncertain, so I coughed again and continued. 'I mean, I have something to say to you first.'

'No.' My wife frowned. 'Me first.'

I knew that look; she was biting her bottom lip, picking off the skin with her front teeth and darting her eyes back and forth at the placid street behind me. She was nervous. I had no choice, and so I nodded, said 'Fine', and followed her into the house. She took my hand, held it hard, digging her nails into my palm as she led me through the front foyer and the kitchen. I looked around as we walked, gazed numbly at the shadows of appliances collecting dust on the counters. The chairs around the dining table were pushed in, unused since Christmas. I couldn't remember the last time we'd had a family meal. No, that couldn't be true – Janet had guests over last Sunday. Isn't that right? Not family but guests just the same. I wondered where the children were; they should have been home by now.

We made our way to the bedroom and I dropped my wife's hand; I had to wipe the sweat left over from her fingertips on to the sides of my trousers. There were flowers in the bedroom balanced on top of Janet's nightstand: pink orchids that Janet must have bought for herself. Everything was pink, a colour I had always found nauseating and that I'd had to live with for seventeen years, since before we were able to have Lindsay and Devon. Janet thought we would never have children. She was obviously wrong. The colour stayed; she said it was good luck.

'Come sit, Jay.' She took a seat on the edge of the bed, and I had to turn away because even her face was flushed pink.

'Janet, I really need to say something first.'

'Lindsay is pregnant.'

I pretended not to hear. No, never mind. I must have *mis*heard. My eyes half-closed, half-zoomed in on my fingers reaching for the closet light switch, tightening their grip around the white plastic knob.

'Jay?'

I flicked the switch up and down, up and down, hypnotised by the pattern of light across my feet.

'Jay?'

'Yes?'

'Did you hear me?'

'No.'

'Turn around.'

My fingers had lost most of their colour by now. I forced myself to turn around, to look at Janet. She extended her arm to pat the square of quilt beside her thigh, her forehead crinkled into concern. I stuffed my hands into my pockets and focused on the dust ruffle, on its intricate design of folds and wrinkles, strawberries and creams.

'Lindsay is pregnant.'

I told my wife to shut up, please. Thank you. I looked at her sitting tall and erect on the bed.

'But Jay, what are we going to do?'

We. I shrugged and turned around, refaced the closet doors. I ran my fingers up and over the wood shingles; it sounded like a soft heartbeat. *We.* What are *we* going to do? There was no way that I could leave. Not tonight. Not at all.

Fuck, Lindsay.

'Jay!'

Janet was now at my side, inspecting my bleeding fist, inspecting the closet door, hollowed in the middle by a dark open hole, with jagged splinters pointing inward. Her eyes were wide, her skin pale. 'I'll go fetch some bandages.'

I nodded and inhaled deeply from the sting, cupping my knuckles with my other hand. It was a stupid thing to do, a brash thing to do. I knew better.

Janet returned with the bandages as promised. 'I hope you haven't broken anything this time.' She was tender as she wrapped the open flesh. I watched her eyes, dark brown, long lashes curled down, intent and focused on the task at hand. She was always good with things like that. Always the nurse.

'Thanks,' I said.

She nodded.

I pulled away and patted my fist softly. 'I don't know what came over me, Janet.' I knew that an apology was appropriate, but instead I continued to bow my head, pretending to focus on my wound while stealing glances at Janet through my peripheral vision.

She shrugged her shoulders. 'Lindsay will be home soon,' she said, her gaze still focused on the closet door. 'Devon's going to a friend's house to give us some time. Some privacy.'

'For what?' I asked. 'Doesn't this concern him at all? Does he even know?' Janet frowned at me. I tried to picture my son at a friend's house and felt the urge to punch the closet door again; I never met any of my son's friends. I took a step in front of Janet. 'Devon should be home for this. A family meeting.'

Janet shook her head. 'Lindsay wants to you tell you by herself. She doesn't even want me here.'

The buttons on my shirt constricted around my neck; I tugged at the collar and wondered whether or not my face was turning red. 'Really?'

'Yes.'

'Can't you be here with us?'

Janet took a step towards me and struggled to help undo my top button, her claws scratching my neck; she was only tender when it involved blood or broken bones. I rubbed the skin and frowned.

'You have to do this, Jay.'

'I would prefer all of us to be here. I wouldn't know what to say.'

'You're her father.'

'Isn't this a girl thing?'

'This isn't a *thing*, Jay.' Janet sighed, rubbing her forehead at the temples with both hands. 'Yeah, well, I guess it is a thing. A big thing. A mess.'

'Disaster.'

'You said it.' She took my hands again and squeezed them. It hurt my damaged hand and I thought she should have known better. I looked at the clock behind her head and asked what time our daughter would be home. Janet raised an eyebrow. 'Any minute now. We should go wait for her. Come.'

I followed her out into the hallway, the walls of which were one-dimensional monuments devoted to our children through the years. I froze at a photograph of Lindsay while Janet continued to move past me. I tried to remember when the picture was taken, how old Lindsay was. She looked about ten years old, leaning over a wall at the zoo in front of a rhinoceros sleeping in the distance. I think we were in Ohio. Her curly hair was cropped short, and she was smiling, her front teeth crooked. She was making the peace sign with her fingers. I must have taken the picture although I didn't remember doing so.

'Jay, I hear her car.'

I walked quickly, joining Janet at the front window. We watched Lindsay thank her driver, a girl about her own age with dark hair, in the moonlight. They waved goodbye to each other and Lindsay started up the driveway alone, her thin face focused down on the tarmac as the headlights behind her faded away with the body of the car.

'You ready?' Janet asked.

I shrugged. 'Do I really have to answer that?'

The door opened, my daughter poked her head around the frame, her large pretty eyes aware of our presence in the foyer.

'Hi, honey.'

'Hi, Linds.'

She did not answer, just looked at my wife and me with long, poignant stares. I noticed that she was gripping the door handle so intently that her fingers were turning white.

'Did Janet tell you?'

I nodded. 'Just now.'

Lindsay pushed open the door and stepped inside. She dropped a backpack to the ground and folded her arms across her chest. She did not look in the least bit concerned. 'I want to speak to you alone,' she said to me.

I nodded, flashed a pleading look to Janet who turned away. 'I'll be upstairs,' Janet said. 'Call when you're ready for me.' She kissed Lindsay on the forehead as she walked by; my stomach muscles tightened as I watched the back of my wife disappear.

'Should we go sit on the couch?' Lindsay asked.

'Yeah, sure, good idea.' I followed Lindsay into the living room where her small frame fell into the leather couch. I sat across from her and allowed my eyes to scan her stomach for a sign of life inside, a sign of movement, growth, truth – anything. It looked flat, unchanged, the same as yesterday. I felt a flutter in my chest, a small hope that this was all a misunderstanding, Janet's idea of a sick joke on Dad.

Lindsay puffed out her cheeks, exhaling loudly as though she was bored, waiting for me to speak. I asked her how was school and she rolled her eyes.

I asked how the college search was going and felt my throat dry up: I hadn't thought of college. Would she still be able to go?

'Dad.'

I stiffened. She hadn't called me Dad in years, not since she started high school and the traditional terms of endearment dissolved into *Janet* and *Jay* in passing.

'Yes?'

'Say something.'

'I am.'

'Say something about *this*.' She pointed to her stomach.

I scratched my head, tried to think. 'Do I know the boy?'

'No.'

'Does Janet?'

'No.'

'Devon?'

'Yes. Well, I think so, anyway. Everyone at school knows him. He's that kind of kid.'

'Great.' I leaned back, put my head in my hands, peered at my daughter through my split fingers. She was pulling her hair out of its ponytail, allowing it to fall free around her shoulders. She twirled one piece around her index finger, and then ran the strands across her lips. She looked far away and coy, and almost sexy doing it. It made me aware of the obvious fact that she'd had sex. I told her to cut it out, to leave her hair alone.

'It's time to be mature,' I said. She rolled her eyes. I looked at the clock beside me; it was half-past seven already. I had planned to be on the road by now, nearly to my brother's place in New Haven. My stomach rumbled.

'Do you have somewhere else to be?' Lindsay was glaring at me, reading my thoughts, one eyebrow raised. She looked nothing like her mother. My daughter was beautiful.

'You hungry?' I asked, standing up, stretching. Lindsay hesitated but followed me into the kitchen. 'What can you eat? Eggs? You like eggs? I make a hell of an omelette.'

'Dad you're sweating.'

Lindsay handed me a paper towel. I wiped my face and cringed at the impression it left behind. I crinkled the sheet in my hands and turned away, turned toward the stove.

'Hand me that pan, will you?'

I thought I heard her sigh but she obeyed and the metal pan felt nice and solid in my hand. I turned to get the butter and eggs but Lindsay was blocking the refrigerator, arms folded across her chest.

'I'm really not hungry, Dad.'

There was a photograph of someone else's kids behind her left shoulder pinned beneath a magnet that read: 'The only things I know how to make are reservations.' The kids in the photograph were smiling, teeth missing, shaggy black hair, and, if I had to guess, they looked to be around middle school age. I had no idea who they were or why they were on my refrigerator as opposed to pictures of my own kids, a continuation of the shrine in the hallway by the bedroom. My daughter did not seem to notice my distraction. She herself looked distant.

'You need to eat something, Linds.'

'Why?'

'Are you keeping it?'

'She shrugged one shoulder as if the thought had never occurred to her.

'I guess so.'

'Go sit down, then. You're eating for two.'

She rolled her eyes and shuffled over to the table. I felt her watching me as I opened the door; I left my head inside for longer than necessary just because I liked the feel of the cold across my cheeks, the smell of the cold, plastic and artificial.

'Dad?'

I closed the door and stood erect.

'Do you think I should keep it?'

I carried the supplies over to the counter and began to crack the eggs into a mixing bowl. It took me a moment to answer. I decided to be honest because I didn't know what else to say. 'I don't think you have to decide tonight, Lindsay.'

'What happened to your fist?'

'Accident.'

'Again?'

I didn't answer. I began to pour the liquid eggs into the buttered pan, holding my spatula ready in my good hand. I was enjoying being at the stove. When Janet and I first got married it was me that did the cooking: pot roasts, stuffed chicken, lamb shanks. Meat and two veg, that's what Janet preferred. Whenever I got experimental it wound up in the garbage disposal. Janet was never one for change.

And so it went.

'Does it hurt?' Lindsay asked.

'No.'

'Why do you do it?'

I narrowed my eyes at the pan, the thin yellow coating beginning to bubble gently. I picked up the handle and levelled out the remaining liquid. 'Why don't we talk about you? One thing at a time, all right?'

'OK.' I heard her tapping something against the table but I did not turn around to see what she was holding. 'I don't feel anything, yet.'

I didn't answer.

'Am I supposed to feel different?'

'Are you sure you're pregnant?'

'Of course.' Her voice was defensive, borderline angry.

'I didn't mean anything by it, Linds. Honest.'

'Janet wants me to get an abortion.'

I froze for a moment, my stomach muscles contracting once again. I pictured Lindsay as a little girl, trampling through the back yard in her high tops and jeans. She was a tomboy. She did not play with dolls.

'I think you should see a doctor. And then decide.' I had to force my next sentence: 'Your mother only wants what's best for you.'

'What about you?'

I began to sprinkle bits of cheddar and Monterey Jack into the omelette. 'What about me?'

'You don't get along with her.'

I put down my spatula and faced my daughter. She was not looking at me, her eyes were now focused in the doorway where Janet was standing, her nightgown covered by a faded salmon bathrobe. Her hair was pinned back at the sides, and I couldn't help but notice that she looked much older than thirty-seven.

'I figured it would be OK if I came in now,' she said. She gave Lindsay and me a smile, her teeth clenched. She sat down next to Lindsay. I turned back to the stove.

'Shit.'

'What's the matter, Jay?'

'Nothing. I just ruined the omelette. It's scrambled eggs now, Linds. Hope that's all right.' I finished mashing them up with my spatula until all that was left was bright yellow mush. I turned off the heat and reached for a plate. I was tired of cooking.

'So?' Janet said, her elbows indenting the foam, floral-print placemats. Lindsay was twirling her hair again. I poured some salsa on top of the eggs and carried the plate over to her.

'Hope they're OK.'

Lindsay smiled at me. Janet frowned and straightened her posture, bringing her hands against the table with a thud. 'Did you two come to some arrangement?' she asked.

I nodded. 'She is going to see her doctor. And sleep on it. How are the eggs?'

'Forget the eggs, Jay.' Janet had raised her voice, had changed the tone of the situation so that the colour grey had suddenly flooded the room. It made Lindsay slump down in her chair, which in turn made me angry, clench my fists.

'What's the problem?' I asked my wife.

'Unbelievable, Jay. You're unbelievable.'

'Janet, it's taken care of. No use stressing the kid out tonight. She needs time.'

'You were the one who called it a disaster.'

'Dad?' Lindsay was looking at me with wide eyes, her fingers gripped tight around her fork. Her face had gone pale.

'Linds, I never. Fuck, Janet, why? Why do you have to do this?'

Janet had turned her chair around to face our daughter head on, the legs of the chair lined up and bumping Lindsay's. She took the fork out of Lindsay's hand and replaced it with her own fingers.

'Honey,' she said, the volume of her voice decreasing. She sounded like a child conspiring. 'We need to come to a decision tonight. I don't think you realise what a big deal this is.'

'Janet...'

She waved me away with a nod of her head, furious, flushed, still focused on Lindsay, who by this time had started to tremble. 'I handle this all the time at work. I see it. I know. We need to consider all of the options. The best options.'

I backed up as I watched her speak, my eyes half-closing, half-zooming in on the mole on the right side of her lips. There was a faint trace left of her lipstick, worn off instead of washed off, cracked where chewed. I could not look at her any more.

'Where are you going, Dad?'

'I'll be right back, Linds. I just need some air.'

I knew she needed me. I knew that I should stay. But I left anyway, made my way back through the foyer and out the front door. I sat on the stoop outside, hugging my knees tight against my chest. My escape car, the Jetta, sat still in the driveway as though it was waiting, ready to follow through with our plan. The keys were still in my pocket.

If you are going to leave, go now, I told myself. I stared at the Jetta, turned away, felt my eyes begin to sting, my bandaged fist begin to hurt again. I was stuck here. And my daughter was stuck inside. I laid my head back and allowed it to smack down gently against the concrete while I looked up at the sky, starless and purple, the colour of ripe plums. I thought I could hear the faint sounds of someone crying back in the house, probably Lindsay, probably because of Janet.

Fuck, Lindsay, Baby Girl. You're pregnant.

I closed my eyes, waited for a breeze that did not come. I imagined that I was somewhere in space, flying through a wormhole, passing through time at unrestrained speeds. I imagined that it would feel something like birth, a push and shove effect, being handed to the light. I remembered how I felt when I saw Lindsay for the first time, my first born, my only girl. Amongst the blood and mucus, black and white and sea foam green, ocean waves playing on the nurse's CD player, amongst all of this, I held a star.

I opened my eyes. Nothing had changed in the sky above, in the stale, humid air. Inside the house my baby was pregnant, and in a sense, so was I, so was Janet, and this mystery boy, this popular enigma. Everything had changed. Slowly I stood up, pulled out the keys from my side pocket and walked over to the Jetta. I didn't know where I was going, but I knew it couldn't be far.

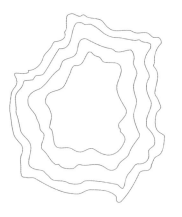

PLOT 8

from the novel The Allotment Plots by Sally Hare

Though Anna's husband Luke was killed in a drink-driving accident on Christmas Eve, he still nags her to tend their allotment in her dreams. One day she sees a vision of him on the plot, in the bed where she scattered his ashes.

'I'm not wearing this, Helen; I look like a prostitute in it.' Anna tugged at the swirly pink Lycra nightmare that was constricting her ribcage like an asthma attack. Her sister dragged the bottom of the dress down to the middle of Anna's thigh, which only served to pull the neckline down past the top of her lace-topped bra.

'You do not look like a prostitute. You look... alluring.'

Anna jerked the neckline up again, revealing a washed-out pair of cotton knickers. 'I look like a prostitute and you know it. It's coming off.'

'Don't you want to look nice? Makes a change to see you in something that isn't, you know...'

Anna poked her in the shoulder. 'Isn't what?'

'Isn't, well, nice and comfy, dear. Now put these shoes on and trust me.'

Anna picked up the sequinned, pointy hen-night horrors between finger and thumb. 'Where do you find this stuff?' she asked, stuffing them back in the carrier bag.

'Well, the dress was British Heart Foundation and the shoes were Cancer Research. Oh, come on, you're not getting into the spirit of this at all.'

'The spirit of what?' Anna pulled the micro dress down over her shoulders and kicked it across the room. 'You're getting this all wrong. I don't want to look alluring. It's just a bloody drink, for God's sake.'

'With an eligible bachelor...'

'Oh, stop stirring. This isn't like you and Max, OK? You may be ready to get out there and shake it, but I'm still...'

'Yes?'

'Look, Diggory is a nice guy, and I let him store a load of timber out the back for a couple of weeks, and he just wants to say thanks, OK? I'm not ready to start making sweet love with the king of the fairies just yet.'

'OK, OK, don't protesteth too much, will you, lady?' Anna tried to pull on a pair of jeans as Helen turned her attention to her sister's hair, twisting it into a tight little bun on the top of her head. Anna batted her hand away.

'That looks like a turd, Helen.'

'Thanks.'

'Oh, I'm sorry. I just don't see this like... like you obviously do.'

Lily ran into the room and picked up the micro dress.

'Oh, you have it,' said Helen. 'It'll fit you a lot better than it fits us.'

Anna helped her daughter's hands through the sleeve holes. 'How is Max, anyhow?'

Helen grimaced. 'He's an arsehole. And a crap father. I mean, goodness knows what state the girls will be in when they get back tomorrow. You should have seen him last time he had them for the weekend. Couldn't bloody wait to get shot...' Anna engaged her automatic Helen filter and pulled on a flowery tunic.

'...Fed them on tinned bloody tuna and oven chips, *again*, and never took them out at all...'

'Mmm, mmm... Oh dear.' Ten past eight already. Anna began to wonder if expecting punctuality from a man who believed in the power of the primal scream might have been a little too hopeful. She loosened the silk scarf that had just been wound around her neck and wandered downstairs.

'...Their feet stank, I tell you, and I swear their hair hadn't been brushed all weekend...'

Lily and Dexter were soon seated, sweeted and genially threatened while Helen continued with her diatribe from the kitchen, reappearing with a bottle of Merlot.

'One for the road?'

'No, thanks.'

While her sister's complaints and the whine from the television dissolved into a sum more irritating than its parts, Anna sank into the tired velour sofa and wondered how best to approach spending an evening with Diggory. His invitation had come as a complete surprise; the last thing she had expected whilst restocking the snack display at the shop. Guilt tickled her spine like a centipede. She knew full well that she would have made an excuse if he had asked her two weeks previously. But the shock of Luke's visit to her birthday party on the allotment had unsettled her; the family had been surviving on shrink-wrapped vegetables ever since. If anyone could explain his appearance then that person was likely to be Diggory. And at least she could trust him not to laugh.

Though Luke had been absent from her dreams since then, he had invaded her consciousness in a far more unsettling way. She was still unsure what Dexter had or had not seen that afternoon. 'Daddy bumped his head,' had now become a permanent addition to his 'Where's Daddy, Daddy gone?' script, but otherwise he seemed the same as ever. She had asked him about it, gently, a few days later, but he had become flappy and sought refuge in repetition, reciting the familiar phrases over and over. 'Mummy fine...' When his voice began to take on its robotic edge Anna knew not to persist. She had hugged him, and kissed his fair hair, and talked his favourite Yoda-speak to make him laugh, hoping that, somehow, Dexter was making sense of things in his own way. This was one applecart probably best left standing.

'...I mean he keeps telling me he's missing me but what he's missing is a full-time drudge...'

Dexter and Lily were playing footsie now, twining their legs together and falling off the sofa. He certainly didn't look too traumatised, though Lily was looking paler than usual. Too much supermarket rubbish.

Diggory eventually arrived at half past eight, by which time Helen had exhausted all Max-related topics and had moved on to a scathing evaluation of the policies of the Child Support Agency and the government's treatment of single parents in general. Anna ran to the door as soon as she saw his thin shadow pass the window, before the sound of the bell roused Dexter to shout 'Not you!' and slam the door in his face. Regular visitors were used to this level of hospitality, but it could cause embarrassment to the uninitiated.

'Evening,' said Diggory.

'Evening,' said Anna with a determinedly unamused smile. Her date had certainly 'scrubbed up'. Under the customary once-black fedora, his lanky frame sported two lurid shirts over a fractal vest, desert-orange combat trousers and Doc Marten boots polished to screaming point. He looked like he might have rolled in one of the second-hand stalls at Redland Green Fair. The air around him reeled with a heady blend of patchouli oil and Lynx.

Anna had never seen Diggory close-shaven before. Though stubble was all part of the uniform for a swag-bag toting, stripy-shirted burglar, Diggory looked more suspect without it somehow. The centipede of guilt began wriggling again. All this effort expended on her miserable ulterior motives. *Because you're worth it*. Then, perhaps she had mistaken his motives too. Helen certainly seemed to think so, performing pantomime winks and nudges behind his back while he bobbed his head and blushed.

'Picton?' he asked, 'or would you rather go into town?'

'No, no, the Picton's fine by me,' said Anna, blushing back. Diggory, she knew, was of a species that best thrived in its native habitat. Dragging him as far as one of the wine bars on the main road might challenge the local ecosystem, she suspected.

'Right. Be good for Aunty Helen, yes? Any phone calls and there'll be trouble. Bedtime at nine and no messing about. Comic in bed at nine-o-o, Dexter, yes? Mum back soon. Lily, you can read till half past.'

They made their way through Cobham in a state of oddly formal politeness, as if all their chats in the trading hut hadn't counted. 'How's Orlando?'

'Yeah, he's cool; had a birthday last week. Haven't seen him much, to be honest – Jade's been touring the festivals doing reiki treatments so they haven't been about at weekends much.'

'Oh.'

The terraces cast long shadows across the narrow streets, the stone and tarmac still radiating the warmth of the day as they made their way towards Cobham Road. Children scooted past on the pavement and teenagers leaned on walls, swearing unimaginatively. The ripe evening air hummed with sticky possibility, and Anna remembered a similar night, long before everything had got so grown-up, when she and Luke had drunk scrumpy from a gallon canister on top of Brandon Hill, only staggering home when the sky paled to peach over the gothic excess of St Mary Redcliffe Church. They had said that they loved each other that night. But perhaps not for the first time.

'How're your kids?' Diggory asked.

'Oh, fine. Well, little buggers, you know, but they've had a tough year...'

Diggory frowned, over-serious and awkward. 'Yeah, right.'

They heard the drumming long before they reached the pub. It rumbled through the soles of their shoes as they turned into the alley beside the allotments, thumping inside their chests by the time they were half way down.

Diggory groaned. 'Shit, I'd forgotten the Farm Fair; it'll be packed down there. Do you want to go somewhere quieter?' Anna shook her head: a dollop of noise and bustle might, she reasoned, grease the silences a little, so she paid two pounds at the barrier and they wandered into the crowd.

The Victorian buildings that comprised the farm and the original farmhouse, now the Picton Arms, sat side-by-side with the Gaudí-esque café at the southern edge of the allotments, all festooned with bunting, and throbbing with once-a-year goodwill. The pub's usual mix of occupants, from the socked-and-sandalled to the muck-wellied, had deserted their usual tables, beating a graceful retreat in the face of this lightly mirrored invasion.

'Pint?' asked Diggory, and disappeared through the wooden gate into the pub garden. Anna found a space on the lawn and waited, watching the ebb and flow of the crowds in the road outside. The fair was heaving with crochet and tie-dye. 'Stalls', that were really kitchen tables or sofa throws spread on the floor, displayed hand-painted plant pots; hair wraps; exotic-looking pipes; herby things in plastic bags. Bell was wandering with her jazz band round the pig sties, their usual fluorescent cacophony jostling for ear space with the samba band swaying past the duck pond at the far end of the farm. A predictable aroma floated in the air. Diggory reappeared with two pints of Old Nodder and they balanced them between the knobbles on the grass.

'Cheers.'

'Cheers.' They sipped in what might as well have been an awkward silence, dragging out the usual suspects of meaningless conversation – parenthood, planting, weeding, chitting.

Potting on.

The comparative merits of bought versus harvested seed...

Another?' asked Anna, and dashed off to the bar, appalled by her unusually atrocious lack of conversation. The pub was heaving; by the time she had secured two more pints and wobbled back through the bazaar of bare legs, spangled Indian bags and personalised tobacco tins strewn over the grass, Diggory was sharing a roll-up with a young man Anna recognised as one of the straggly Jack-In-The-Green dancers on the common. They were having a very animated conversation about the authenticity of Rag over Cotswold Morris, so Anna left Diggory's pint beside him and leaned over the picket fence, scanning the crowd for a familiar face.

Every dangle-limbed tree-hugger in Bristol seemed to have converged on the neighbourhood that evening. Long queues had formed in front of the falafel and vegan curry vans, each establishment slightly dubious looking despite all the healthy ingredients chalked on its menu. There was much chatting and drinking, and marvelling at how a whole year had passed since the last fair, as visitors promenaded in their most faded finery. Anna wondered how many would have to don suits on Monday morning. Or if any secretly read the *Daily Mail*, and got cheap thrills from buying musty-scented regalia from head shops, hiding their guilty purchases under a mountain of M&S tailoring at the back of the wardrobe in their oyster-beige homes. If, when summer came, they told their partners about imaginary squash leagues, while really sneaking out to get changed in public toilets and rub up against flimsy kaftans and scratchy South American shirts. She wondered if the festival junkies knew this, and sniggered at the interlopers' embarrassing attempts to pick up the vernacular.

Diggory's eyes seemed a little red and unfocused when he rested his hand on her shoulder a moment later. He mumbled an apology, then giggled and sipped his pint. Then giggled again. Then squeezed her shoulder and began to roll up, the twist of cling film sitting inside his tobacco pouch confirming Anna's assumptions. 'Don't mind, do you?'

'No, no... Look, Diggory, can I ask you something?' She knew that there was no point beating round the bush. From now until last orders there would be nothing to look forward to but sniggering drivel. Might as well try and wrestle a last bit of sense from him.

'Depends what it is,' said Diggory, chipping bits of dope off the block with his thumb.

'Well, I remember you saying something a couple of weeks ago about going to a drumming camp with Orlando, and you said you saw angels everywhere.'

Diggory sealed the paper and flicked his lighter. 'Yeah, man, awesome.'

'Well...'

'...Yeah?'

'Well...' Anna drank a large mouthful of Old Nodder. Diggory inhaled deeply on his joint.

'...Yeah?'

'Well, what did they look like?'

'Look like?' he hiccupped, neck as stiff as a bamboo cane, chin tucked on to his chest.

'Yeah, I mean, did they look like, well, angels in pictures, or people, or what?'

Diggory exhaled loudly and offered the joint to Anna. 'You've never seen one?'

She waved it away. 'I don't know. I don't know what I've seen. I mean, what have you seen? You don't look like a Christian, so how come you've seen angels?'

Diggory leaned in close and squeezed her shoulder again. 'God's a state of higher consciousness, you know? Any person can reach it. Don't need organised religion to mediate for you.'

'Eh?'

'Well angels aren't solely a Christian thing. They've just nicked them and made them exclusive. Like Yule.'

Anna frowned. 'Right.'

He inhaled again, leaving Anna waiting long seconds before continuing. 'I mean, after the Atlantean Civil War, right, the destruction created an enormous, like, shift in Universal energies – sort of cast a Veil over Gaia for thousands of years. Taken all this time for the karma to balance again, you know, for the Veil to shrink enough for the angels to come back through.'

'I see.'

He squinted down at her. 'Do you? What do you see?'

Anna was losing patience. 'Never mind what I see. What did *you* see? I mean, are you always seeing them? Or was it just the Drumming Camp?'

Diggory drew back and gave her a superior look. 'Why are you so interested in angels all of a sudden?'

'*Diggory!*'

He waved the roll up under her nose and grinned. 'Well, they're just, like, there, you know? You can just see them.'

'*But what do they look like?*'

Wandering Jazz staggered into the garden playing a discordant chorus of 'Colonel Bogey' and Diggory frowned. 'Well, like angels,' he bellowed over the racket.

Anna folded her arms. She had finished her second pint and felt a strong desire for something small and neat in a crystal glass. 'I mean, white, in floaty dresses, red with little horns, *what?*' she screamed.

'Well, they're more of a feeling really, you know, like, an aura.'

'A shiny light?'

'Misty, you know, kind of spectral.'

'But do they have faces?'

Diggory laughed. 'Don't need them, man, that's just the prison of the body...'

'OK, no faces. So you can't... can't recognise them at all?' The sound of 'Colonel Bogey' shrank to a belching grumble as Wandering Jazz made their way into the lane behind the farm. Diggory didn't seem to notice.

'Recognise what?' he shouted.

Anna brought her voice to a stage whisper. 'You know – the angels.'

'Course you can!' he shouted back. 'I mean, I know when I've seen an angel right away. Unmistakable.'

'But they don't look like people?'

Long, long pause again. 'People?' At least he had finally noticed the band had gone and stopped shouting.

'Yeah, like... I don't know... Like your dead granny or something.'

'Oh, no, that's not angels. That's ghosts.'

Anna's teeth were starting to grit. 'What's the difference?' she hissed.

'Well, your angels have never been incarnated as people. They've always been angels.'

'Right. Well what about ghosts then?'

'What about them?'

'Have you seen any ghosts?'

Diggory sniffed. 'Oh, no, man, you don't want to go believing in ghosts. Load of nonsense.' He leaned back against the wooden fence. Anna grabbed the joint from his fingers and took a large drag.

'What do you mean, load of nonsense?'

'Well, the spirits of the dead just, like, become one with the spirit of nature, you know? No such thing as bloody ghosts.' Anna finished the joint and ground the stub beneath her heel. Diggory paused before reaching for his papers again. 'You're all right, are you? I mean, I know you're, like, coming through your trauma and everything, but you are all right?'

'Fine. Bloody marvellous. Look, Diggory, it's been nice but I've just remembered I've got to get back now.'

'But we've only just got here! What do you need to go back for? Sit and chill, you know? Have another...'

'I, erm... I... I've just remembered I've left something in the oven.'

Diggory frowned. 'Can't you ring your mate up and get her to sort it out?'

'No battery!' Anna shouted, waving her mobile phone and slipping through the gate before he could spoil her escape plan by offering the use of his own. 'See you later! Thanks!'

She elbowed her way through the crowd with unbecoming violence, glaring in all directions and muttering furiously under her breath. Stupid hippy. Stupid useless bloody hippy. What could she do now? She sniffed back frustrated tears, realising despite her anger that the only stupid person in this sorry affair had been herself. Stupid to think Diggory was capable of talking sense about anything. Stupid to be so single-minded that she might have led the poor sod on. Stupid to make such a big deal of getting drunk and nodding off and having a nightmare. Stupid, stupid, stupid, stupid, stupid.

She retraced her steps up the overgrown lane beside the allotments, grateful that the Samba band seemed to have packed up. It was still quite light, though dusk had begun to creep in amongst the trees and bushes lining the path. Her head was swimming with beer and dope, swimming like it had done on her birthday. Oh, you idiot, she thought. Poor old Diggory. For a second she considered returning to the garden, to apologise and explain that there were no hard feelings, that she was still in a state after all these months...

'Anna.'

A voice she knew well. She turned, knowing that there was no one behind her.

'Luke?'

Silence. 'Luke? Is that you?' A flash of something amongst the trees, the check of a gardening shirt. She ran to the fence and peered through. 'Luke?' Nothing but the allotments stretching over the horizon. Her fingers found the gate key in her pocket, and for a second she tried to fumble it into the lock. But just for a second.

'You're pissed.' she said to herself. 'You're pissed now and you were pissed then and you are a big mess. This is not real. It has to stop'. Slipping the key back into her pocket, she ran the last twenty yards to the main road, where reality waited for her in the rumble of the traffic and the sound of a hundred Bruce Forsyths wittering through open windows. Stopping only for a large bar of Dairy Milk, she whistled 'Colonel Bogey' all the way home.

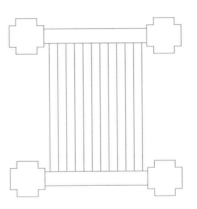

APENTI'S LUCK

from a short story cycle by Lucy Hewitt

The steps must be swept, the floor scrubbed, the chickens fed, the fish cleaned and gutted and the stew cooked. If Ese hurried, she could finish the chores before it got dark. Not so long ago, she had felt proud when her friends visited the house. She wanted to feel that way again.

Ese quickened her pace, putting her hands up to steady the fish basket on her head. She ignored the heaviness of her school bag and the burning sand between her toes. The village was quiet – people were still at work in the fields. Three goats had gathered on the path. Two of them head-butted each other, while the third chewed on the spiky leaves of a toppled palm.

The door of the house was open, but she couldn't see her mother moving about inside.

'I'm back,' she called. There was no answer. Ese sat on the step and placed the fish basket in her lap. Four mackerel lay at the bottom, their scales glittering blue, grey and black. She would make a good supper, the best they'd had for a week. If she paid attention and didn't leave any bones in the fish or let the yam boil dry, then maybe she could make things better. Her father had been unlucky lately. She could change all that. Ese pictured the family laughing and joking together, her mother sitting next to her father and Kwame relaxed and happy. If they tasted her food and forgot about their worries, she was sure this would happen.

A shadow fell across the step. She looked up to see her mother.

'Save one for tomorrow. We'll have to make do with three fish today.' Her mother frowned. She handed Ese a knife for the fish.

Ese noticed her hem was ripped and she was not wearing a headscarf – she looked plain without it. Lately she had been going for days at a time without one. Her wispy curls were lank and knotted. Ese would wait until she had finished the chores, then offer to oil and comb out her mother's hair.

Ese reached for a fish. Laying it flat on the stone step, she placed her thumb over its eye so that it could not watch her. Ese hated this job. She should do it quickly and try to forget about the mackerel's oily gaze. She picked up the knife and scraped off the scales. Slotting the knife tip neatly beneath the fin, she pushed down hard to crack the spine. Ese flipped the fish over and did the same on the other side. Its head came off with a crunch. The eyes had clouded over, their knowing blackness giving way to a milky sheen. Careful to avoid the grey stomach sac, she cut along the side of the fish. Using the blunt part of the blade, she eased out the intestines and removed the blood clots. She picked up a second mackerel and started again.

Apenti slipped the spare key out from beneath the flower pot. It clicked satisfyingly in the lock and the front door swung open. It was safe. He knew the nuns' house was empty. The fat Sister had gone on an errand and taken the others with her. Apenti had wanted to shout and clap when he saw the four-wheel drive turn out of the compound in a cloud of dust. As the odd job man, he was always expected to be hard at work. 'The fence beside childcare is broken.'... 'Make sure you remember to paint the blackboards in the school rooms.'... 'Don't forget to fix the window frame in the guest chalet.' With Sister Pauline around, even a small nap in the middle of the day was impossible.

Apenti fished in his pocket for a cigarette and held it up to his nose, sniffing at the warm tobacco. His match spluttered and weak flames lapped at the paper. Ah, that first deep breath. He pressed his lips together, holding the smoke in his lungs until it turned hot and fiery.

He walked into the kitchen and shoved the window open so forcefully that the shutter bounced against the wall. The fat Sister would not be back for hours, but she had a keen sense of smell. He'd heard her with the volunteers the other day: 'You two stink of fags. Your teeth will fall out and your hair will turn yellow.'

The one that reminded him of a plump chicken said, 'My hair's already yellow, Sister Pauline.'

Later, in his van, Apenti had laughed at that. The albino in the next village had yellow hair, but with a rusty tinge. This *obruni's* hair was like a field of guinea corn ripening in the midday sun.

He hawked up a ball of phlegm and rolled it around in his mouth. As he flicked some ash into the flower bed, he heard a thud. A mango had fallen, a lucky one to have escaped the eyes of birds and children. On the way home he'd pick it up for Ese and Kwame. He didn't often bring them gifts. It would be a relief to see Kwame smile. The boy blamed him. Ese didn't, she could see how hard he tried.

He tossed his cigarette butt out of the window. There was something shiny on the ground next to the mango. A trick of the light? No. It sparkled again. He pulled himself on to the ledge and jumped out. He could do with some luck. Abena had been getting suspicious. She was always asking him about his wage: where was it going, why wasn't it lasting as long as it should?

A watch. It had a gold strap with tiny links that slithered and clinked as he stroked them. He flipped the watch over. The words: *Ann, a gift for your twenty-first birthday, love Mum and Dad*, were engraved on the back. Apenti mouthed the sentence to himself. Yes, the volunteer girls. But which one was Ann? He couldn't remember if she was the plump chicken with coconut-milk skin, or the scrawny brown goat. Apenti slid the watch into his pocket. It rested against his leg, heavy and full of promise. For the first time in his life, he felt rich. As he swaggered back to the house, the watch swung loosely against him.

The blank television sat in one corner like a sulky child. Apenti twisted the volume dial until the table beneath it buzzed and throbbed. Leaving it to chatter to itself, he returned to the kitchen. The cupboard contained two boxes of cereal and some bottles of beer. STAR – that familiar gold label. Apenti smiled. The old nun was always drinking it. He clicked the cap off with his teeth. A soft rush of fizzy bubbles surged into his mouth and frothed at the back of his nose. He emptied the bottle in several gulps. Then he walked through to the lounge, flopped into a chair and rested his feet on the carved wooden coffee table.

'We've waited for you.' Abena's mouth was thin, unsmiling.

The room smelled of fish and yam. Whitebait, snapper or mackerel, they all tasted the same.

'Sorry,' Apenti told his wife, and slipped off his dusty flip flops. The plastic T-bar in the middle had worked its way free. He needed a new pair but there were ways around these things. He would go about bare-footed for a while.

Ese grinned at him but Kwame didn't look up. They sat in a circle on the floor, the big metal pot resting in the middle. He held up his bowl for Ese to fill. She did it slowly and he saw that she picked out some of the biggest pieces of fish. 'Did you get paid today?' asked Abena.

He scowled at her. 'Not now,' he said, flicking his eyes in the direction of the children.

She sucked at her lips and stood up, spilling her stew. Kwame winced and turned away. To create a diversion, Apenti clanked his spoon noisily against the rim of his bowl, scooping up the last bits of white flesh and leaving three transparent bones on the side. The spoon scraped across his teeth and he dropped it with a clatter. He reached out a hand to Ese and smoothed the soft skin of her cheek.

'Thank you,' he said, and walked out.

In the brief time he had been in the house, the sun had sunk. As the last of the light vanished, he imagined the huge red ball cooling in the sea, ready for the new day tomorrow. He climbed into the van and made sure to slam the door. The soft leather of the seat welcomed him, confirmed his presence. Before the intention had formed, his hand was in his pocket, checking the weight of the watch. Its winding device dug into his palm. He brought the watch out, stroked it and restored it to its resting place. The ignition key turned stiffly and the engine coughed, then died. After several goes, it settled into an uneasy rattling. His foot reached for the clutch and he felt something soft squish beneath the pedal. Peering down, he saw the remains of his mango, its stringy tentacles spilling across the floor in a mess of bruised skin and juice. He kicked it to one side.

As he drove away, he imagined the taste of beer in his mouth, the feeling of it warming his body and dulling his mind. The heaviness of the house began to leave him.

Ese stood on one leg, folding the other beneath her, stretching the tired muscles. The candle flickered as one of its waxy walls folded.

'Bring me the clothes for tomorrow's wash, then get ready for bed,' said Abena.

Ese went to fetch the washing basket from her parents' room. Her father lay on the bed. He grunted and turned over. He hadn't spoken since he got back. They'd heard his van stop outside and then the staggering steps as he found his way to the house. When he came in, Kwame and her mother pretended he wasn't there. Ese was the only one to greet him. She had been rewarded by a brief pat on the head and his warm, lopsided smile. The familiar smell was on his breath.

Her father's trousers lay in a heap beside the bed. She should include them in the washing pile. Grease marks and spilt liquids had stained the cotton. Something heavy landed with a clunk on the floor. She looked down, expecting to see a tool from his work box. But instead of rust and grime, there was polished metal. A lady's watch. The delicate gold leaf around the edge was etched with tiny flowers. She had never seen anything so lovely. Her hand hovered, not yet daring to pick it up. She pushed the questions aside. This would mean an end to the money problems. It was what they had been waiting for. Tentatively she reached for it, her fingers connecting with the sleek glass face. Ese cupped it in her hand like a pearled oyster before sliding the watch back into the pocket. She folded her father's trousers and left them at his feet. The washing basket was heavy but she skipped and danced across the room with it.

'You are too cheerful my child, too carefree and that's a fact,' said Abena.

'Luck waits around each corner. That is what they tell us at school. We should be ready for it.' She squeezed her mother's leathery hand.

'I hope you are right.'

The hot sun poked a cruel finger into Apenti's eye. Abena had let him sleep for too long. The rest of the family were up. He swung his legs over the edge of the bed, trying to ignore the pounding in his head. His stomach lurched and he retched some of last night's beer into his hand. When he looked up, Abena was standing in the doorway. She shook her head rudely.

'What is it, woman?' Apenti muttered. He wiped his hand on the sheet and leant down to look for his trousers. All of his waking moments were taken up with explaining or hiding from her. He would never have guessed she could become this person. Sometimes his friends mocked him: 'Apenti, you have married a snake. One drop of your wife's venom is enough to wither a man's treasured parts.' What had happened to his laughing girl?

'What is it? You ask me what is it, when your children are out selling iced water for their school fees. You know Ese might not make enough to go next term. Do you want your children to be like us?'

Even though he had heard this before, he was surprised by the bitterness in her voice. Where was respect for him, her provider?

He lunged at her and pinned her shoulders against the wall. 'Never speak like that,' he shouted. 'We've been unlucky, that's all. It doesn't mean I've given up on my dreams.'

Abena's eyes were wide, the whites bloodshot. Her bones were fragile beneath his hands. He turned away so that he did not have to look at her.

Ese tapped her fingers against the dashboard in time to the song in her head. The passenger seat was springy and she bounced up and down. These were her favourite times. Father would drive her to school, well, nearly to school. He'd drop her at his work and she would walk the rest of the way. She was lucky. Most fathers didn't have vans. Kwame used to get a lift too, but nowadays he insisted on walking. Ese liked being able to talk to her father without having Kwame there, scowling.

Ese nudged her father so he would look at her. His face was sad today. She could not think why; money wouldn't be a problem now. She bit her lip to stop herself from telling him she knew. He might think she was prying. It was enough that they shared a secret. After all, he could not keep quiet about it for long. Maybe he was waiting until the watch was sold.

As the truck rattled into the compound, Ese heard shouting. It was not the usual children's shouting. This was a woman's voice. Her father stopped the truck and turned off the ignition. Sister Pauline was in the middle of the yard. She was holding a little boy by the neck of his T-shirt and bawling at him. Next to her were the two women from England. One was fat with red skin and parrot-yellow hair, the other more like a skinny brown monkey. The boy was sobbing but she could not hear what he said.

Ese opened the van door and climbed out.

'Thief,' Sister Pauline yelled. 'After what this woman has given you.' She flapped a hand at the fat one. 'After she helped you with your reading. Well?'

'Not me, not me, not me,' the boy sobbed. His words ran together the way her father's did when he was late home. She recognised him as Patrick.

'Go.' Sister Pauline pointed. 'I'm sick of you.'

Head lowered, Patrick began to run blindly, stumbling and tripping on the uneven ground.

Her father was still in the van. Ese waved at him but he looked past her. He wore the same expression as when her mother shouted at him. It was as if he were living in a far-away land.

Apenti counted the last of his *cedis* on to the counter. The fat Sister wouldn't miss him for a while. There was too much else for her to think about. He swilled the *apetiti* around his glass and watched the clear liquid swill up the sides. She had caused him a problem. If he returned the watch to the plump chicken, they would wonder why he hadn't said anything that morning. Of course, the boy might have stolen something after all. It could have had nothing to do with the watch. Then Apenti would look foolish, trying to protect a proven thief. They might think he was in on the boy's secret. The fat Sister didn't like him anyway.

Abena would have known what to do. It was one of the reasons he had wanted her in the beginning – that cleverness. He had been too young and stupid to realise such women cause difficulties. It was a relief that Ese was not clever. She would make a good wife one day, eager to please and happy. He had done well there, in spite of her mother.

'Another.' He pointed at his glass. 'I will pay you next week.'

The watch felt heavier than it had done the day before. Apenti was aware of it in his pocket, a spiteful, skulking thing. He should get rid of it.

The shadows in the bar merged with the light and confused his eyes. Dark shapes perched like vultures around the room. They didn't have heads or eyes, just brooding black bodies that melted into nothing, or swelled like waves above his head. Their voices chattered faster than he'd thought possible, then slowed and distorted like a broken radio. His head was too heavy to lift. Something glinted in front of his eyes. It weaved in and out, making patterns, hypnotising him. It was soothing. He rested his head and closed his eyes, but the gold reflections pressed through the lids and dazzled him. There was something familiar about what he was seeing. If he focused hard, gold turned into flowers and leaves. The flowers' stems were spindly and weak.

'That's a fine piece of jewellery you have there, Apenti. Fit for a rich woman. Do you have a rich woman?' There was laughter, loud in his ear.

He saw Abena's terrified face as he pinned her against the wall and the sobbing, stumbling boy. Wherever he went, he brought trouble and disappointment. 'Take it. Take the watch,' he said and rested his head in his hands.

Deep, like a voice echoing in an ocean cave, he heard the words, 'A very generous gift. I never dreamed you had such riches to give away.' He felt an arm across his back and smelt the reek of week-old sweat. He turned away from the booming laughter and vomited weakly. His stomach was cramped and knotted. He neither knew nor cared where he was.

'What did Patrick take?' Ese asked Adua, after school. Adua lived in childcare with Patrick.

'He says he didn't take anything.'

'Do you think that's true?'

Adua shrugged. 'I'm not sure – it's a strange thing to steal. I don't think he knows how to tell the time.'

Ese stared at her. 'A watch,' she whispered. 'It was a watch?'

'Kwame, Ese, go and look for your father please.'

Ese stood by the door while Kwame finished his homework. He threw down the book and glared at her. Then he stomped out of the house. Ese ran along behind. Please let Father be working for Sister Pauline, she prayed.

Kwame pushed open the wooden door to the bar. They peered through the sweaty bodies and thick smog of smoke. Ese stared at Mr Omboye's pigeon-claw hands and tried to avoid looking into his red, sunken eyes. 'My father,' she muttered and stopped. He was there in front of her, slumped across the table, arms cradling head.

'Father,' she whispered. 'Wake up.' There was no response. She could smell the strong sugary fumes even though his face was turned away.

'Father, please.'

Kwame pushed her roughly out of the way. 'Get up,' he said and pulled at Apenti's arm. 'Father, get up.'

Deprived of something to lean on, Apenti slid sideways and fell to the floor like a sack of rice. Two men got up from their stools and walked over. They each took one of Apenti's arms and dragged him from the hut. His feet trailed in the dirt behind him. A gash on his heel exposed meaty red flesh. The men waited for the children to follow and gestured at them to swap positions.

Kwame and Ese began to walk home, pausing to ease the pain in their shoulders and shift their father's weight. After a while, they stopped for a rest. They tried to prop Apenti up, but he kept toppling over. Ese hated to see her father helpless, lying on his side like a newborn animal. They tugged him into a kneeling position but could get no further. Ese was too short to lever him up and he was too heavy for Kwame to lift alone.

'You wait here,' Kwame ordered. 'I'll get someone to help.'

Ese sat down next to her father. There was a dark patch around his crotch and a splatter of yellow vomit down his shirt front. She shifted so there was more of a gap between them. She reached up to wipe her dripping forehead on the back of one hand. The heat closed in. It clung to her like the gasps of a sweating, panting animal. She took a deep breath, but that didn't help.

A brown nanny goat wandered over. It stopped and began to chew on her father's trouser leg. The sound of gentle chewing and the persistent tugging at his clothes roused him. He lifted his head, tried to focus his eyes and wagged a finger in the general direction of the goat.

'Good luck is just around the corner,' he said. 'I know it.'

Ese shooed the goat away. Then she got up and brushed the earth from her legs. She pressed her knuckles into her eyes trying to rid them of that dry, aching feeling.

It was time. Ese began to walk. The darkness closed around her, soft and comforting. When she turned, she could see the vague outline of her father, silhouetted against the trees and bushes.

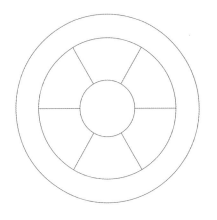

FIVE POEMS

by Carole Humphreys

The COMPAQ Wireless Mouse and Her Mate

He lies there upon the flatbed scanner –
a mouse-transceiver upon a piece of technology
that's passing time in energy-save-mode,
while being used as a coffee table.

He reclines there without purpose
and he's nothing without his wireless mouse mate
and she feels redundant without him.
It feels like death

when neither one of them is in operation –
he mourns, knowing she's been in the wars and lost
her protective cover; her intricate workings
are embedded with dust

and her batteries are dying. Interdependency –
hit his 'connect' button, his blue light will blink
until her corresponding button is activated. And theirs
is a ballet of a blue light twinkling while she,

in a red blaze, dances on hyperlinks. A romantic radar,
he finds her, and is joyful. Her red light
relays her pleasure until, at last,
her batteries die and she is lifeless and grey.

And his blue light is flashing as he pines. He becomes
a plaintive lighthouse throughout the black of night;
ever seeking a lost vessel. Off and on, never
diminishing.

I eventually notice his distress; hit 'connect'
and retry her dead batteries. There is just enough juice
for her to reply and then I grant them the long sleep
of tragic lovers.

Caesar Sends a Telegram after the Battle of Zela
Veni, Vidi, Vici.

I weathered out the winter with Cleo.
Come summer, my thoughts turned to fighting –
a need to flex other muscles. Pharnaces of Pontus
was a stubborn foe, no pushover; his army

matched mine to the last. Failure, an alarming thought,
were it not for my dogged determination
to get the job finished. A bloody mess – my men
reduced in number. No need to tell the Senate the facts.

His Gift of White Lilies
Flores Para Los Muertos

I have kept his gift of white lilies. I watched their passing,
saw them droop and dry, until all that was left was skeletal,
white petals and tentative threads. I saw the leaves turn brown,
losing the will to reach out or curve; they're now bedraggled.
But nothing has fallen – not even the black stamen, once so proud –
now lowly hung. Everything clings, hanging from vertical stalks.

He wonders when I'll dispose of the dead lilies – like there's a rush
to disturb dust on the dresser. I say that I like them more now;
I love to watch the shadows they cast, the way their vitality
has shrivelled – in death, their beauty is almost ridiculous.
They give me solace, and while I admire them in their wretched state
I know I am thinking of my own worth.

Lizzie Siddal's Cradle

My fingers follow the grain;
there are no splinters here,
just soft oak and honey hues.

My hand moves from wood
to Belgian lace, smoothing
the white pillow –

this is where her head should lie.
I imagine feeling her warmth
in the soft hollow my hand makes.

I rock the crib, sing *hush, little Rose,*
and whisper to visitors who call,
asking them to come on another day.

I need to be with her a while longer.

Dancing Bear

You like my soft paw shuffle, my groovy,
on-the-spot Samba; or is it my sashaying hips
in my attempt at a quick step
which prompts you to call for more?

Your cameras click and whir.
As Rana tugs the rope, I follow my nose –
this boy is my puppet master.
My toothless smile must mean I'm happy.

You're taken with the Bhangra beat,
clapping as the rope chafes me. My feet stagger
through Tchaikovsky's *Waltz of the Flowers*,
and you laugh. You're going to love my Rumba.

THE UNINHERITABLE HOUSE

from the novel by John Kefalas

One

Skinny-dip

The piano jangled into life. An imbalanced life at best – one afflicted by the signs and strains of age because not all of the keys moved. Some were slack enough to be blown into action by the slightest draught or breeze. Others were arthritic, resisting movement – obstinate.

Yet everything asked of the old instrument it delivered, along with a heavy dose of irony that mocked all but the most suitable music. Fish's music was suitable because he made it suitable. He knew how to exploit the piano's idiosyncratic resonance, how to play to its insolent comedy. He knew how each tone was like an arrogant child, announcing itself distinctive and unique.

Today the music was medicated – decongestant octaves in the left, non-drowsy thirds in the right – soothing. On any other instrument it would have sounded banal, but on this gross heirloom it had the fulsome density of a baroque continuo – harpsichords, viols, recorders, all consorting under the lid like a gathering of disagreeable aristocrats. Fish listened intently to the sound. Taken seriously, the out-of-tune instrument had unsettling depth. Its skewed harmonies sang an anxious song: a song of tension, a song of immersion, like how a deep-sea diver might feel when the ocean above begins to press with psychological as well as physical weight.

Fish had been in the sea that morning; wading against the high notes, swimming through tangled waveforms. He'd been in the sea because he liked it there. But it hadn't been *his* sea. *His* sea was a warmer, stewing sea, a thickly strung, bass sea. Today's sea had been a cold, forbidding sea, not the blue Aegean that laps warmly without explosion and uproar. Today, in the North Sea, he'd have been dead in fifteen minutes, because it was a grey, refrigerating sea that beckoned skinny-dippers every New Year's morning and the lads from the student block had insisted he went along.

They were in the water before him. 'Make a dash for it, man!' one of them shouted, so Fish backed himself up along the glazed expanse, making his leg go like a bull readying to charge. 'Eh toro!' yelled the American, and Fish sprinted at the water, the soles of his feet slapping the packed surface, the water ricocheting up his calves. 'Uughhhbrrrr!'

The others howled –'waaaeeeooo!'– then swam towards him and kind of mugged him. 'Get iz head in!' shouted the Yorkshire one, and the three of them leaned on him and he went under.

He'd snatched a good breath so he was quite relaxed about it. Let them drown me, he thought, sitting on the seabed, arms folded. It was easy being on the seabed. His eyes were closed but he could still see crabs and jellyfish (big man o' wars) and seaweed, coiled up like charmed snakes. The pushing had stopped and he felt himself rise a bit because of the air inside him, so he blew some out and settled back on his bum. He wasn't feeling cold now, because it was hot from something crude that was burning and making everything look as bright as Christmas. *He* was still down here somewhere, Thimio, sitting on his bum on the seabed amid the brightly burning oil.

Fish heard the muffled voices of the others and felt someone grab hold of him and try to lift him out. Now it was their turn to be worried: payback for all the crap they'd given him.

'Are you OK man?'

Fish surfaced, staggered out of the sea and collapsed on to the furrowed sand, landing in one of the puddles left behind after the tide had gone out. He propped himself up, arms stretched out behind him, trying to catch his breath, as the wind bleached his hearing and the sea sneezed spray against the distant pier.

'Ah, come on man, you can't be getting out already!'

'Give us a minute!' he shouted. That was when he noticed the elderly folk in bathing costumes, stepping through the ankle-deep shallows like tentative flamingos. That was when he made the comparison, and wondered what it would be like to linger on that beach for half a century and watch the one group turning into the other and the other becoming no more. 'Difference', it seemed, was little more than a matter of shape and posture – of melody and tempo. But not of impulse, not of *theme*, for they'd all come with the same thing in mind – to assert their continuing presence in the world and make themselves known to the New Year.

Fish broke off from playing to let out a sneeze. He closed the piano lid, tightened the belt of his dressing gown and made a mental note that having a cold was a great excuse for another week off lectures.

Two
Woodwind Debacle

In his symphony seagulls shriek. The music makes curved Vs the shape of wings.

Fish opened his eyes – more gulls, stuttering like abandoned oboes. A grey light bordered the curtains. He yawned and scrubbed his scalp. The music pad was still open on the duvet, the pencil where he'd left it. He gave a sniff but nothing budged. His head felt bunged up and his eyes were hurting from the pages, which he'd put together cheaply out of photocopied reductions – twenty-two staves crammed on to an A3 sheet and a hundred run off for free on the staff photocopier using Cardigan's repro code. The lines were tiny. Notes ran along them like industrious ants. He turned the pages, conjuring the music in his head, gauging the effect as each phrase, gesture and seagull scrolled by. He stopped, crushed his eyes into a blink and sighed. There was still plenty to do, not least a batch of instrument parts to finish off before the run-through on Friday.

Outside, the sparrows were twittering. They were having their daily debacle. The sparrows made him feel good. Everything made him feel good. He was feeling good about the music and the gulls and the sparrows. Even the noise of the heating system, traipsing around the student block like a charivari, seemed to be a cause for celebration. He was happy because when he added these things together they created a kind of glow; a being-alive glow that he'd translate into string flourishes to corrugate the air with, and woodwind debacles to wake up to, and brass jabs to grip snow with.

He reached for the jiffy bag on the floor by the mattress and pulled out the wad of paper from inside. The bulldog clip holding the pages together was at full gape. He eased it from side to side, but it slipped free with a rip that took bits of torn thesis with it. 'Shit!' He threw away the cover sheet and read the first paragraph of text. He couldn't see anything wrong with it. It seemed like a perfectly OK piece of work to him. Except for the contamination. Red ink! The bloody hand of Professor Cardigan!

Fish flick-booked the pages, made the red glyphs dance like abstract animations. He pictured the old fart in his office, marking essays, his specs sliding down his sweaty nose, fingers juggling the ubiquitous Bic like it was a part of the mechanism of his mind. Fish's work always came back bloodied after a bout of cerebral coitus with Cardigan. The Marks and Sparks Knitwear Chair in Musicology was an intellectual stud, who wielded his meaty brain like a pedagogical penis, entering the minds of his students, splattering his contents everywhere. Cardigan was a scrawny, undernourished little man. His face bore the rouge brushwork of part-time alcoholism and his ankles were like ladies' wrists, which made his socks go crinkly, and Fish couldn't stand the guy.

Three
Bechstein

It had been her way of saying he was adopted, that they'd been abandoned together, him and *it*. The grander of the two babies for the tea dance season, the lesser, forever.

It – the grander one – would have been difficult to miss, stationed at the far end of the church hall with its lid open like a mouth. But the lesser baby had a mouth too, and it had opened it, and its cry had bombarded the strings, causing them to sing, like eerie, harmonic ghosts – part human, part wound wire. 'Oh Dear Lord,' were the words that sprang to Greta's lips as she'd peered inside. 'What greater wonder,' she later proclaimed, 'than for a childless piano teacher to deliver herself a babe from out of her very own Bechstein?'

Very funny! If it were really true that he'd been abandoned, *and* that she'd found him inside her piano, then how come 'things' hadn't happened? How come the police hadn't been involved? But Greta insisted she hadn't reported it, hadn't said a thing to anyone on the afternoon she picked up a certain screaming child and carried it home to her three-bedroom semi and did thereafter what she claimed had been 'simple' – looked after it, without telling a soul, not even Thimio.

To Fish it all sounded implausible. Made him seem implausible, especially when later the story changed to the one where she and Thimio had longed to adopt a child and had waited with their names on the register for the chance of a newborn. That story was probably true, mostly.

When he was four Greta taught him to pray. She said that prayer was a bedside lamp that you could switch on any time. He prayed but he didn't see any light. He heard things, though – sounds, noises, music. He wrote them down. Compositions! A pile of them had grown like a hedge. Greta did the trimming.

It was in the tiny back room of the house where Greta Fisher LRAM ARCM did her teaching. A concert hall made for two. He'd been her star pupil, her Little Sonata. Stevie was the audience, listening from the passage and rocking at his own tempo, then stopping to press his face against the glass door. Stevie still did it even when he was in his teens. If practice went well Fish liked Stevie. If it went badly he hated his stepbrother's dumb skull. Then he'd play Schubert because he knew Stevie hated the sound of Schubert. Together him and Schubert could get Stevie so worked up on the other side of that door.

Greta had taught him well. Technically. But she'd played him too, like a set of variations – inverted him, changed his signature, altered his tempo – so that whoever he was never quite made it as far as the fingers. At least not when they played other people's music. With his own it was different. But Greta had been *in*different She'd messed him up more than she needed to.

One afternoon she'd shown him a note. Handwritten. It was the afternoon when she said she would tell him a true story about himself. He wondered how many other stories there might be. She said the note from his real mother was real:

> *sorry can't keep it sorry*

Four
Pointless Symphony

How to cook a symphony? *Tum tee tum tee tum?* Sounds dated. Why bother? But he does. Despite it being pointless. Despite it being the least fashionable thing to do on the entire planet. Despite the chances of anyone ever hearing it being zero.

There was a symphony lodged in his brain – his symphonic brain that played a mind that had aeons in it.

Cardigan was holding up Fish's score between his thumb and forefinger, like a dirty pair of underpants. Fish was telling the class how Britney's album had inspired him, because her shit was daubing the magnolia every night in the student block and it had grooved its way into his thoughts. Why wasn't it symphonic to have the vinyl of his thoughts grooved in a Britney-magnolia-cool sort of way?

'Misogynistic,' explained Cardigan.

'Bollocks!' countered Fish.

One thing was certain, things were going to be no drum machine now that Cardigan had it in for him.

*

In his symphony the tap runs piping hot for the first two inches then lukewarm for half an inch before going cold.

Fish was in the tub – knees up, shoulders under the water. The objects on the windowsill were addressing him: Gel Spray, its label turned towards the wall, was spurning him. Shaving Mirror, all steamed up like a huffy spouse, was standing at an oblique angle, trying to stop him from getting a decent view of himself. Nasal Spray was cannier – on its back, puffed-out from dispensing remedy. Moisturiser was keeping itself to itself at the rear of the sill. Maybe it was the kind of product that was ill at ease among more gregarious types.

Fish pushed a wave of water over his belly to warm it. His skin shone like an exposed sandbank. He had no idea how those cosmetics had come to be in his bathroom. Perhaps they'd always been there, because they were covered in that damp stuff that collects over time and looks like snot. Perhaps they were refugees from a world of bottled disenchantment; an oppressed community, enclosed within the grotto of the window recess, with the broken light from the chipped glass lending an ephemeral timelessness that they'd otherwise only get in adverts. Toothbrush and Toothpaste were different. He could relate to them, huddled together inside the cup like blood brothers, their parents (Dental Floss and Mouthwash) long gone. They issued stern reminders – that it was vital to brush regularly, which was what Thimio always said, because he had no teeth of his own, only a little container.

The bathwater was tepid. Fish climbed out. The water drained off him like a flow of ideas. He dried himself, brushed his teeth, and sat on the edge of the bath, trimming his softened toenails, picking at them like tricky adhesive labels. The student block was quiet now, apart from the distant aerosol of traffic.

He pulled the plug and the bath guzzled water: a glossolalia that he'd have to roll ball bearings down cardboard tubes to replicate. Then a sordid gulp and a slake too great for the bath's narrow throat made the last dirty suck go all the way down without a breath. Uncharted symphonic waters, these.

Five

Epic

He reckons he has one more night in the Union bar before they tumble to his pass being void. The early evening soaps get projected on to the wall above the spirit bottles, which makes the actors seem epic. The giant image shows their epic facial wrinkles, which makes him love them. The volume is turned down because music is played over the PA. Sometimes there's an inappropriate combination, like when a war is shown on the news and it's reggae that's playing. That one makes him cringe and feel sad and embarrassed for the crudity of accidental juxtaposition.

Tonight he's forced to watch eleven female backsides because there's a salsa class on. As the music plays, two world leaders are standing above the bar at lecterns, smooching politics at one another and smiling for the cameras as a war gets shown between-times. Female backsides are multifarious, he notices, being mindful not to stare. He's attracted to one in particular, which is reasonable odds in the scheme of things, he reckons.

Sometimes it's the mattress that gets the better of him. Tonight it's the noise of the pipework that's heating up his imagination. He's nocturnal – like Thimio – out of bed, sitting at the piano, headphones on, a cup of water and a packet of Chocolate Eclairs to hand. The suck of one lasts till around bar forty-three, which, despite what the sleeve note says, he can only partly attribute to Schubert because mixed in with it are particles of late night chatter coming from other rooms and from the road outside. The combination makes the night feel epic.

Most of the next day he spends writing. In the evening he realigns the underlay because the pieces have shifted – the edges having crept up the skirting to leave random gaps on the floor. The piano holds the middle piece in place. It's a heavy bastard, that piano. He sleeps with his body partly under it: sometimes head first, sometimes feet, depending on how he feels. Sorting the underlay is displacement activity because he's due to visit Stevie and is putting it off.

Six

Thimio

Psaraki! In his dream Thimio was calling him. It meant 'little fish'. He missed Thimio. His adoptive father's death had seemed unreal. Left them all at sea. The memory of him floated like oil. On the telly there'd been a plume of smoke from a ship on stilts.

Fish tried to resurrect Thimio in the pages of books, the ones he brought back with him on shore leave and used to store in Fish's room – under the bed, in the corner by the window, on top of the wardrobe. They were the collected wisdom of twenty years in the Greek merchant navy and another ten on North Sea rigs. Fish never knew Thimio's exact line of work. He was always simply 'on the ships' or 'on the rigs'. The vague idea that Thimio was an engineer rotated somewhere in the back of Fish's mind like a propeller.

Gleaning the man's occupation from books had been fruitless because their topics were too diverse. There were titles on astronomy and stellar navigation, the history of jet propulsion, post-war European history, classical philosophy. Half were in Greek, the rest in English. Works of fiction were in the minority: *Don Quixote, Tropic of Capricorn, Kon Tiki*, novels by Kazandzakis and Patrick Lea Fermoy. Thimio had been in the habit of storing away each clutch of books as he unpacked his case. He'd climbed the stairs with them concertinaed between his big hands, humming quietly like a distant helicopter.

Shift work had made Thimio nocturnal. Sometimes at night the pungent aroma of Greek coffee would wake Fish and make him turn on to his front. To coffee Thimio used to add Nou Nou, a brand of evaporated milk that came in tiny cans and which he kept in titanic quantities inside the kitchen cupboard – not stacked neatly, but piled like rubble.

When he was home, Thimio did most of the cooking. *Spanakopitta, pastitsio, gemista, keftedes.*

Thimio always brought gifts: tubes of chocolate medallions for him and Stevie, and something in a box with a ribbon around for Greta.

Fish tried to itemise Thimio: a pumice stone for tackling hard skin; the smell of meatballs and oregano; a jar of vanilla; instruction in how to crack open the salted pumpkin seed called *pasatebo*; packets of *masticha*; ways of turning department stores into tongue-twisters – 'Woolwuthers', 'Littlywoods'.

Thimio was anti-monarchy – anti any monarchy, even the nice English one. On Christmas Day when Greta watched the Queen, Thimio would exit. Fish would stay with Greta, watching and listening for what the little woman in the two-piece suit did that got Thimio so steamed up. Thimio hated the Orthodox Church too. 'Their hands are not clean over the junta,' he'd said.

Only now did Fish realise what an inordinate amount he knew about Greece for someone who'd never been there. He treasured this knowledge. It was his antidote to Greta. With Thimio there'd been no complex counterpoints, no interpretive conundrums. He'd been straight as a *zeïbekiko* – the showy dance he used to do for them on the little stage of the bay window. Its intermittent rhythm summed Thimio up – there even when not, present despite the pauses.

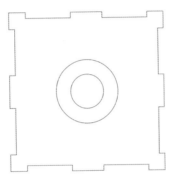

SHARK BAIT

from the novel by KM Kernek

My last rational thought when I left my girlfriend for the final time was: glad to be going. But, then again, timing is everything. I say 'rational' because it wasn't until sometime later that I started thinking judiciously again. But I was glad, because I needed a change of pace. My whole life had gotten a little samey. Lana wasn't too pleased with the entire thing. Her eyes were lightning: eyes that could zap you with ten thousand volts in a millisecond. I shied away from them then, but I never could meet her gaze.

'Well, fuck you, too,' she said.

I started to leave before she could pull herself together enough to throw something hard at me like I deserved. She didn't even know half the truth.

'Stupid shit,' she said. I couldn't tell which one of us she was referring to.

We'd started going out almost two years ago. Long enough to know we sucked together, but too long to call it off. The whole faulty thing is that the momentum made it feel like it was fine, when it wasn't; and it had only gotten worse when I'd let my addiction get the best of me.

See, now, I pretty much run the pool scene around here. All the bartenders know to send me the best fish for a tip in the winnings. The lowlife bars crawling with as many slimy cockroaches as real insects are my kingdom. And that's where I'm heading now. It just happened to be my goddamned luck that Lana chose this night of all nights to dress up and go to dinner with me. It'd have been nice to be asked, but she wanted to celebrate on a night she knows is Rusty's, and I don't care that her leather-bound daily planner had a birthday cake sticker on it. What the hell, I said, and stormed out under those lightning eyes and the stiff breeze from a closing door.

To Rusty's, I went.

Rusty and I go way back to the beginning of the beginning. I helped him with a few faulty toilets and he taught me my trade after-hours on a crummy table with ripped blue felt and mismatched balls – which was entirely appropriate considering the source.

Rusty is the John Wayne of pool players, resourceful and cagey. He stands a startling six-foot-seven with sticking-out bones someone could pick teeth with. I always picture him in my mind's eye with a cue held in each hand like a pair of shotguns and some John Ford backlighting.

He showed me the stunts early on, claiming to see some talent in my black heart. Not knowing any better, I joined him at the tables, drinking his proffered bitter and nearly choking when I saw him make those balls stand up and do the hula. I sucked up everything he said like the dumb kid I was. He taught me the value of gambling. That was twenty thousand bucks later and eighteen months ago.

Shit. A lifetime ago. You could say that I lost a fortune in the following months because of cocksuredness, but I say I was saving lives. My own.

In the whirlwind months following that first night at Rusty's, I developed a system. Rusty says a system can't fail. Keeping under the shark radar meant planning and, when that failed, a quick stop at the bar to distribute some greenbacks to the other side of the counter.

I started out scoping the bar scene. My only requirements were dim lighting and cheap beer. There were plenty of dives that made the list. I made a chart for every place: when I'd visited, who I played with, how much I won or lost by, and the chump's reaction. The key was to avoid being recognised for what I was, so I couldn't play against regulars – guys who were most likely to remember me. First-time arrivals were an easy target. but didn't pay the rent. No, the money was in the risks. It was hard at first to pick out a fish. He had to be dressed a certain way, pace the table a certain way. Bigger money could be found if he had a chick to show off to. No drunks, no women, no one on social security. I only broke the rules once; and to this day I wish I hadn't.

When I arrived at Rusty's after the break-up that night I was greeted with a cold one and a table in the back without having to flash anything but a smile. Apparently Rusty was doing something in the kitchen, which made the whole place stink like a Zamboni. I heard someone holler to him that Teak was there and his grunted reply.

My preferred table in the back was free, so I set about racking. I reached the balls and lined up my break. A pair of legs wrapped tight in fishnets and a mini walked into my sight down the cue. I followed the legs to her clingy top, pausing for a generous look before meeting her eyes. I kind of expected a blonde, but a brunette would do. She gave me the greasy eyeball before going to an occupied table and sitting next to a wimpy guy with glue in his hair who was, incidentally, glaring at me. Across from the couple was a huge guy with a pinky ring, and chest hair peeking over his loosened collar.

Yikes, I thought, whistling through my teeth as I focused on my other set of balls. I had to regroup for a minute before I smacked the cue ball hard and fast, sending it down the felt right into the nerd's palm. I hadn't noticed him get up.

'Hey,' I said.

'Maybe you should keep your eyes on the table. It would improve your aim.' His lip was curling back on the right side to show gold fillings on some generally yellow teeth.

'My aim was fine. Like the lady.' I caught the cue ball en route to my head and put it back where it belonged. This time I shot it right away, clearing real estate in double time. Nerdly leaned his hand against the balls I'd so carefully prepared, knocking them out of alignment just before the white blur sent them careening randomly.

He was really starting to annoy me. Not seeming to mind, he took a cigarette from a metal case and flicked a lighter on it for emphasis. I laid the cue on the green felt. I wanted to be amicable, but I also wanted my hands free.

'Look, fella, if you got someplace to be I'd totally understand. Run along.' I was a little too comfortable here, a little too bold for my own good – made that way by months at the top of the game.

'Why don't we see if your balls are as good as your bark, puppy,' Nerdly said. He looked down before looking up, making his innuendo clear.

'Sure, why not?' I shrugged. 'Maybe Bruiser over there could help you.' The man with the ring rearranged his bulk on the bench, paying more attention now. I wasn't about to back down; the brunette was watching. 'I'll even make it easy on you and let you break.'

His sneer displayed more espresso-stained enamels and swollen gums. The look told me two things I didn't want to know: first, that he was reasonably capable, and second, he knew I was; that is, he knew who I was. But I wasn't about to let on so I mocked him instead.

'You should let your dentist get a look at those pearly yellows, bro.'

His smile shot away – which reminded me of my newly ex'd – and made my spinal muscles charlie horse. I looked at the stakes to remind myself what the point of all this machismo was. She wasn't helping. She was looking at a prep playing with the juke in the corner. It made me look at Nerdly and wonder why.

It wasn't so much that he was like a nerd, or smart for that matter. It was that he stuck out in a dive like Rusty's: his shirt had started the day ironed, his haircut had cost upwards of seventy dollars. He was a priss without a prayer of beating me. That identified and my confidence restored, I spread my hand towards the cue in a gracious gesture that reddened his face further. He flicked ash on to the floor before he punished the cue ball into the rack, which broke beautifully. I had to nod with appreciation. He sunk the three and five, and pushed the seven towards the back corner. His only problem would be the eight – which is most people's problem – that was butted against the bumper.

Nerdly looked exceptionally pleased with himself as he lined up. I took a look around the bar. I didn't need to watch his next shot, or his second or third shots either. After the break the balls become a treasure map complete with dashed lines and an x-marks-the-spot over the eight ball. The prep at the juke-box had chosen a raucous dance remix that belonged in a club rather than in a quiet, smoky bar filled with a collection of has-beens. Those has-beens were sneaking looks at us for the entertainment value. They didn't really care who won. I gulped down some of my pint.

The brunette was still avoiding our table and purposefully sipping her drink – a bright green concoction that I felt sure had enough sugar to give cavities to a horse. It was the same green as her eyes. She had harder features than I expected in someone with that body. There was something in her jaw that said she had muscles there from clenching. I returned my attention to the table in time to watch the challenger crush the four into the side pocket and the thirteen he had combo'd off of into the corner one.

'Bad luck, friend,' I lied. There was no luck, good, bad, or other, only fairly adequate playing and sucking, which he just had. I moved him out of the way with my cue before he'd stood up from his shot. Off-balance, he shoved me away, which only caused Newton's third law to send him tripping out of the light of the table lamp.

'You don't touch me.' He was in my face, trying to burn me with his glare.

'Yeah, yeah, hot stuff,' I said before I lined up my shot, butting him over with the end of my cue. I knew I had about a half second before he'd come at me, so I looked and loosed without thinking. If he was boiling before, I didn't know what he was doing now as my purposefully tricky shot made it safely to its destination. As I moved around the table, I spared a glance at the lady just to make sure she wasn't bored. She wasn't. Her eyes caught mine and she smiled. There was something curious about that smile, but I didn't allow myself the time to ponder because I didn't want to wreck my concentration. I deliberately took my time clearing the table, proving what I had known, what Rusty had seen when he took me under his wing. I was the best.

'Well, that was fun, boy,' I said, my head ducked under the lamp to reach my hand farther across the table. The light ruined my vision. I couldn't see anything beyond the green felt and wooded border. A hand came from the darkness, gripping my wrist. My first thought was how Nerdly's hand had gotten so huge. My second was *ouch* as my head slammed into the light in my effort to resist the pulling. I didn't really have a chance. I was already sprawled on the table, a little dazed, when I realised what was going on.

Nerdly's friend grabbed my belt with his free hand and yarded me off the table to the ground. I tried to stand up, or strike, or yell but every attempt was taken to mean I wanted to be kicked, so I stopped. I'm sure Nerdly laid a few extra on just for fun. I twisted out of the way of a kick aimed for my head and simultaneously kicked Bruiser's knee. His right leg crumpled, sending him towards Nerdly. Nerdly tried to step aside and the distraction gave me a chance to get up. I put a fist in the punk's nose, feeling a satisfying crunch as I connected. I glanced around the room to see where everyone else was. No one was stepping up to help me out; not that I expected it. We were only on first name basis with frequent nightly dates at our favourite place. I was too good for them.

'You ignorant—,' Nerdly said through bloody lips. He made a few swipes at the drips; then put his hands up boxing style.

'Going to try it, rich boy?' I replied. I should have kept better track of where his burly better-half was. I didn't see him on the ground. He must drink his milk to get bones of iron like that. That's when he smashed the bottle over my head.

I remember thinking, if I ever see you again I'll put a cue right through your ears – I figured it was the path of least resistance. That was my last coherent thought as they dragged me out the emergency exit to the gravel where I was kicked until my lungs felt crushed and my stomach roiled. I puked beer and acid, then dry-heaved. My head felt like someone was screwing a vice tight across my temples. My vision started to tunnel. At the end, Nerdly gripped my ear and pulled up so he could look me in the face. My eyes were already swelling and that combined with the tears made him a blob with vocal cords.

'*That* was fun, you little shit. You don't know what's good for you. Next time, don't look at my girl.'

I would've said something scathing, but all I could think was that this was my day to be called names. And part of me wished that I hadn't played so well. He dropped my head and put his heel to my right hand. He pressed my fingers against the uneven rocks. I think I yelped, but I can't remember. I do remember blinking and seeing two pairs of pants and one pair of legs walking away before I blacked out.

Groggy only covered about half of it when two guys from the bar pulled me to semi-standing. I was dragged between them and laid on a sticky table. The bartender brought me water to wash the blood from my mouth and some ice. I put the ice on my right hand; the skin was already tight with fluid. I was angry at these jokers who were crowding me and asking me if I was all right when I was, but hadn't bothered to help when I wasn't.

'Sure, I'm all right,' I said, pulling my arm away from somebody doing amateur doctoring. 'They're gone, aren't they?' My swelling lip slurred my consonants.

Rusty pushed through the crowd. All the patrons thought I was the entertainment, even the prep-city boy from the jukebox. Rusty was wiping his hands on a shop rag. It wasn't clear which got cleaner.

'You shouldna bothered with him, boy.' He said it without a hint of familiarity or concern.

Well, damn you, too, I thought. I struggled to a seated position. Rusty pulled out a pen-light and shone it into my eyes. Whatever he could or couldn't see satisfied him, and he moved the hand holding the ice bag to examine the injured fingers.

No one argued with Rusty. He had random shit locked away that could be misconstrued as genuine knowledge. He'd never gone to school, made money taking it from suckers, and bought this hole so he could pretend legitimacy. That's all I knew about him, which meant it was about twice what anyone else knew.

He picked at each of my fingers, watching me wince at different degrees. 'You'll play again,' he said.

'Good.'

'More'n you deserve.' Rusty turned and started back to the kitchen.

I manoeuvred myself off the table, glaring at those who tried to help me. I staggered after him.

'What's that supposed to mean?' I'd tried to put some conviction behind my words, but they still came out slurred and hoarse. 'You let those thugs in here.'

On that, Rusty whirled around. 'Look, bucko, I don't *let* anyone in. They come in. I don't see a sign on the door that says minors and sons of notorious gangsters, and their bodyguards, and their girlfriends not allowed. You're a shallow cuss to have tangled with 'em and that's your own dumb fault. Go home and clean yourself up. You're givin' my bar a bad reputation.'

I wondered how the bar's reputation could possibly get worse when I felt hot from all the eyes on my back. I was going to be nursing a lot more than my physical wounds, seemed like.

'I don't have a place, Rusty,' I said in a small voice. I could imagine Rusty's eyes making a full revolution before he said, 'Come upstairs.'

I knew from previous experience that upstairs was a converted dance loft. It had its own bathroom off the stairwell, so he could hold up in there without much problem. His bed was on the stage in the corner, separated from the open space by a black screen painted in faux oriental-style birds and grasses. The central bar had become a kitchen of sorts. Overhead glass racks now held pots, the fancy column originally meant for hard-alcohol stored accoutrements, staples and one or two post cards from the Middle East.

He'd kept the sub-bar mini-fridge and dishwasher and some bar stools. The sound system and crazy lights still hung from the ceiling. I suspected he used them as a kind of fitness regimen because he rarely had company, and none of them possessed that female inclination to dance. The place was dingy, but clean enough, like downstairs. In the only corner with windows, he'd put a pool table. His worsening arthritis kept him from playing much; maybe that was why it was here: a trophy from a tournament in Syracuse. He prided it over life.

There wasn't much in the way of furniture. A Goodwill sofa was pushed against the back wall, but it did little to ease the largeness of the space. I'd slept here before, during marathon training sessions that took all night.

Rusty went to the bar and grabbed a first-aid kit. 'Sit,' he directed. He administered some cleansing balm on my open cuts from across the bar. He never got too close.

'Who'd you say those thugs were?'

'Part of bad news.'

'I can take it,' I said, then winced as he patched a particularly painful section of my cheek.

'You shoulda let him win.'

I harrumphed, letting him know precisely what I thought of that.

'That should do it till the next time you let someone give you a facial,' he said, separating himself and putting away the first aid.

'Thanks,' I said, adding in my mind 'for nothing'.

'There're some blankets in the closet.' Rusty turned, making it clear that his hospitality had run out. I would have been offended, except that I was used to it.

'Why aren't you telling me? Don't you think I've earned it?' I said, pointing to my face with my crippled hand.

'Look, I tell you, you go searching for trouble, you come back dead, that's with a capital 'K' for killed.' He walked out of the bar and straight to the bathroom.

I hadn't really thought about it in those terms, but it did sound like something I would do. I'm not so much a punching bag when I have better odds. I'm actually kind of handy.

I eased myself off the bar stool and hobbled to the closet where I found some blankets. I recognised them; I even recognised the way they were half-folded, half-crammed into the space. I took a look at my new living quarters, thought about my roommate and suddenly missed Lana.

I climbed under the covers, hearing the shower running, and thinking of my ex-girl with the lightning eyes. Then, I thought of the smirking brunette. I wasn't a fan, but I felt that I could be. I even fooled myself into thinking she was impressed by the way I handled Nerdly, until that last part. But I'd find out who they were and act accordingly.

I only woke up once when I heard Rusty crack the rack. Two or three balls thunked into the netted pockets. I rolled over.

OUT OF THE WATER

from the novel by Rachel Knightley

Twins and central characters Daniel and Orla McManus deal with their separate theatre-based catastrophes before being rudely interrupted by a real one.

It was hard to tell which were the child's real arms inside the caterpillar costume, but judging by the speed with which Laurence was marshalling him towards her, Orla assumed they were the ones in the handcuffs.

'We have a situation,' said Laurence, apologetically confirming her suspicion. It was clear on closer inspection which were the caterpillar's real hands: they were the only ones turning purple. *The stage manager's job*, Orla inwardly recited as she gazed upon them, *is to make sure no one else panics.*

'Five minutes, Will,' she called, giving the caterpillar an encouraging smile and beckoning him to follow her out of the auditorium.

In front of the stopped audition – a stage full of about thirty children who had been interrupted mid-'threatening stance' and were not sure if they were allowed to move yet – Will Openshaw, the artistic director's head inclined; lips pursed under his moustache. Will famously believed in the importance of a united front amongst the staff, but his facial expression made it perfectly clear he wanted to throttle Laurence, whose loping steps Orla heard behind them as she steered the child out of sight towards the locked door of Will's wife, Dr Openshaw's, teaching room. After a short search of her increasingly overloaded key ring she found the right one and switched on the lights, first to the main room, then to the small room behind the folding wooden doors that was the painters' toilet and shower room.

'What's your name?' she asked as she perched on the lid of the toilet and located which of the eight arms to examine.

'Matthew,' the boy mumbled, obediently responding to her gesture to be seated on the edge of the bath. There was no way the costume could come off before the handcuffs without ripping, and having been with Dr Openshaw during its construction Orla knew how arduous it had been to make. Not to mention expensive.

'Been in the youth theatre long?'

'A few years.'

'Long enough to think you own the props as well as the place, huh?'

'Was bored.'

'Not bored now though are you?'

'No,' he admitted.

'Nor bored enough to look for the bloody key before you tried them on,' snapped Laurence. Matthew's antennae drooped over his bowed, brown and green velvet head. 'And then I've got bloody Sasha spending too long complaining to me about being short staffed to notice what the kids are doing with the props.'

Matthew laughed. Orla said nothing but continued to squeeze soap under one of the cuffs.

'As if she thinks the louder you complain the more efficient you're being.'

Unlike you of course, Orla thought and just managed not to say it. All of it was true but she was disappointed in him for saying it now. Laurence was right about the props mistress – Sasha was Orla's least favourite thing: a faffer – but Orla agreed with Will: there wasn't any good in allowing students to hear things they weren't ready to hear. Seeing staff disagree would give them a little initial fun, amuse them for a few minutes, but every time it happened was a notch further away from their believing adults were united, in control and had a good reason for everything, which was a luxury to be maintained for as long as possible. Childhood was like having a good stage manager: you had the right to the illusion of order being preserved.

'Orla, that piano still hasn't moved,' said Will, suddenly looming in the doorway.

'All by itself? You do surprise me,' she mumbled hypocritically, in the caterpillar's hearing. Without getting up from her knees she turned to face Will. 'I prioritised this. And it is an hour before we do any music.'

'Half an hour now.'

'What?' She checked her watch. He was right, and she'd not even managed to get one wrist free yet. Will left, having made his point, and she continued to soap in silence, pushing the child's skin back through the handcuff, millimetre by slow millimetre.

'Continue.' They heard Will's command as he arrived back on stage, his usual dignity unscathed. The recitation of 'The Walrus and the Carpenter' began again from the top, with Will's occasional shouts of 'Project, Sam, don't shout,' or 'More revulsion please, Katy.' Laurence wandered over to the shower radio and tried to tune it. There was a snatch of Mozart interrupted by, 'This is the news from BBC Radio Three on September 11th, 2001. A pl—' Laurence got bored and twisted the knob again and the news was replaced by Robbie Williams's *Millennium*.

'You don't hear that song so much already, do you,' Orla said as chattily as she could, her voice straining but determined to make conversation as she wrenched at the manacle. 'I mean, talk about a short shelf life.' She smiled at Matthew, who smiled back politely, but he was eleven and probably had no idea what she was talking about. It didn't matter – as long as he was interacting.

'Where would he have got the bloody handcuffs from?' asked Laurence, fiddling inexpertly with the other cuff and illustrating his despair by talking as if the child couldn't hear him.

Orla shrugged. 'Most things are in a theatre somewhere; the danger is being bored long enough to look. Isn't that right?' The caterpillar nodded gratefully. 'Maybe next time I'll get you building a prop, rather than forcing me to rescue you from one. How about it?' The caterpillar nodded harder.

Will's head appeared around the door again, off-duty politeness having somehow crept in. 'I've called Joanna down from the sound box to supervise in there. Look, if there's any chance we're going to have to call nine-nine-nine, we have to make the decision now.'

'Ambulance?' asked the horrified caterpillar, looking with new interest at his narrow metal prison.

'No, no. Just the fire brigade. It's not worth waiting, is it Orla?'

Orla felt an invisible camera panning in on her, as she stood at the centre of the bathroom surrounded by caterpillar, colleague and artistic director all looking to her for a meaningful decision.

'What we need is something to hammer it through,' said Laurence.

'What?' Will, Matthew and Orla chorused.

'Well not a hammer, obviously.'

Panic gave way to lateral thinking. 'Give it a rest the lot of you,' Orla said, 'and help me soap the left handcuff. And, Will?'

'Yes?'

'As you're here...'

Surprised, Will walked in to join them in the small bathroom. Orla smiled politely at his co-operation and stationed him behind the child's shoulders to pull, with Laurence's hands around the cuff to loosen it. At her nod, they forced the metal bracelet past the thick part of the hand.

'OK Matthew,' Orla said as she sat back on the toilet lid so she could look straight – and calmly – in the newly panicky face. 'What we are gong to do, is we are going to pull very hard. It can't do you any damage because we've got the bracelet over the bone already, but it might pull a bit. So, you're just going to be really, really brave for a second, alright?'

Matthew nodded again.

'Laurence and Will are behind you; I'll be here. On three. One – two – three!'

They pulled. There was a small squeak, which was the boy and not the handcuffs, and Orla shot back into the sink. 'Excellent,' she said, subtly checking her elbow for blood. 'We're half way there, one to go, so—'

'Hello,' said a voice from the toilet door. Orla's conversation froze midstream.

'Hello,' they all said, picking themselves up as if stopping games at the madhouse when someone uninitiated had come to look through the screen.

'I was looking for Will,' Andrew said politely. 'The piano isn't where I expected it to be.'

Orla tried to keep the small groan inside her mind from creeping as far as her vocal chords. She'd forgotten he was the session pianist. She tried to remind herself that Andrew's song-writing partner, Mark, being her boyfriend didn't make Mark's outburst, or his storming out of the band's last rehearsal, in any way her fault. But she was still mortified by her immediate exit after him. What must Andrew think of her?

'Per – um – haps you'd join us?' she asked.

Andrew looked at the handcuffs. He didn't ask how it had happened. He just looked firmly into the bewildered eyes of the caterpillar and broke into a smile.

'It's all right,' he said. 'I'm a builder.'

'Well we've cancelled tonight's performance and it's about an inch deep,' said Finbar into the theatre's mobile phone.

Daniel paused in his mopping to concentrate. The artistic director of the Verray Devil was making his telephone call perched on the edge of the bar, as being the only dry place in the building. The producer's reply was probably shouted, but Daniel couldn't hear as it was drowned out by the speakers of the huge, wall-mounted television screen they'd just had installed and which was currently stuck on the French news channel.

Finbar had been cheerfully polite so far. There was nothing else to do what with the water coming down the stairs from the auditorium.

Directors shouldn't have to mop. Daniel stuck to that core belief, but didn't have a choice for now, and certainly didn't complain. If he complained about this it would decrease the value of his complaints when he was actually directing.

'Yes and the television's stuck on a fucking French news channel.'

Daniel straightened up, to make sure he still could. He looked down, at his wet-look jeans – genuinely soaked – and around at the pub. At least the Verray Devil itself was starting to look all right again. The Devil's Theatre upstairs was a mess. To think this place could exist by the Thames for hundreds of years and the one flood he'd had to deal with in nine months of working there was caused by defective toilets. He returned to his mopping.

'Of course we're suing the plumbers,' Finbar said. Then, 'Oh fuck.' Daniel shot up from the floor. It wasn't the language; he barely noticed that. It was the sudden and complete sincerity behind it.

'Ed, can I call you back?' Finbar was staring at the screen and hung up too quickly to have listened to the answer. 'Danny, look at this.'

Daniel dropped the mop without much reluctance and joined him under the screen.

'Do you realise what this means?' Finbar asked.

'Not entirely, it's in French.'

'Look, arsehole.' There was clearly something in the world Finbar did not consider funny. Daniel looked at the TV screen. It looked as if a comet was going into a tower block. It was because of Finbar's reaction, not any belief in the possibility of what the world was starting to realise, that Daniel worked out what he was seeing. 'Do you know,' said Finbar, 'what this is going to do to business?'

'Isn't that a bit insensitive?'

Finbar turned to look at him, or through him, or didn't know where to look at all. 'Clearly you don't,' he answered. The images of the World Trade Centre began over again.

'And, push!' Orla shouted. The piano tilted, paused and crashed on to the first step.

'Argh. Shit.'

'Now.'

'Fuck.'

'Give it a rest, Laurence; you sound like a new play. And, now!' Another shunt. 'Ouch! Sorry. One more to go.'

'Fnnahhgh!'

With a final clunk and shake of wood on wood they had reached stable ground. Panting but smiling, Laurence and Orla stared at each other over the top of the piano on the stage. It was positioned in the left wing, just poking out on to the stage. Orla cursed herself for not having done as Joanna had suggested before Dr Openshaw went away, and getting her to nag Will more enthusiastically to cut spares for all the keys. But the one to the side entrance from the auditorium was probably in New York by now, and there was nothing she could do about that. She was only dwelling on it to stop herself thinking how quickly the other handcuff came off once Andrew arrived with his drill. At least with moving a piano she hadn't been able to dwell on anything beyond staying upright. Now they had finished and so was the defence from memory.

'Time, Ash!' she called.

'Thanks,' said Andrew from beside the stage. Orla hadn't realised he was standing so close: last time she'd looked up he'd been talking to Will at the back of the stalls. She remembered her first gig as stage manager and realised that Andrew's calm had been to remind himself as much as to instruct her. It was only nine months ago and she was already bossing him around with the unshakable confidence she had so aspired to. She'd never dreamed it would be so fragile a façade.

'Positions.' The collection of students fell silent at the first plosive; at the end of the word they scattered. In the lighting box, Joanna would be putting down her paper and beginning. Orla looked up. She could see two heads on the other side of the box's window, both black, although that could just be the light. The taller one was probably Will and she wondered if the students knew.

Laurence passed a coffee from the urn to Orla and the two of them sat in the back row of the stalls, sipping, watching and glad it wasn't them any more.

It was nice being back at the Academy. She was still based in Firwood because of Mark and Ash Groove, so most of her jobs were a long commute. Even on regional tours – the biggest she'd got so far – she insisted on not being away more than a week without one night at home. The acting ones, of course, could be anywhere.

The next part was a group dance, with Isabel, the ballet mistress, bark-
ing orders that didn't interest her, and hadn't even when she was a student. Under the cover of darkness, Orla's eyes wandered to Andrew. The small light attached to the piano spilt a little on to his face, long with tiredness from the night before. She realised they hadn't started packing away much before two in the morning.

'Look at that girl's wig,' Laurence whispered in the darkness. Orla grinned and glared at him simultaneously. They had to stop giggling, fearing Isabel could hear; a terror neither had ever quite grown out of. The chorus was as-sembling; Will, Orla and Laurence made their way into the stalls and Andrew sat down at the piano. She watched his long fingers and the grace of the droop of his wrists over the keys. She had instinctively trusted his precision with the drill, as close as he had been to the skin – and to Dr Openshaw's caterpillar costume.

He saw her looking and she glanced away quickly, then she listened more and looked back again. He nodded in return.

'He's good, isn't he,' said Laurence.

Orla nodded, not wanting to say anything that might come out over-the-top.

'Better than Harold.'

'Yeah.' That she could safely respond to. Harold was forty, smelt of moth-balls and got cross easily. He lived with his mother in the converted windmill on Moor Road. Technically Harold was almost as good as Andrew, maybe bet-ter, but his demeanour was that of someone who could have been a profes-sional and knew it and had to carry the knowledge with him every day of his life, particularly through student auditions. The thought scared her. Maybe that would be her and acting in twenty years.

The dance piece ended and the lights came up. In the ensuing coffee break, Orla was surprised to find Andrew wandering down to join her, instead of hanging around at the back with Will and the rest of the staff, whom she still couldn't help thinking of as the grown-ups.

'Quite an interesting emergency you had there,' he said. Orla tried to think of a reply, shocked that he seemed to want to have a conversation.

'Laurence wanted to hammer it through,' she said.

'I didn't,' said Laurence. 'Not with a hammer anyway. And Orla was bright enough to work out how to loosen it...'

'I only got one hand out.'

'You did very well – and I'm not easily impressed,' said Andrew.

'That I do know.'

'How's the make-up design going?' he asked.

'I'm getting a lot of practice – Will's springing a dress run and walk-through on everyone who's cast tonight, after you've gone. You're not obliged to stay. Wanna stay and watch?'

'I'll stay and help. I mean, it's clearly entertaining.'

Torn between thanks and sorry, Orla settled for, 'I'll just go and put this back.' Going to throw away a plastic cup rather than talk to someone she had known for ten years seemed a bit rude to her once she arrived at the bin, but the embarrassment had been unbearable. He'd made it look so easy. Andrew had removed the second manacle in half the time it had taken her to pick up the detritus from the messy removal of the first, then everyone had wandered off back to the day as planned. She tried not to think about how much of every-body's time she had wasted on something as daft as rubbing soap on to a small child in a room to which Will shouldn't even know she had the key.

'Would you like to give notes, Will?' Isabel enquired sweetly, her eyes directed to the sound booth. A panicked low-level twitter skated across the group.

Hearing this echo of their own days in the youth theatre, instinctively Orla looked at Andrew and they smiled in recognition. Everyone was always scared of the ballet mistress, but though Will's manner was friendlier, they now re-alised he was harder to please. Being a former student wasn't enough to get you approval: once you graduated he only took you back if you were useful.

'Yes I would.'

The pause stayed as long as it took him to leave the booth and walk down the back stairs, returning to the studio through the main door.

Laurence had to go over to check with Andrew that the piano was up to spec and Orla decided to go with him. She sat on half of Andrew's piano stool, the rehearsal forgotten; they were colleagues – friends? – on their own terms again.

'Will,' Joanna stood in the doorway, her face blank.

'Yes?'

'Telephone... New York...'

Will's expression turned from pleasant recognition to concern as he registered Joanna's tone. He strode to the door. She stood back respectfully and then followed him out of the room.

LOVE'S LIBELS LOST
from the novel by Carin Lake

Araminta stood at the window, naked under her red satin negligée. Another half an hour and the children would be home from school. Surely Hunter wouldn't be late! Her eyes scanned the bedroom, checking everything was in place. Champagne on ice: tick. Rose petals scattered over pillows: tick. Hunter's favourite Chris De Burgh CD ready to play: tick. New and rather naughty set of lacy underwear laid out on bed: tick, tick, tick.

The crunch of wheels on gravel called her attention back to the window. There was the little red Toyota with its suggestively dented rear bumper, backing urgently into the driveway. Araminta pressed *play* and wrestled with the champagne bottle. Footsteps thudded up the stairs. The door was flung open. Hunter leaned against the doorframe breathing hard, a film of perspiration coating his rugged features. His steel grey eyes widened as they took in the scene.

'The Lady In Red,' sang Chris.

'Pop!' went the champagne cork.

'Happy Anniversary, darling,' said Araminta.

Without a word Hunter advanced towards the bed. He unbuttoned his shirt, revealing first those curling golden tendrils at the top of his chest and then, as the shirt fell away, the rippling muscles beneath. He unbuckled his belt, unzipped his zip and let his trousers fall to the floor. Ridding himself of his boxer shorts was more of a struggle as his excitement mounted. He stood before her in the full, proud glory of his manhood. Then he reached out for the pale pink knickers that Araminta had so carefully arranged on the edge of the bed. He fingered them lovingly a moment, savouring the textures of silk and ribbon and lace. Then, balancing first on one foot and then the other, he slowly pulled them on.

I thought if he bothered to read the book at all – *Life's A Drag*, my third novel – Henry would be touched I'd renamed him Hunter. It had been a pet name between us in the early days, the days before marriage, before children – a time I now look back on as a golden age of innocence when being together involved nothing more complicated than a bit of chasing and catching and a lot of *Oohs* and *Eeks* and *Aahs*. Putting the name in the book seemed a kind of in-joke, if you can have an in-joke with your ex-husband. As it turned out, maybe you can't.

Apart from that one name, which only Henry knew about, I'd gone to a lot of trouble to change identifying details. Actually I thought I'd done rather well. Araminta had a touch of class, more substance than my own name, which is Suzy. And Henry should certainly have been chuffed at the physical write-up I gave him: the 'steel grey eyes' are in fact a wishy-washy though not unattractive blue, and I doubt he can remember when his muscles last did anything as definite as ripple.

As far as I was concerned there was nothing to suggest the book was anything other than a work of fiction. I ABSOLUTELY DID NOT (as certain people have suggested) intend to embarrass Henry or his new wife, Belinda Blenkinsop MP, Shadow Secretary for Legal Affairs. The whole, horrible mess the book landed me in really was a simple mistake – a mistake that came down, after all, to just three words out of a hundred thousand.

Three words. That's all it took for Belinda – happening to pick up the book in a rare idle moment between committees and press conferences – to claim not only that she recognised Hunter as Henry but that friends, relations, neighbours and colleagues did too. They were appalled, according to Belinda. Henry was a laughing stock, now known from Westminster to Surbiton as the Dorking Drag Queen. His reputation was in tatters. He was held up to Ridicule and Contempt. And, worse, their marriage, so Belinda insisted, was now perceived as a sham: *her* reputation, too, was at stake.

The three words that caused such outrage? 'Little', 'red' and 'Toyota'.

I should have noticed, I suppose. I didn't, for the very reason the car caused all the fuss: it's so much a part of Henry it just fades into the background. Why Belinda hadn't bought him a nice shiny BMW is anybody's guess; she could certainly have afforded it. Possibly she saw the usefulness of Henry's scruffy comprehensive-teacher image to the cuddly, caring new face of her Party. Possibly – I say it a little doubtfully – she loved Henry as he was. For whatever reason, one year into their marriage he was still driving here, there and everywhere in his little red car with its bashed-in bumper, casually referred to by me on page twenty-three and instantly identifiable as Henry's by all who knew him.

As I say, I should have noticed. I should have changed it. I could so easily have made it a blue Renault or a racing-green Astra. Admittedly, I was under pressure at the time. Tom and Katie both had chicken pox and the au pair had suddenly remembered an urgent appointment back in Slovakia. I can find excuses. But if I'm honest I guess I just got lazy.

So what? you might well ask. What does it matter anyway? What if your husband *is* taken for the original of a bodice-ripping hunk with creative sexual habits in a soon-to-be-forgotten work of light fiction? Isn't it really just a bit of a laugh? Has the woman no sense of humour?

Well no, she hasn't. There was, for example, the time Henry failed to recognise the latest Leader of the Opposition at one of their interminable fund-raising parties and, thinking the good-natured chap standing next to him looked as out of place as he, Henry, felt, suggested the two of them slope off to the pub before they got stuck with the speeches. (Belinda didn't talk to Henry for the rest of the evening, so he told me when he popped round the next day to pick up Tom and Katie.)

And then there was the time Tom was going through that irritating practical joke phase and took his fake adder along for the weekend to Belinda's house in Oxfordshire. He sneaked into Henry and Belinda's en-suite bathroom and artistically arranged the snake in the sink with its head poking out of the overflow, adding the classic cling-film-over-the-toilet trick as an hors d'oeuvre. Unfortunately Belinda had given the master bedroom to their other houseguest, her old friend the Attorney General, and even more unfortunately Tom didn't realise until... No, don't even go there – as Tom assures me he said to the Attorney General just before...

Anyway, take it from me, Belinda has no sense of humour.

The first I knew of the Toyota Trouble was a phone call from Henry. He didn't pick a good moment. Katie and I were in the sitting-room on one of our frequent hamster hunts, the ones that start with her sidling into the room murmuring 'I only let him out for a moment' and end with carpenters taking up floorboards and plumbers dismantling washing-machines.

I was lying on my stomach peering under the sofa and Katie was looking under the cushions and snivelling more and more loudly as Einstein failed to appear. The phone rang somewhere near my ear. I reached out a hand and felt around for it on the coffee table. Under the sofa, behind several sweet wrappers and a Lego brick, something moved.

'Hello?' Through the dusty gloom I could just make out a little, twitching nose.

'Belinda's gone ape-shit!' Henry's opening words.

I considered the unattractive picture this conjured up. 'Well, Henry,' I said, swivelling round on my stomach and wriggling towards Einstein in a non-confrontational way, 'you did choose to marry her.' A reasonable observation, it seemed to me: it wasn't, surely, for the Wronged Wife to provide new-relationship counselling for her ex-husband. I'd have said more but at that moment Einstein ran out from under the sofa and simultaneously, right on cue, the door creaked open and in pranced Madonna, our tabby cat. Einstein froze.

'What am I going to do?' Henry had adopted that plaintive, little-boy-lost tone I knew so well. Meanwhile Madonna was hunkering down to pounce, bottom wiggling in readiness. Katie, clutching a cushion in her hands, let out a wail. There was only one thing for it.

'Chuck the cushion at her!' I yelled.

'But Suzy,' Henry sounded put out, 'she's really upset.'

Katie threw the cushion at Madonna, who jumped sideways with an expression of indignant surprise. Einstein scuttled back under the sofa. I sprang up from the floor and made a left-handed lunge for the cat who slithered out of my grasp, scratching me hard in the process.

'Bloody cat!' I screamed.

Henry's tone was distinctly huffy now. 'Well, Suzy,' he said, 'if that's your attitude there's no point talking further. Just make sure you do something about your book!'

'What?' It was my turn to be confused.

But he'd hung up.

Clarification came two days later. I'd sat down at my desk with my first cup of coffee and was busy pondering whether to set my next novel in a massage parlour or a merchant bank when the phone rang.

'Erm...' said a male voice.

'Rory!' It had been a couple of weeks since I'd spoken to my editor from Passionfruit Press. 'How're the sales figures?'

'Erm, that's not quite... not quite...' For someone who makes his living from words Rory is endearingly inarticulate.

'Press coverage? Media tie-ins? Deadline for next manuscript?' I thought

I'd help him out.

'No.' Rory was quite definite. 'Actually, Suzy, it's your ex-husband.'

'Henry?'

'Yes!' Rory seemed pleased we understood each other so well. 'He's suing us for libel!'

'What?'

'Libel,' Rory said more loudly.

'No, I mean... *Henry?*'

'Yes!'

'It's a joke,' I said confidently. 'Naughty of him to send it to you. Ignore it.'

'It doesn't sound much like a joke. And the letter's not from him. It's from his solicitors.'

I sighed. 'I expect Henry's been talking to some of his mates in the Queen's Head again. Don't worry, Rory, I'll give him a ring.'

'No!' Rory sounded alarmed. 'No! You're not allowed to speak to him.'

'Says who?'

'Says our lawyers.'

'What?' I said again.

'Meeting at their offices tomorrow, nine am. Bring anything relevant with you.'

'Like what?'

'Erm...' There was a brief silence. Then he said, 'Goodbye.'

I got up at seven the next morning to prepare for the meeting. I decided my usual style (which I like to think comes across as carefully judged artistic disarray) wouldn't do. Businesslike efficiency was called for. I scrambled through every wardrobe and chest of drawers in the house and came up with a pleated grey miniskirt I'd bought from Topshop about twelve years ago when I was still temping in the City and a red and white striped shirt of Henry's that he hadn't taken when he moved out and that I somehow hadn't got round to giving back to him or throwing away. I pulled my hair back in a ponytail, put on my reading glasses and took a look in the mirror. I'd do.

I kissed Katie and Tom and gave Carmen, our latest au pair, an encouraging pat. I issued reminders about hamster food, football boots and the difference between fabric conditioner and bleach and left the cosy chaos that is our breakfast table for the humming hell that is the tube.

I hadn't joined in the morning commute since about the time I'd bought the Topshop skirt, and I'd forgotten quite how Hades-like it is. Still, one of the advantages of being a novelist is that every experience is a research opportunity and the journey proved full of story lines that I stored away for possible future use. For example: efficient, businesslike but quirkily beautiful young woman lands in lap of burly Afro-Caribbean builder and despite his initial surprise ('Fuck, lady!') love ensues. Or: efficient, businesslike, etcetera woman engages in sparky conversation with grey-haired businessman who's reading a surprisingly interesting article in the *Daily Telegraph* and despite initial (no doubt sexually charged) tension between them ('Why don't you buy your own bloody paper?') love, of course, ensues.

All too soon it was time to emerge into daylight and enter the glass and steel tower that houses Passionfruit's lawyers. I spotted a familiar tweed-suited figure sitting on a sofa on the far side of the atrium. I walked over with a confident stride.

'Rory!'

Rory looked up at me through his little gold-rimmed spectacles. He has a Young Fogey style that makes him look like a cross between a twelve-year-old boy and a favourite, pipe-smoking uncle; often I can't decide whether I want to mother him or sit on his knee. He shuffled himself up to a standing position. I stepped forward expecting a hug but he stuck out his hand rather awkwardly instead. A man in a suit and tie stood up too.

'This is Frank Lloyd, our Finance Director,' said Rory.

I held out my hand. The man took it in a limp, unenthusiastic grasp.

'Suzy Stephens,' I said. 'Pleased to meet you.'

Frank didn't comment. He dropped my hand and looked past me, over my shoulder. Turning, I saw an elegant blonde coming towards us, wearing a black trouser suit of such pressed perfection I immediately realised not only did I look like I'd raided the dressing-up box but I was covered in cat hairs.

'Estelle Smythe,' the vision introduced herself. 'Shall we go up?'

In Estelle's tenth floor office three chairs had been set out in front of a huge wooden desk which was empty apart from a computer screen and a single file. We sat down. Rory slumped in his seat. Frank clicked open his briefcase and took out a notepad and a calculator. Estelle positioned herself behind the desk and opened a file. I fished around in my handbag and took out a biro.

'So,' Estelle said brightly, turning over a couple of papers. 'Letter from solicitors acting for Henry Stephens and his wife, Belinda Blenkinsop... their client seriously defamed... will provide statements from numerous acquaintances claiming to have recognised him in the book... reputation severely damaged... pupils now drape Ann Summers underwear over his desk... lost all authority... career at an end.' She looked up at me enquiringly. 'What do you say?'

'I can't believe it!'

'Awful, isn't it?' said Rory, slumping down further in his chair.

'No,' I said more firmly. Rory's defeatism was starting to get on my nerves. 'I mean I *don't* believe it. Henry can handle kids. If they left knickers on his desk he'd just raise an eyebrow and say "Not my colour". And of course it's not the end of his career. He's a brilliant teacher.' I paused. 'Henry just wouldn't do this. It doesn't add up.'

'I imagine his wife isn't too delighted,' said Estelle dryly. 'The picture portrayed in your book isn't quite the right image for a prime minister's husband.'

'But Belinda isn't prime minister!'

'Not yet. But I imagine she thinks she might be one day. I'd say she's the kind of woman who looks ahead.' There was a pointed silence while we all considered the kind of woman who doesn't look ahead.

'Can't I just say I'm sorry?' I said.

Estelle consulted her file. 'An apology is certainly part of what they want. But it'll take rather more than that to get them to go away.'

'But if I explain it was just a silly mistake?'

Estelle narrowed her eyes. 'What was a silly mistake?'

'Putting in the bit about the Toyota.'

Estelle looked weary. 'You knew Henry had a red Toyota?' she said.

'Yes, of course...'

'With a, what did you call it, "suggestively dented rear bumper"?'

'Well, yes...'

'And you knew other people would recognise it as Henry's car from that description?'

'I suppose so, but...'

She cut across me. 'No, we can't just say it was a silly mistake.'

Frank's finger was poised over his calculator. 'So what's the damage?'

Estelle rifled through her file. 'They're looking at a substantial six-figure sum, but I hope we can get away with a little under a hundred thousand. Plus a full apology. Plus obviously we pulp the book.'

'Pulp my book?' I wailed.

There was another silence. Rory put his head in his hands and rocked to and fro. Frank looked down at his calculator and then up at Estelle. 'And the alternative?' he said.

Estelle closed her file. 'The only alternative here would be justification.'

'Meaning?' asked Frank.

'Meaning we prove the allegation that Mr Stephens enjoys dressing up in women's underwear is true.'

Which, of course, it was.

IF THE SHOE FITS

from the novel by Emma London

One

Anna

My friend Clarissa always says if you want something doing don't ask anyone, just do it yourself. A fine sentiment coming from a person like her who has no hesitation in going up to complete strangers and asking them to change her car wheel, or could they possibly give her a ciggie as she's *gasping* for one. Clarissa is always like that; she says one thing but does totally the opposite. Like arranging to meet me for a drink in a crowded Camden pub one Sunday lunchtime and simply not turning up. I sat there for an hour, had two half lagers, and then left feeling like a complete fraud who'd only pretended to be meeting someone. I went away empty handed. Alone and friendless.

Sorry Anna but Finbar rang and I had to see him, she said.

That's all right then.

Just do it yourself. Well that is what I decide to do. I wait for the children to leave for school on their first day of term, Maisie all excited because she was going into Year One (so there, ner ner ner ner nerrr). I make myself a strong black coffee, get a fat pad of paper and sit down at the kitchen table. A LIST, I write. I will take good old Clarissa's advice and do it myself. I will change my life.

I continue to write:

1. Reflexology
2. Hair Cutting
3. Reading
4. Writing
5. Education

That makes me feel better. When I was preparing for my A-levels (twenty blinking years ago) I was very good at writing lists concerning all the studying I needed to do. It took up my most of my time. I didn't have any time left to study.

  6. Stop writing lists.
  7. Stop seeing Clarissa.

My list has started to look a bit negative so I add:

  8. Skipping.

Finbar is one of those men who has charisma. Clarissa loves charisma and will swallow it whole when given a chance. Finbar is canny like that; he offers her a spoonful, gets her hooked and then disappears for weeks at a time. Not that Clarissa mopes around; no, she has far too many interests for that. She has a new career every year, it seems, and that is the reason for my list. I have no career. I have children.

I happen to like my children, but that is no excuse, says Clarissa, and in a way she's right. Because they grow up and leave home and then they don't waste your space or your time and only occasionally waste your money and you are left with empty bedrooms and no career.

I need a career.

My husband wants me to do what I want to do. We don't need the money because Adam has his career. He goes out to his office and comes home and shares the domestic stuff and laughs with the children. He's sorted. He can say at parties that he's a Trade Mark Attorney, and people look interested and don't glaze over and rush to get a drink somewhere as far away as possible. I dread the question: *What do you do?* I do children, that's what I do. Did. Now that is all changing because I'm getting myself a career.

The phone rings and I reluctantly leave my list to answer it. The sitting room is cold and I am slightly miffed that I've been interrupted. It's Clarissa.

That's just typical.

I hear you want a job, Anna, she says. Fenella needs a secretary to help her with her admin and...

She warbles on in her arrogant voice, while I wonder what Ned wants for his birthday tea. Ned who is just about to be fourteen and is in love for the first time with Samantha. She's a sweet enough girl, but so young. How can they know what love is, and what do they do with all this emotion? On Ned this heady emotion is erupting in spots, and on sweet Samantha it hovers over her translucent wrinkle-free skin attracting other, older, Neds and making my little boy wretched. My baby.

Hmmm, I say into the phone during one of Clarissa's brief pauses.

Clarissa arrived in my life when she came to my Grammar school in the Sixth Form. She took one sweeping look at the girls in green on offer and plumped for the one who scrambled in late. The tall skinny one with short mousy hair and skeleton earrings. Me.

There is another lull at the end of the phone.

Thanks Clarissa. I don't want a job. I want a career, I say.

Silence. You could practically hear her mind computing this new information, chewing it over and spewing up the right answer.

You'd better go to university then, Anna, she says.

I think about this for a second, mumble something inaudible even to me and say goodbye.

The phone is placed safely back in its cradle and I return to my list.

The problem about finding oneself a career, at the ripe old age of thirty-six, is that it has to be the right one. One that is interesting, stimulating, challenging and applicable to a more mature person. I don't fancy being the tea lady in a successful office, where my pushy boss might be only a few years older than Ned.

Just the other day Tom, my other son, declared I should be a racing car driver when I was hurrying through rush hour traffic, as I do every Tuesday, and I had just overtaken a dawdling driver too hesitant at a junction. When I told Tom I was too old he explained that I could do anything I set my mind on, repeating Adam's phrase verbatim.

Thanks, Tom.

No, Tom, she can't, interrupted my pragmatic daughter Maisie, she's too wrinkly.

No she's not, he replied, anyway she looks like one.

What did *that* mean?

I do have a great leather jacket with zips and subtle stains and a few discreet studs. It's more biker than racing driver. Adam bought it for me after I'd had Ned. I loved being a mum but I did not want to *look* like a mum.

But what have I set my mind on?

Number One on my list is reflexology.

Elizabeth, Clarissa's mother, is coming round. She once did a course in foot massage.

Almost the same thing as reflexology, darling, she says. I'll show you.

Elizabeth had Clarissa during her first brief marriage and this infant was dragged through the other marriages like an inconvenient antique travel case. Clarissa was abandoned at boarding school, she claims, and often hadn't realised her mother had moved again, let alone married, until the start of the summer holidays when the car pulled up outside a different house containing a different man. Elizabeth spent the first eighteen years of Clarissa's life trying to shake her off and for the past eighteen years Clarissa has been shaking her mother off. This is why Elizabeth calls me. She doesn't know where Clarissa is half the time, but she knows where I am. There are only so many times Adam can lie and say that I'm out.

Tonight all the children have, for once, gone to bed early. I think this is a sure sign Ned is maturing until Adam admits to having promised him a trip to the cinema if he went upstairs with Tom and Maisie before Elizabeth arrived. This is Adam being supportive and it makes my quest for a career feel even more desperate.

Elizabeth arrives glowing.

I am very lucky with my mother; she keeps a discreet distance, loves my children and offers us holidays when we've all forgotten to have one. As punishment for having the perfect mother of my own, I seem to have acquired Clarissa's. One day I'll start calling her Mother.

Elizabeth loves having a mission and helping me find a career is now her sole responsibility. She thinks. She looks very professional with her canvas black bag embroidered with multicoloured butterflies, full of intriguing plastic bottles containing pink and purple liquid. She takes them out and lines them up in rows on the coffee table, ready for battle. She also produces a CD, the cover of which is awash with watery swirls and hippy rainbows.

Pink Floyd? Adam asks facetiously.

Elizabeth gives him one of her I-killed-Jesse-James looks and hands him a £10 note.

Get us something fizzy, darling, she says in *that* voice while nudging him out the room. Adam is always obedient when it comes to Elizabeth (aren't we all); he glances sneakily in my direction and contemplates raising an eyebrow, but daren't do so, so waves a hand instead.

Be quiet when you come in, Elizabeth tells him.

She makes me lie down on the floor, thrusting an old deflated cushion under my head. This is depressing; I haven't vacuumed for a while. Under the sofa there are neat clumps of congealed blue wool from Ned's new jumper, the one Samantha likes, and the carpet has moulted and spewed bits of red everywhere. It doesn't feel terribly hygienic down here. Elizabeth doesn't notice. She tucks an invisible strand of hair behind her ear and takes the top off the first bottle: Peppermint Foot Lotion.

Where's your CD player? she asks.

The CD is called *Sounds of the Sea*. The waves are slapping the shore, the wind is groaning softly and the occasional bird hiccups. I lie back and shut my eyes. This is relaxing. After the initial feeling of tickling, I begin to enjoy the sensation of Elizabeth's surprisingly strong hands stroking my feet. I feel better than I have all week. I open my eyelids a fraction to watch her at work.

Elizabeth changes her hairdo frequently. When I first met her in the early eighties she had an elegant French plait of light brown hair, with the odd strand painstakingly placed at regular intervals around the periphery. After a while the strands overtook the plait in importance, and eventually the plait disappeared altogether.

Adam slips back in and places a large glass of Cava by my right hand. Bliss. The liquid tastes gorgeous, the sea sounds inviting and even Adam quietly giggling in the background doesn't upset my equilibrium. Elizabeth must have given him another of her looks because he suddenly shuts up and goes and sits in the far corner pretending to read a book. But even from my point of view I can see it's Ned's German Grammar book. He doesn't know any German.

Clarissa always maintains Elizabeth's hairstyle fitted the husband, but in *my* experience this isn't true. She has had half a dozen totally different hairdos since I've known her, and only two husbands. The three previous husbands had been discarded before I came on the scene. Gerald was around until the Kings Road shop opened and Elizabeth was a curly blonde then. Malcolm married the blonde and it was at their first anniversary party that Elizabeth appeared with short black hair. I was married myself by then. Elizabeth went a lurid red for a while, sporting bunches like Ginger Spice, much to Clarissa's fury. But now fast approaching seventy she has returned to the more sedate bun, her natural white is beginning to appear and it deflates me. I always felt Elizabeth's fight against age and conventionality was a beacon for us all to follow. Her acceptance of the inevitable is too grim.

At least she's still trying to organise my life for me; through the post this morning arrived the prospectus for the University of West London. Opened but not perused. This is the Elizabeth I have come to love and cherish; the Elizabeth who hasn't changed. I know that Elizabeth knows that I know she sent off for that prospectus. We don't mention it.

Why not try for Oxbridge? Clarissa had said on the phone earlier.

Not helpful Clarissa.

Maybe I too could learn to massage feet.

I imagine myself at a party.

Hi, my name's Anna and I'm a foot masseuse.

Or perhaps: Hi, my name's Anna and I'm a reflexologist.

That sounded like a proper career. I would be interesting.

It's not just a massage darling, Elizabeth explains, it can also aid digestion, headaches, circulation, in fact health in general. All through the feet, darling. All through the feet.

I must say I am feeling pretty damn good. I suspect the Cava is helping too.

Elizabeth opens her second bottle of magic cream. She has a look of intense concentration on her face. This bottle is called Blackcurrant Foot Balm and the globular content is mauve. It smells like the tongue-red ice lollies the children insist on having; sweet and medicinal. Elizabeth is now pummelling my big toes rhythmically and I am almost in a trance. Elizabeth asks Adam (there's a love) for more Cava, which surprises me as I'd forgotten he was there. He fills up both our glasses and I realise I am pissed.

Suddenly there is a loud and totally unexpected squawking on the calming CD. The tranquil moment is lost in an instant. I start giggling hysterically and Adam gags on his mouthful of beer. Elizabeth jabs my foot with a spiteful nail (shit), which causes me to knock my drink all over her new bag full of potions. Even Elizabeth, not renowned for her sense of humour, laughs grudgingly.

I'd forgotten about the neurotic whale, she says.

Monday morning and the children have gone to school; packed lunch for Tom (but no tuna please, Mum) £1.50 for Ned (is that all? Stingy) and two pieces of fruit for Maisie (not apples, no way José). Adam has gone to work (don't forget your briefcase my dearest). I begin to imagine bulk-buying Peppermint Foot Lotion and Blackcurrant Foot Balm, ordering white crispy laundered sheets, awaiting my clients, helping them on to my firm massaging bed... My clients.

Instantly this career fantasy flounders. Who will these clients be? Where will I find them? Will the feet be sterilised? How do dentists do it? Do they look into unknown mouths and fiddle in those dark, damp orifices searching for pus and rot and pungent things? Surely feet are as bad, if not worse, than mouths. I imagine flaky corns, knobbly bunions and yellow, gnarled toenails. No. I don't want to be near just anybody's feet. No no no. Feet are personal and smelly and they are NOT sanitary... I cross Number One off my list.

Clarissa is on the phone, yet again. She's put out that Elizabeth came round this weekend. She thinks it's *her* mission to sort me out. Why can't they both leave me alone?

Your mother never had a career, she snaps.

This is true. Even after my father died my mother decided not to work. She received a small pension and was content to concentrate on her ghastly teenagers. We were all still at home then.

I am icy on the phone.

I am *not* my mother, I say.

Clarissa hangs up. This is not a good sign; it means she will be round later. Have we split up? she'll say.

Adam and I thought we were going to have a quiet night.

I met Adam at one of Elizabeth's weddings. Her fifth to be precise. My husband sometimes speculates on the amount of money spent on her wedding cakes over the years. I don't like cake, much to Adam's annoyance; he could talk about cakes, biscuits and chocolate all evening and cannot believe I don't share his love for all things sweet and sticky. I used to get a basket of fruit for my birthday when I was a child because my mother realised that cakes left me cold. I could talk about fruit all evening.

Adam was the son of Malcolm's accountant and was invited only because there was an embarrassingly large number of single women on the wedding list and no single men. He was dismissed instantly by Clarissa that morning because he didn't arrive in a smart car. He drove a battered Land Rover then.

Anna, sweetie, Clarissa announced, accountants are *the* most boring people in the world, therefore the son of one will be even more so.

I started to protest, on Adam's behalf, but with Clarissa it's rarely worth the
effort. In the end I was rather grateful for that particular snap decision. I had
sampled one of Clarissa's cast-offs already and it had been a painful experience.

THE SEAHORSE

from the novel Learning to Swim by Kate McEwan

The doctor is surprised that I know about the seahorse when he shows me the pictures of Ma's brain. I suppose the whole hospital is talking about the stupid English tannie[1] who's so backward she's never even seen a television. Well, I may be stupid, but I'm not a fool. The nicest thing about the doctor is that he keeps reassuring me that there was nothing more I could have done to help Ma. At first, when he began to ask all those questions about when it began and how she changed – ticking my answers off against a long list – I thought he was blaming me for not doing anything sooner, and that he might even tell the police. I was so scared that I might let out something that Ma wouldn't want other people to know, something that would get us into trouble. When you live with a mixed-up person for a long time, you begin to forget what's real.

But Ma is not mad! The results of all the tests are back from the laboratory, so the doctor can rule out the things she hasn't got and confirm what he says he suspected all along: something called Alzheimer's disease. He says it's a new name for an old illness, but I don't care: her disease has a name; she's not mad.

'So you won't lock her up in Valkenberg?' I have to be sure, for Ma's sake.

'Valkenberg! You mean the mental institution in Cape Town... is that why you didn't call a doctor?'

I just nod. It was one of the reasons Ma made me promise – when she was still able to think for herself.

'Don't worry, we'll look after her. And I think you've done a truly fantastic job looking after her all on your own, Miss van Niekerk. Tender loving care is the best treatment for her condition until research...'

'It's Miss *Fischer*,' I say. 'My name is Fila... er... Mina Fischer. My mother married again.' I sound like an idiot, interrupting him like that, but I have to put him right. I was never a 'van Niekerk'.

'Ja, well, no, fine. I'm sorry about that, Miss Fila-Amina Fischer,' he says,

---

[1] Aunty. Afrikaans term of respect for an older woman

sympathetically. 'My parents got divorced, too.'

I want to explain that there was no divorce and that it's plain Filamina, but Pa always called me 'Fila', and Ma 'Mina' and sometimes it felt as though I was two different people. But I don't say anything. What does it matter, now, anyway?

'Come round to this side of the desk,' says the doctor, 'and take a look at your mother's CT scans.' He has a little television on his desk that he calls a computer. He fiddles with a flat sort of typewriter and a brilliant red, green and blue picture appears on the screen. 'There, this is a good slice – can you see how the cortex, that blue stuff, has shrivelled up inside her skull?' He goes on about tissue loss and nerve cells dying and blocked messages, but I'm not really listening. I am looking at a picture of my mother's brain. I am looking *inside her head*. I am looking into the place where she thinks and dreams and keeps her secrets. How can a camera do *that*?

The doctor is still talking excitedly as he flicks through the pictures. I haven't taken in a word. It's nice to see someone so passionate about his subject; Pa was like that when something interested him. I try to pay attention.

'Here, this is the one I'm looking for – the inner surface of the temporal lobe. This is the clincher. Now, it's not terribly clear unless you know what you're looking for, but can you see this small grey area inside that fold, down there, a sort of seahorse shape?'

'The hippocampus!' I almost shout the words. So Pa was right, after all.

Now the doctor is really impressed. 'Spot on! It's always the quiet ones, hey? I bet you were top of the class at school.'

'It was my father, not school,' I say. 'He was an autodidact.'

The doctor looks at me a bit strangely. 'Ek sê;[2] an autodidact, hey?' he says, pretending to be impressed, but I can see he doesn't really know what it means. (He may be a doctor, but he doesn't know *everything*.) The hippocampus, he explains, is where Ma's problems started. As it started to shrink, it became more difficult for her to make new memories. That's why she forgot things and her stored memories of the past became mixed up with the present...

His words buzz around the hot room, but I'm remembering Pa coming in all wet with spray and smelling of the sea one wintry Sunday evening, and clumping straight through to the kitchen where Ma is heating up the dinner and helping me learn my four times table.

---

[2] I say

THE SEAHORSE

'I'm an autodidact!' he shouts. 'It's official! The mayor himself told me.' Pa sometimes took the mayor and his friends fishing in the bay on his day off.

'I'll autodidact you if you don't get those wet boots off my kitchen floor,' Ma says. 'What's an autodidact when it's at home, anyway?'

'Wait, I'll show you...' Pa tries to pull off his boots on his way to the sitting-room for the big, fat book that always sits on the little stool beside his chair: *Webster's New International Dictionary, Second Edition* – thicker than my hand can stretch, with 604,000 words that weigh almost fourteen pounds on Ma's scales with the brass weights.

Boetie comes running in to see what all the fuss is about and everyone waits until Pa hops back, one boot on, one boot off, and thumps the dictionary on to the kitchen table. The man at the library said he could have it, after the roof leaked and ruined the cover and left a rusty stain running down the picture of the aardvark. Pa turns the tissue-thin pages carefully as he runs his finger down the columns of As.

'There it is: "au-to-di-dact – one who is self-taught"; from *auto* plus *didaktos*. The Greeks said it first, of course. See, what did I tell you? All you need to get an education is to be able to read and to want to learn.'

'Ag,[3] Frikkie, never mind self-taught; *you* should be a teacher. You know something about everything, and the kids would love your stories.' Ma has nothing but respect for teachers. She always takes their side if we get into trouble at school, even when they smack our legs. But she's right about Pa's stories: he can make ordinary, boring things seem magic, and magic turn into something you can see and touch.

'No, man, they'd never have me with only Standard Four. A little knowledge is a dangerous thing, as they say. And, when you're a teacher, you have to tell stories the way other people want them told, not your own way. Anyway, teaching is hard work, and work is for people who can't fish. I'd rather wrestle with a Great White every day than face a class of pikkies[4] like Fila, all chanting, "Four fours are eighty-two, three threes are six"...', and he prances around the kitchen in his socks, pretending to read from my book of tables, while Ma flaps after him with her oven-gloves, laughing and shouting, 'You know nothing, you silly autodidact!' and 'Don't listen to him, Mina, he's telling you all wrong!'

---

[3] Oh

[4] Small children

Pa reads *Webster's* every night, as though it were a novel. He likes to learn a new word every day. He has other books, too, in the little bookcase he calls his library: books that people gave him, or that he bought in jumble sales, or from the bookstalls on the Grand Parade in Cape Town. A lot of Pa's books are about animals or fish or birds, but most are about history. He says that if you want to find out what's going to happen next, you have to check out the past because it takes people a long time to stop making the same mistakes.

'But always remember, Filatjie, that you can never rely on just one person's story about what happened. Everyone sees things differently, depending on what they believe.'

'Does that mean that people who write history books are telling lies, Pa?' Telling lies was a very big deal in our house. 'Tell the truth and shame the devil,' Ma always said. If you did something wrong, you got into trouble; but that was nowhere near as big as the trouble you got into if you told a lie. Ma once beat Boetie on his bottom with the back of the clothes-brush for lying about where he had been. And he wasn't allowed out for a week for not coming home on time.

'Hmm,' says Pa, 'that's a ticklish one. No, not lying *exactly*. There's always a good reason for why historians believe what they do, so they can't help telling it like they see it. But if you want to make up your own mind about why things happened, then you have to add a good pinch of salt to everything you read, and spread your net wide to try and catch the truth.'

He thinks for a bit, and then he says, 'Truth is a tricky thing – it's like when Ma looks into a mirror and says, "My hair looks terrible, today". But when I look at her, all I can see is how beautiful she is. So we don't always see things as *they* are, we see them as *we* are. Sometimes the truth is staring us in the face, but we just can't see it.'

'But if she can't see it, then what Ma believes is also true. For her.'

Pa bursts out laughing. 'Filatjie, you're a philosopher already! It's a shame you have to go to school and be taught what to think. Ja, you've got it; that's my point exactly: truth is different for everybody. But what we believe changes the more we learn. So the important thing is to keep an open mind, and for us to keep telling your mother that her hair looks better than Jackie Kennedy's.'

Over Pa's desk, in a postcard-sized frame, is a quotation by a famous scientist that he asked Ma to type out for him at work:

Learn from yesterday, live for today, hope for tomorrow. The important thing is not to stop questioning.
– Albert Einstein

You could ask Pa anything. He always took your questions seriously and made you feel clever for asking. Like the day we found the seahorse.

Sunday is Pa's only day off – unless the southeaster blows too hard for the boats to leave harbour, or his back is hurting him. Sunday mornings, while Ma is at church and Boetie is at Sunday school, is *our* time. I'm too young for Sunday School and Pa doesn't go to church often. 'God isn't in a building with fancy windows,' he says, 'he's everywhere. I prefer to save up all my sins and confess them to Father Doran once a year; it's more fun for him that way. Anyway, Jesus was a fisherman, he'll understand about my day off.' We sing 'All Things Bright and Beautiful' to make the tunnel walls echo as we walk through the sandy subway to the beach, swinging my tin bucket and fishing-net between us.

'Gently, Fila, gently. How would you like it if someone came along and poked *you* in your tummy?'

'I'm just playing, Pa. I'm not hurting it.' But I pull my finger free of the sea-anemone's pink tentacles and climb on to his lap, letting my bare feet dangle in the rock-pool a safe distance above the spiky sea-urchins that line the bottom. The tide is way out on this breathless Sunday morning. The sun still has to burn off the last of the mist from the Hottentot Holland Mountains across the bay. Along the rocky shoreline, the brown people are collecting mussels. Around us, a sparkling rock-pool world glints with treasures for Pa and me to find: mother-of-pearl shells, tiny periwinkles smaller than the nail on my pinkie, skeleton shrimps that you can see right through, scuttling crabs and starfish of all colours and sizes. Barnacles and limpets hiss in the sun so that it sounds as though the rocks are breathing. I wriggle off Pa's lap to chase a speckled klipfish with my net. But it's too quick for me and all I catch is seaweed. Seaweed with something pinky-brown in it; something with a long pointy nose.

'Pa, Pa, look what I've caught! Is it real?' I whisper in my excitement, afraid to raise my voice in case the magical creature disappears or changes into something ordinary.

'A seahorse – now that's a *very* special find, Filatjie. You don't often get

KATE McEWAN

Hippocampus capensis this far south. They live way up the coast in the Knysna Estuary. Maybe it was chasing shrimp or plankton and got washed out to sea.'

'But I thought seahorses were only in books – like unicorns and mermaids. I didn't know they were still living.' With feather-soft fingers, I uncurl the seahorse's tail from the seaweed and scoop him gently into my bucket to see him properly. He bobs upright in the water, no bigger than Pa's thumb. The fin on his bumpy back flutters like a fairy's wing as he propels himself around the bucket. He is the most beautiful thing I have ever seen.

'He doesn't look anything like a hippo, Pa.'

'*Hippocampus. Hippo* means horse; he's half horse, half monster according to the Greeks.'

'He's not a monster! How could they say he was a monster!'

'No, but it's a real mix-up, the seahorse,' says Pa, peering into the bucket with me. 'Look, Filatjie, he's got a horse's head... and a curly tail like a monkey... and see the way his eyes move backwards and forwards like that? Just like a chameleon. He can change colour like a chameleon, too. And what about his armour-plating?'

'Like a dinosaur?' I ask quickly, desperate to contribute something to the construction of this wonderful creature. Pa has told me all about dinosaurs.

'Ja, you're right, good for you! Like a stegosaurus. And yet he's perfect, hey?'

'Just perfect,' I breathe.

'And do you see that little pouch under his chest, like a kangaroo's? That means it's a boy. The mommy seahorse lays her eggs in there and it's the daddy who gives birth to the babies. *Hundreds* of them, poor little chap. But he keeps them safe in that pouch until they are big enough to swim on their own.'

We crouch over the bucket, the spring sunshine warm on our backs.

'What was it like when I was born, Pa? Were you there when I came out of Ma's tummy?' I know this story, but I want to hear it again.

Pa puts on a sad face. 'Ag, Filatjie, they don't let men into the delivery room at the hospital. But I would have been right there in the waiting room if you had just stayed in long enough for me to get back from catching snoek in Walvis Bay. You were already almost a week old by the time Ma managed to get a telegram delivered to the coastguard to find me.'

'What did it say, the telegram?'

'Girlie. Early. Perfect. Hurry home.'

The seahorse pirouettes gracefully around the bucket, his head held high.

And I want him to be there forever. 'Can I keep him, Pa? Please? I'd look after him... I'll get him fresh seawater everyday... and I'll catch shrimps for him... please, Pa?'

'Ag, no, my little one. It wouldn't be right. He's a fish, not a pet. Catching fish to eat or make a living is one thing; taking them out of their natural habitat just to provide us with entertainment is quite another.'

Pa hates any wild thing kept in cages or fish-tanks. Ma often says how she'd love to have a canary because they sing so beautifully, but he says she'll just have to make do with his singing, instead. And when a boy at school gave Boetie some stick insects and a praying mantis, Pa made him let them go in the garden, 'where they belong'. I know he's right about having respect for nature, but...

'Oh, Pa, *please*? I want him so much.'

'Ag, Filatjie, would *you* like it if you had to live in a small glass room for the rest of your life, and could never run outside and play?'

'No, Pa.'

'And how do we know his wife isn't waiting for him out there in the bay? They mate for life, you know. There may even be babies in his pouch...'

'OK, Pa. We'll put him back. I don't want to keep him any more.'

Pa strokes my hair and smoothes a curl back behind one ear. 'Anyway, you don't need another seahorse, my skattebol.[5] You've already got one... two, in fact, right inside here.' And he taps my head just above my ear.

'No, Pa!' I protest, giggling, and shake my head away from his prodding finger. Sometimes it's difficult to know when Pa is joking, but this can't be right.

'It's true, 'strues Bob. There's a bit of your brain shaped like a seahorse that's also called a hippocampus. I was reading about it, just the other day, in that magazine that Dr Farrant lent me – you know that nice old bloke from Norman Road who comes fishing with us sometimes? It said that if we didn't have a hippocampus, we couldn't make any memories and so we'd forget how to find out way home.'

'What are memories, Pa?'

'Now *that*, Filatjie, is a very good question. Let me think a bit.' Pa leans back against the rocks and stretches out his long legs. He lights up his pipe and takes a deep, thoughtful draw, then lifts his face up to the sun and closes his eyes.

5 My treasure

KATE McEWAN

The little lines at the corners of his eyes are pale against the seaweed-brown of his face from years of squinting to see which way the fish are running. I look out to sea. The tide is turning, and every now and then a wave sprays against the rocks at the sea's edge. The brown people are silhouetted against the sky as they walk towards Danger Beach. They look very small from this distance.

Suddenly Pa opens his deep-blue eyes and sits up. 'Memories are the story of your life. Memories are who you are. They're your own personal history recorded in your brain. Every time you do something or see or smell or hear anything, it makes a memory, a kind of thought-picture. And all these memories go into the little pocket of the hippocampus in your brain to be sorted. They swim around in there, slippery as fish caught in a trek net. Some sink to the bottom and those are the things we forget – because it's impossible to remember *everything*; we'd go mad. Some swim away to other parts of the brain to wait until we want to remember something and pull them up to the surface. But it's the hippocampus that decides what we'll remember, and what we'll forget.'

'I'll always remember the seahorse.'

'Ja, me, too, my skattebol,' say Pa.

We carry the seahorse to the end of the rocks and carefully tip him into the sea to find his wife. The brown people are almost out of sight, now.

'Where do they live, Pa?'

'At the bottom of the ocean. They hang on to seaweed with their tails...'

'No, not the seahorses. I mean the brown people who were collecting mussels down here just now. Look... over there...'

But the brown people have gone.

Pa looks puzzled. 'I didn't see anyone. Only you and me. That's what's nice about coming down here so early.'

I know he's teasing me again, but it's getting too hot to argue. We walk back along the rocks to the seawall of the Ladies' Pool, to meet Ma and Boetie for my swimming lesson.

STILL LIFE

from the novel by TRC Martin

Whichever way he went, he always managed to walk past Tink's house. When he got there, he'd stand around outside for a while like a teenager then walk home. It was his circuit. Tonight was no different.

The house was in the middle of a crescent, between two small hotels. He stood at the bottom of the steps and peered up at the brass panel where the buzzers were. It was smudged and tarnished from a day's use. That'll be clean by midday, thought Tamby. His phone rang.

'Camden?' It was Mike McAdam, his Chief of Station. Camden was Tamby's codename. All the agents currently operative in London were named after parts of the city. The names were changed each quarter, or each security breach, whichever happened first.

'Putney?'

'Why are you standing outside her house?'

Still facing the building, Tamby stepped off the pavement, walked backwards across the road and stood under a tree. 'Hey, Putney, c'mon, I only just got here. You know my habits. Why are you checking up on me?'

'Why?'

'I'm just doing my job, same as usual.'

'After today, you're asking me why I am checking up on you?'

Tamby headed back down the crescent, towards the park.

'Good OK,' said McAdam, 'you just keep on going, keep on walking.'

'I'm walking,' said Tamby. Up in the sky above his head, the CIA satellite was making binary code out of his footsteps. Agents were tracked via their mobile phones, just like everybody else. Tamby had read somewhere that this did not increase an agent's vulnerability as I-Sat was unhackable. His eyes darted over his shoulder, half as a joke to himself, half not. 'You just happen to be awake?' he asked his superior.

'The operation is closed, you know that,' McAdam said.

'So you get someone to call you if I go for a walk?'

'I care.'

'Define closed.'

'You were at the meeting…'

'Not officially.'

'…and at the meeting, we discussed that it was all closed, put to bed, for the files, fifty years.'

'But starting from when?'

'From buh-bye.'

'No natural wrap-up?'

'Are you drunk?' McAdam asked.

'It's a possibility,' Tamby said. 'Are you?' He had reached the park. The site had originally been a foundling hospital, back when they still had foundlings. Now the flat, hemmed-in playing field was dominated by one of those safe playgrounds known as a recreational area or kidspace, the kind of place you couldn't help thinking about paedophiles, where nothing worked or was any fun. He jumped the fence and stood on some woodchippings, hypnotised by the primary colours and half-sizes.

'I am not,' McAdam replied. 'Define drunk.' He chuckled to himself, slightly away from the mouthpiece. Tamby liked the sound, it was like a trained walrus calling for a fish; a natural, college-kid's laugh. This was not surprising. In general, Mike McAdam was a thickset old man with thinning blond hair and a moustache. If skinny meant had a lot of excess skin, then McAdam was skinny, especially around the face. He had the look of someone Tamby might have seen fishing on the canal; inexpert, content. But that attractiveness, that generality, was McAdam's life work: Full Body Camouflage had been his area of expertise before returning to operations. Aside from teaching Tamby at training camp, McAdam had taken his highly classified, laboriously Zen method of 'no-disguise disguise' to secret military training camps all around the world. He called it The Morph; they had worked on Tamby's Christian-who-likes-sailing persona together.

He liked McAdam, or admired the way he did things, and had known him for a long time. And yet, when Tamby had realised that there was something about the meeting earlier that day that he didn't know, the only thing that really linked the two men had gone. Trust. He still admired the man, but as far as the laugh was concerned, it might as well have been straight out of the manual.

'Are kids afraid of paedophiles these days?' Tamby asked.

'No.'

'Tell me what happened at the meeting.'

'Why did you put Smee in hospital?'

'To protect her, of course.'

'After we'd just agreed she didn't need protection?'

'Yes.'

'A grave error of judgement, Camden.'

'Not at all.'

'*Qui sème le vent récolte la tempête*, don't you think?'

'I do, I couldn't agree more, Sir. Been thinking that a lot recently?'

'Oh, you're an artist!' replied McAdam, tapping some background object in mock applause. In training, Tamby's specialisation had been a particular form of cold combat known as The Verbalise. It was a potentially lethal method of manipulation that came naturally to Tamby, having been based, as far as he could see, on that ruthless Southern politeness which his mother and her friends used to share over morning cocktails. He had been practising it earlier that evening with Inez Fabian.

'Well, don't take this the wrong way,' Tamby persisted, 'but you got the promotion? I love coincidences; they just happen.'

'The wit. I was always going to Paris when this wrapped, you know that.'

'I know, I know. I'm kidding. You wanted your baguettes, we didn't find anything, they aren't lunatics, case closed.'

'I didn't say they aren't lunatics.'

'It was a trick question, I was testing to see if you'd defected.'

'To the FBI? Is that all that's left?' McAdam whistled through the gap in his teeth.

'Oh, Putney Bridge, you tell me,' said Tamby.

'Me and you got on this wagon trail too late. Especially you,' said McAdam.

'So tell me why we're pulling out. Does Tink even know we're not there?'

'Scotland Yard have got their regular celebrity division on her, as you know. It's all she needs. The FBI is satisfied – thanks to all your great work I might add – that she's got nothing to do with the lag.'

'Was this before or after the material was analysed by the Directorate? Only if it was after, they've been speeding things up a lot back home.'

'Yeah, I know, you said that at the meeting too. What's that noise?'

Tamby had been fiddling with one of the chains on the rope bridge. Without noticing, he had started swinging the whole bridge, making the chains jump and strain. He stopped the bridge and headed out of the park towards Russell Square.

'Are you OK? How's the patient?' his superior asked.

'Is this line secure?'

'Yes, we're fine on this one. We're trying out those double blind connections; you never know.' Double blinds were the latest thing. Science & Tech had been working on a computer which invents a computer which invents an encrypting code. Reports were saying it could be the big breakthrough. Tamby admired the tech guys' frontier spirit. He wished he had a little bit more of it himself to help face the next day's news. Early rumours weren't starting out too well.

The street cleaners were already circling in Russell Square as Tamby headed down into the darkness of Montague Street. Something hadn't felt right about running Smee down, but he hadn't been able to say what it was. The walk was supposed to help clear his head, but he was using all his energy to get an answer out of McAdam about the operation.

'I don't know how she is,' Tamby replied. 'How is she?'

'She's fine. She hasn't changed. She's probably not fine. It was a risk.'

'Now standard procedure is a risk?'

'Congratulations.'

'I suppose so. Aren't you tired yet?'

'Are you finally going home?'

'Yes.'

'I don't want another call.'

'Why are they pulling the operation?'

'We are. *We* are pulling the operation because there's nothing more, nada, done. Even if there was, you neutralised it.'

'It'll be interesting to find out who's pissed with me tomorrow morning.'

'Pissed *off*, Rupert, darling,' McAdam drawled in an English accent, chuckling again. 'The parents? MI5? Say hello to the British Museum from me.'

Tamby waved through the railings as he walked past. 'How many fingers am I holding up, Putney?' The line went dead.

TWELVE POEMS

by Lawrence Pettener

Sarajevo

The cleaning lady in the launderette is from Sarajevo;
her eyes look out from somewhere older than she is,
and her voice has a sad, Scouse-like lilt, as though

she is singing tears: *I don't know why is it*, she says,
that one sock is left by the people, always. I speculate
aloud, that this is the minimum sacrifice

demanded by the Goddess of the washing machine.
She nods, appreciatively, with a faint smile; her eyes
seem to fix on the idea as I say it. The washing machine

behind her pounds on with that timeless, tabla rhythm
like that produced by *dhobi* washerwomen in India,
and we both sway ever so slightly.

Selling Celebratoriness
to the English

Picking your nose after chopping chillies
is more than a wholefood alternative
to cocaine. Garlic's good

for occasional treats, but if you want
the real thing it's got to be chillies.
Some nights,

I buy my girlfriend a vindaloo;
afterwards, I thrash around
while she licks

my nostrils clean out, my limbs passive
graveyard petals. She scratches
at my hairline

and my pelvis rocks me into waves
whose edge I ride, wavering
and flailing

between focus and abandon,
before coming
into a full-on sneeze.

Hummingbird

I had been at the mini World Music Festival
in the Brussels park for two or three hours
before I realised that something was amiss.

I didn't know what it was at first, but then it came
to me: no one was hiding behind a mobile phone.
I had lost an English friend when she got the latest,

tiny new mobile. She had shrunk herself down
to the size of a hummingbird to fit her mouth
and ears to it; nobody saw her after she got that phone.

Magpie

I was looking out my window as I always do
on my birthday, looking for an indication,
a flavour of the year ahead – a curiously
shaped cloud, say, or bird behaviour.

Outside, a magpie landed on my motorbike.
Hello, Mr Magpie, I sang at him.
He looked mischievously at me,
then another landed – two for joy.
Then another – three for a girl. I was
looking for a girlfriend, so I was happy
to leave it there, but then another landed.

When the fifth, sixth and seventh
appeared, I started to sing the 'Magpie'
song. I had the impression
they were all looking at me,
but I couldn't say for sure.

I glanced away momentarily.
When I looked back, they were crowding
round the bike – I counted twenty-four.
They seemed to be organising – two
on each handlebar-grip, and most of the rest
on the kick-start mechanism. Two were
hot-wiring the ignition.

I legged it downstairs in two leaps. My bike
was revving up nicely as I flung the door open,
and as I reached the pavement the bastards
were banking round the street corner. I blamed
myself for shining up the chrome the previous day –
the day before my birthday.

Cante Jondo

Tak-takatak, tak-takatak... *Oye!*
Eso es! Yes – this is it: *Siguiriyas*
unfolds from its own centre. We are implicated

deeply, all of us. I am here with Maria, my housemate
from Galicia. It is *demasiado*; we like it too much.
We survive intensely until the interval

like wound-up cats. It begins again
barely visibly, in near-total darkness –
a minute action born from intention, stage right –

a foot pointed outwards, posturing precision,
inevitably: *dance, sex, tragedy*. The séance
feel of the moment erupts into ribaldry

and lightning for the spine. I shatter
like a brandy glass with shards flying inwards.
No, I am not all right. Later, at home,

I translate Lorca roughly: You can have
your psyche torn apart by authentic Flamenco.
Hombre, tell me about it.

This Tap Behaviour

As I close my door, my psychotic neighbour
bangs the wall just once to let me know he's in.
I move to fill the kettle. He goes at his taps
with a hammer, or fists perhaps.
It disconcerts me mildly, though this

is the light end of his range – he runs
to shouted threats, fists ground in my face
in the street. I call it obsessive compulsive,
this tap behaviour – a colleague said it must be.

One night last week, his tap seemed to stick –
he may have left it open, I thought, unusually.
A long, pining whine keened high through our shared pipes
like sacred music. I imagined him stopped still
and listening to it too – there was no noise

coming through, just this plangent song of water,
a plumbed release of pressure. After all that had flowed
between us had run off like so much dismal news,
we would still need to control the outflow.

Yat Kha

Yat Kha are the best Mongolian punk band
I've ever seen; the only one, in fact. And since
we're talking facts, they're neither punk
nor Mongolian; they're unique. Listen,

they're from Tuva next to Mongolia,
three days' haul from Moscow – far out indeed.
Heavy versions of traditional folk songs
and covers of western rock classics

are thrashed out on goat-hair violins,
drums, and Albert's electric guitar.
Albert's throat singing is what wings this band
out. Lemmy, Barry White, anyone

is falsetto compared to this. Close your eyes,
and a herd of Hondas, Yamahas
or Suzukis are calling out to each other
as they graze the steppe.

With fuzz-box and phase, and seemingly
from nowhere, winds skirl by the carved horses
on the Tuvan instruments. The crowd, aged
from nine to ninety, goes wild. Albert smiles

and makes deadpan comments between numbers,
a Steppenwolf in biker's leathers. We
drink Guinness afterwards, at the bar – not quite
as wild as fermented mare's milk vodka.

Late Shift at the Schopenhauer Café

My LED clock was broken; 6.66, it said.
I'd be damned forever if I arrived late.
A pubic calligraphy on the side of the bath
said: *Clean the bath.*

I watched a black and white cat
use a zebra crossing on my way to work.
It struck me that here was the one place
where it would easily get knocked down.

The out-turned legs of lads
walking past the park stated openly:
things are just the way they appear.
At the children's play area, white swans

with their beaks tucked in behind their necks
were plastic carrier bags.
Outside the café, I saw a motorbike
that ran on blood; or that's what was written

on the panniers, in large red letters –
I didn't see what its owner was like.
At the café in my break I typed *Nothing*
into Google, and got a million sites.

Low Doors

When I see a couple of cats
and I guess she's fucking him and she
or both of them are using a cat-flap,
I know this is paradise

every older cat has dreamed of all their lives.
Past and future brushed to both sides
like an outmoded flat cap,
and they're *there*, with nothing to hide,

to lick pussy, endlessly. And beyond,
the air is blue with screams and squeals
and is everywhere, and is gone

Wild Life, April, England

Winter was just three weeks back
when I told a Broadmead beggar –
'Change? Yes please, love,
I'll change into a butterfly.'
She fluttered her long lashes and said:
'Why not open that bottle of wine?'
Without hesitation I declined,
kept it bottled.

A post-party park. I waken
into wild life; a cat trickles by
like a stream of consciousness.
Birds chirp, oblivious.
Trees are ringed by croci,
nature's graffiti,
voting for the all-night party:
'Spring is here, OK!'
Bees are fuzzy headed,
jasmine-tranced.

Anglo-Irish

When I took words for my toys, my father said
he didn't know where it came from; forgetting,
no doubt, having heard me gloss *The Times*

upside-down to him at four years old
while he tried to read it. Our dark bookcase
towered with books: battles, the years they were fought,

and the names of the victors; there was no poetry.
My family claimed to know nothing about poems,
but some would talk about men having had

'enough Guinness taken to choke a horse.'
My father would hold forth on wars; when I tried
to agree on a given point, he would tense

his shoulders and attack; it defeated me, each time.
The one gift he bought me in my adult life,
and late in his own campaign, was a book of war poems:

we debated the merits of Owen versus
Rosenberg, heatedly. I struggled to get him
to write a message in it; the white pages failed

to flag some resolution before retreating
to a close. In the end, he softened under pressure.
Almost relenting, he took up the pen.

Euro Paean

Bonjour, Monsieur –
avez-vous un Euro, s'il-vous plait?
Non, parce-que je suis Anglais.

PARADISE ALLEY

from the novel for teenagers by Christopher Pilditch

It's Midsummer's Night, June 21, 1978. A storm is raging through the forest outside my bedroom window. My name is Paul. I'm sixteen years old. Rain is pouring down like silver bullets, thudding into the trees, pouring off their trunks. Drains hiss and gurgle and overflow, flooding the lane and filling the ditches. The sky lights up and thunder shakes the foundations of de Havilland Cottage, where I live. Wind slams the outhouse door and the garden gate; roof tiles clatter, newspapers and tin cans fly about in the empty village road beyond the hedge. Twigs break from nearby oaks and beeches and fly against the house, tapping on my window pane as if they are trying to get into my room.

I stare out of the window, my chin in my hands. I'm thinking. I feel calm.

Over the din, I can hear the TV. Mum and Dad are downstairs watching *Dad's Army*.

I'm thinking about Mrs Williams, my Geography teacher. She's skinny as a plank and as miserable as a Leonard Cohen song. And she's a crap teacher. She gives out all this homework and doesn't mark it. She says she's been too ill to cope since her husband walked out on her. I don't blame him.

When I leave school I want to be an archaeologist. Mum and Dad took me to the Tutankhamen exhibition in London last year, and now I'm mad for it. I need that Geography O-Level badly or I can't study archaeology. Mrs Williams has let me down. My first exam is in a week.

I make up my mind about what I'm going to do about it. Just to see if it works. I'm sure it can't.

I climb into bed with the storm still raging outside. I'm going to dream about Mrs Williams. I know that sounds crazy, but there's this thing I can do with dreams.

It won't work. Dreams don't come true. You can't hurt someone just by dreaming about something happening.

That night when I'm asleep, there's a road accident in Brockenhill. A woman is run over by a drunk in a stolen car. He loses control on the flooded road and mounts the pavement. She ends up sprawled across the bonnet and he rams her into a tree and nearly cuts her in half, according to the rumours flying around school the next day.

No one can say why Mrs Williams was out in that storm. She was just out there, walking. Wrong time, wrong place.

People tie flowers and teddy bears to what's left of the tree. Not me, I'm too scared to go near it.

Anyway, I've already seen the bend in the road and the demon standing beside the tree, beckoning to the driver with a crooked finger. The demon I invented in my dream.

I don't go to the funeral. I'm scared I might meet it.

A couple of years later, they'll change the shape of the road, straighten out the dangerous bend, build a skateboard park beside the lane on the spot where she died, call it Paradise Alley. You've got to laugh.

The Geography exams work out fine, of course, and I qualify as an archaeologist. I get married, have a son. I consider myself a lucky man. I travel to interesting places, sometimes uncovering priceless treasures, including a scroll from ancient Babylon about demons and demon hunters. I didn't know what it was at first but when I began to decipher it I realised what had fallen into my hands. I studied it for days, alone in my tent, and I realised that fate had sent it to me.

I stole it. I learned its secrets. I still have it.

Now I'm hiding out in the forest. I'm waiting to catch and kill one. A demon. You don't believe me. Why should you? There's no such thing as demons. And dreams don't come true.

Do they?

June 13, 2007 – 8.47 am

Will thrust his fingers through the chain mesh fence surrounding the school yard and squeezed them into fists until his knuckles went white. He stared out, imagining what being in prison was like.

Twenty metres away, Dean Cunniffe was pretending to have sex with the wire fence. Will didn't like Dean and Dean didn't like him. Dean had said things to him about Father Christmas at primary school and he'd never forgiven him.

That morning he'd stared into the mirror. Staring back was a human runner bean. He'd stood there and thought about Traynor. She liked him, but only because of Paradise Alley. Traynor was skinny but she was nice with it. Sixteen and scary-looking. It suited her.

A man came along the pavement. He looked like a professor. No, he looked like Dad. Mid-thirties, neat hair, same long stride, pressed trousers, same permanent sun tan, same worried look. He watched the stranger walk across the road and into the bus shelter opposite where he stood looking at some graffiti, nothing clever, just a symbol. Will saw it and thought of Traynor again.

Somebody had sprayed *that symbol* on the school gates, in Paradise Alley, on the post box and on the hole-in-the-wall outside the Co-op in Brockenhill, on the gates to the Rufus Arms Hotel, everywhere. Everyone was talking about it. Everyone had their suspicions.

At the end of the road where the trees began he could see the entrance to Paradise Alley, the ornate ironwork framing the tall metal gates. Through those gates was where he wanted to be, not locked up in here like a monkey in a cage. He could see the end of the half-pipe, the ramps set out across the tarmac, the fun-box and the melted remains of the litter bin.

A narrow, leafy lane cut away behind the bus stop. 'No Through Road' it said on the sign. Down at the far end was where he lived, where he came from, where all his family had come from for ever. De Havilland Cottage with its creaky floors, low ceilings, shiny antique tables and chairs, wobbly walls, dust, dark corners, the ancient central heating system that kept him awake in the winter, the tiny windows that never let in enough light on hot summer days like today.

Dad was away on a dig. He'd packed his bags and left suddenly a week ago, ruffling Will's hair like a kid where he sat at the kitchen table. Palestine. Interesting place for archaeologists, Dad said, but the way he'd said it wasn't convincing. Dad never ruffled his hair normally.

An old woman was glaring unpleasantly at him through the fence. It was Edna. A large ruby glowed like fresh blood on one of her gnarled fingers. Her glasses hung from a string round her neck beside a small crucifix. They sat together on top of her enormous tits like a yacht moored in a beige harbour.

'Any message for your mother?' she demanded. She talked too loudly. He was glad the fence was between them.

'Sorry?'

241

'I'm meeting her in the tea rooms in ten minutes.'

She leaned on her black walking stick, waiting for an answer. Then she pulled out a small silver box and snorted a pinch of something brown up each nostril.

'Can't think of anything.' A dark trickle of snot appeared on her upper lip.

She gave a grunt and stumped off with fussy little steps like she was constipated. From behind she looked like a garden gnome in a pink shawl with grey straggly hair and a knitted hippy shoulder bag. She stopped and blew her nose on to the pavement. Then she wiped her face on the back of her hand, mumbling to herself as she walked past Dean Cunniffe. She glowered at him and he stopped having sex with the mesh fence.

June 2 – 10.22 pm

Delia Bentley realised it was exactly twenty-four hours since she had packed a suitcase and got on the train out of London Waterloo. At last she had had a reason to return to the Rufus Arms Hotel.

Giant moths had fluttered inside her from the moment she had sprung awake the next morning. All day her stomach had churned with something that could only have been cold revenge. All day she had wandered through the empty shell of the disused hotel, exploring behind curtains and under furniture hidden by dust sheets. Everything seemed smaller, lower, shorter and less interesting than it had been when she was a girl. She had uncovered broken mementos and discarded items from the time when the hotel was full of paying guests – chipped teacups and torn menus, murky, silver-plated spoons and soiled napkins, a toothbrush, buttons, a lost earring.

There were spiders in the bathrooms, and big, brown cockroaches patrolled the walls in the kitchens. She had heard mice scampering behind skirting boards, and rats scratching in the ceilings.

But she hadn't dared to go up the narrow stairs to the top floor, to the little attic room she had occupied as a child. That was where it had all began. It would have been too difficult, too painful, right now. It could wait. Now that Aunt Agatha was dead, she'd have all the time in the world to do that, and without Aunt Agatha's whining voice ringing in her head.

She watched the last remnants of daylight fade behind the line of old trees and the summer sky turn to the colour of ripe plums. For an hour she sat by herself in the darkness. Silence oozed from the thick walls of the hotel. In the lobby the grandfather clock tick-tocked the hours and minutes into slow, equal pieces.

When it chimed eleven-thirty, she stood up and crossed the empty dining room in the dark. The floorboards echoed to the beat of her leather shoes.

It's time, she thought, as her heart began to race again.

She pulled the spray can from the pocket of her coat hanging by the door, knelt down and sprayed a large pentagram on the wooden floor. When she had finished, she stood up to admire her work, twisting the skull ring on her finger until she felt her knuckle crack.

She opened the French windows and walked out on to the overgrown terrace. There was a symbol sprayed on the wall beside her, the fresh silver paint translucent in the moonlight. They were all over the village. She gave a grim smile and took a deep breath and gazed up at the velvet, cloudless sky. Cool air filled her lungs. The stars looked down on her. Then she went back inside and closed the windows behind her.

The main entrance door opened and closed with a reverberating clatter, and footsteps in the hall hurried towards her.

Lucinda came in, out of breath. She looked thin and ill. She always had, ever since Delia had rescued her in a moment of weakness from the homeless shelter in Battersea. Her pale face was long and serious. Her eyes bulged. Delia regretted the day she had clapped eyes on this pathetic creature.

'Well?' she demanded. 'Did you get everything?'

Lucinda held out a large cloth bag as if it were a dead animal.

'Why are we doing this?' Strands of escaped hair hung across her face. Her voice grated like fingernails scraped down a blackboard.

'I've told you a thousand times.' Delia took the bag from her. It felt heavy.

Lucinda's hands fluttered in front of her grey cardigan.

'I don't even know what Edna did to you.'

'It doesn't matter what *she* did to *me*. *That* was a long time ago. What I'm going to do to her is what matters now.'

Delia took a leather-bound book from the bag and opened it. Lucinda stepped closer. She could see an old-fashioned drawing of a tall creature with horns. It looked like a woman. There was one word – QUINTESSIMA – in a scroll around its head, and more Latin writing on the opposite page.

Quintessima looked tall, elegant and angry, with a forked tail.

'Is that Latin? I didn't know you could read Latin, Mrs Bentley.'

'It isn't and I can't.'

'So what is it?'

No answer. Lucinda began to tug at a strand of hair hanging across her face.

'How d'you know your spell's going to work, Mrs Bentley?'

Delia had never summoned a demon before, but she didn't want reminding. All she had was this book. She began to scan the familiar words on the page, but none of it seemed to make sense. It was as if she was reading it for the first time. Her irritation was suddenly swept away like a leaf in a storm and a new feeling exploded into her guts, raw fear twisting through her like an eel.

She closed the book with a snap and emptied the bag on to the floor. Herbs tied in bunches, incense sticks, candles and holders, cook's matches, a small brass incense burner on a chain, and a long dagger with a carved wooden handle tumbled out. She arranged the herbs at the five points of the pentagram. Henbane, restharrow, ragwort, hemlock and lavender.

The smell of lavender transported her back to that Midsummer fete on the village green in Brockenhill. She saw Edna sitting at the cake stall like a self-satisfied toad with her best smile and a piece of chocolate gateau in her hand.

That smile. That smug expression. That look like butter wouldn't melt in her big, fat stupid mouth.

She remembered the scream as the stone hit home. She remembered the tears and the shouts, people rushing about and the blood on Edna's face and hair and on her summer frock. She remembered being led away by Aunt Agatha, bony fingers digging into her shoulder as she was marched along the road, her nagging voice darting through her brain like a knitting needle.

You're disgusting, d'you hear me? What would your mother say if she was still alive? Treating your sister like that. And on her birthday, of all days!

She saw herself locked in her room, sitting at the window in the top of the hotel and straining for the sounds of laughter on the green. Later in the evening, in the distance, she would hear children's voices singing 'Happy Birthday'. Then she would bury her face in her pillow and angrily pound her fists against the mattress. Edna, Edna, always Edna.

She found her fingers had tightened around the handle of the dagger. She spun it towards the ceiling. Lucinda let out a shriek. It landed with a thud in the floorboards, the blade shimmering like a granite headstone in a thunderstorm.

'Light the candles.'

Happy birthday, dear Edna,

Happy birthday to you...

Delia watched as Lucinda knelt down and opened the matchbox. She looked like dead Aunt Agatha, her face caught for a moment in the moonlight as she glanced nervously at where the knife had impaled itself in the floor. The matches spilled and snapped as she ran them along the box with shaking hands. One by one, pinpricks of candlelight caught in Delia's green eyes. They sparkled with contempt.

'Now light the incense. Get a move on. We don't have all night...'

Thin, smoky plumes rose into the still air. Everything flickered orange and yellow. Inky shadows danced like ghosts in the four corners of the room as if trying to escape through the long windows into the night.

The clock chimed a quarter to midnight and the eel rose suddenly in Delia's throat. She swallowed it down hard, her head pounding, her hands cold and slippery.

June 12 – 11.02 am

At break, Will found Traynor sitting on an upturned milk crate, her back against the canteen wall. From the window above came the clatter and smell of school dinners. Chips and curry and aluminium pots and pans. By herself, as usual. Reading a skateboard fanzine. As usual. Smiling to herself. As usual. She was holding it end on and looking at a double page spread, her head tilted sideways, her black fringe hiding one of her eyes. Spiky hair gelled up like a punk. Today it was hennaed. Sometimes it was a blonde streak. Sometimes a green streak.

'Love it. Luvvit, luvvit, luvvit!'

He fetched a crate and sat down.

'What you looking at?' He leaned closer. He could smell patchouli. She was wearing a white wristband with 'Live Strong' on it.

It was a picture of Bam Margera. Viva La Bam. Bam Margera, world famous skateboarder, just standing there in the world famous beanie, not even on his board. Traynor was looking right into Bam's eyes and Bam was looking right back up at her. Will felt annoyed. He couldn't stop himself.

'Jesus, Tray, not *him* again. Can't you think about anyone else? You're stupid.'

She put the fanzine aside and studied his face.

'What's with you, dude?' She tried to sound sweet, to ignore whatever was making him like that. 'Good weekend? Been down Paradise Alley? Didn't see you there...'

'Didn't feel like it.'

'Thought you were mad for it.'

'Whatever.'

'Hey, come on...' She stuck an elbow into his ribs.

Half of him felt good. Half of him didn't.

Then Traynor said, 'OK, me having a mega-crush on a skinny American dude with a stupid name is stupid. Me going shopping *all day* Saturday for a present for my mum when she doesn't even like me and when I could have been in Christ-air heaven is stupid. Having to wear this shitty uniform all week is shitty, shitty stupid. Me being a stupid, nosy cow and making you tell me why you're in such a mardy mood is shitty stupid. Happy now?'

She picked up the fanzine and turned the page, staring at the lists of boards for sale.

'My dad's gone again,' he heard himself say.

'At least your dad comes back when he goes.'

Will felt his face start to burn.

She thought for a moment. 'He just let them put the cuffs on and then he walked out of the caravan without a word. He never did give a shit about anybody except himself. He sends letters from prison but I'm not allowed to read them. Mum burns them.'

She stopped talking and looked down at the fanzine.

He glanced sideways at her. Her eyes were shining.

She closed the magazine and sighed, and they stared out into the dark spaces between the oak trees beyond the fence. He could feel her shoulder nearly touching his and it felt good to be sat there without saying anything.

The bell rang. She put the fanzine in her bag and stood up.

'Come on,' she said, 'We'll meet after school and practise some slides, and, hey, I've found the weirdest place... wicked rails.'

'Where?'

'Let's just say... meet me by the gates of the Rufus Arms, Will. Four o'clock, dude. Be there or be square.' And she loped off round the corner. She looked quite curvy from behind. Tall. Maybe things weren't as crap for him as he thought. Maybe he should just try growing up a bit.

June 2 – Midnight

As the clock struck midnight, Delia rose to her feet. She opened the book and took a deep breath.

'Quentschlimah nah endo maneh!' she said nervously in the tongue of the Old Religion, running her finger across the page and hoping she had got the difficult words in the right places. 'Be summoned from whatever cold or fiery place holds you. Seven times I call you, command you, summon you to stand with us, seven times I command you to come forth from the dark stars of the night. Quintessima, sister of darkness, servant of Methuselah, come forth! Quintessima, I call your name!'

The foundations of the Rufus Arms Hotel started to shudder. It felt like an earthquake. Horrified, Delia dropped the book, her heart thumping. She found she had put her hands over her eyes and couldn't open them. Lucinda whimpered once, loudly, like a puppy caught with a half-eaten slipper. She cowered against Delia's legs.

The French windows burst open. A large object crash-landed into the room.

Everything went horribly quiet. Then something started to creak. With an effort, Delia managed to open her eyes. She peeked between her fingers.

It stood there smouldering, its breath green and thick, its squat body the colour of an enormous bruise in the light of the candles. It looked around with bloodshot, ferocious eyes, its neck creaking like a pair of new shoes as it turned its head from side to side.

'Bloody hell, I wasn't expecting *you*!' exclaimed Delia.

NIGHT AND DAY

a short story by Nazalee Raja

There once was a girl who fell in love with a man while she was a student before she became a woman. She married the man and had a daughter, and found that love did not give her the happy-ever-after she had promised herself as a girl.

Night followed day. Day followed night.

The woman with the girl locked inside her resolved to begin again with a new life. She cherished her daughter and hoped this would sustain her. She became obsessed with cutting the split ends from the girl's hair. She never knew how long she spent at this, or realised that it was her small way of reducing the brokenness in her life. She knew only that it soothed her.

There once was a boy who wanted to be a writer, who grew up to be a man who wanted to be a writer, so the man became a teacher. He told himself this job would support him, and his wife and his daughter, while he composed his fiction. He knew it would be hard to provide for his family with his imagination. Man cannot live by writing alone. He told himself this, but teaching demanded all his time and energy and left him with no time to think.

Night followed day. Day followed night.

The man's creativity slowly shrivelled up and withdrew into the hard, acidic core of him, where it tormented him with pinpricks of doubt about who he was and what he was doing with his life. The words he had once thought would express his inner passion now congealed inside him, filling him with bile. His sourness about himself expanded and filled his life, blurring his vision until everything looked grey, even his wife and child, until he and his marriage were both mere husks.

There once was a girl who was truly loved by both her parents. She knew this because they told her so as they sat her down and explained that they were getting divorced. Daddy was moving to another home as soon as he could afford one. In the meantime, Daddy slept on the sofa, and the air between her parents was purple with bitterness. They agreed they had lost their way – to each other, but not her, they assured her.

The girl was a romantic, a gift from her mother. She wanted her parents to live together and be there to read her to sleep.

Night followed day. Day followed night.

The girl's sanctuary was her imagination, a gift from her father. She invented stories about the world outside her night-time window. She told these tales to her father before he bid her goodnight, hoping to change the future and make him stay, like Scheherazade cheating death with stories. Each evening, she recited an instalment of the story *Night and Day*:

Once upon a time, there was a young god with golden hair and a sunny smile who fell in love with a mortal maiden with long, dark tresses which fell to her knees. He courted her, until she fell in love. They were ready to live happily-ever-after, each fulfilled by the love of the other, and would have done so but for his father.

There was a rule in those times against mortals, who were few, and gods, who were many, falling in love and being happy. The young god's father was furious and accused the maiden of corrupting his son.

To punish her, he took the couple to stand trial before the king of the gods, as was the custom in those times. There the young god and maiden both vowed to love each other forever. The king of the gods knew the rules; this pairing could not be allowed. Yet he pitied the couple and disliked the father.

To teach him a lesson, the king of the gods decreed that the young god would henceforth be called Day and bring light to the world; the maiden would become an immortal called Night to bring it rest and darkness.

The lesser gods responsible for pulling the sun and moon across the sky were idle and neglected their duties. This punishment would bring consistency to the world, and deprive the jealous god of his son.

Moreover, it would give the lovers the chance to meet: once when Night turned to Day and again when Day turned to Night. To this day, the sky is red at dawn and dusk because of the lovers' ardent embrace.

There once was a girl who told a story about the creation of night and day to show her father the power of love. One night, after the vivid red, mauve and orange had faded from the sky, she heard a tapping at her window. Outside, a maiden with long, dark tresses pleaded for the girl's help. The maiden, Night, said the girl had guessed the truth, and now held the power to break the spell. The king of the gods had decreed it. The lovers could be united, at last, if the girl said the word.

The girl, being a romantic, liked this idea. Yet she worried that the world would end without Night and Day performing their duties. Plants would not grow. People would not know when to sleep. Sadly she told the maiden she was sorry, she couldn't agree.

Day followed night. Night followed day.

The girl continued to use her imagination. It became her greatest friend and consolation.

There once was a boy who wanted to be a writer, but this desire was suppressed in the man he became. One day it was revived by the daughter he'd created. Following her example, he began to write again. At first, his words were inanimate, but he persevered until he'd coaxed them back to life, and after a while, they gave him new life.

The man gave up teaching and worked in a supermarket, where he sat at the checkout planning his stories. His writing became a means of self-realisation, and his creativity matured when he remembered what he had loved about stories as a boy:

You can lose yourself in a story, but you can also find yourself.

Day followed night. Night followed day.

The man, inspired by his daughter's story, left one of his own for his wife to find.

There once was a girl who fell in love with a man who wanted to be a writer. The girl became a woman in love with a man who wouldn't write. There came a day when she could find no more split ends. She knew it was time to find her new life.

Day followed night. Night followed day.

The woman came home one day to find a present waiting for her from the man she had loved. She read it with a fast-beating heart. She understood: he had returned to her. It was a story about two people falling in love; a story as old as night and day.

THE FOREVER TRAIN

from the novel English Machismo by Shane Roberts

The train station is just up at the opposite end of town. I go through the door and into the ticket office, looking around. There's a sort of indoor bench where some people are sitting with suitcases on the floor next to them, looking up at this big, black screen with shining electrical letters on it. The screen shows the names of loads of towns and cities – Skegness, Lincoln, Mablethorpe and some others. A lot of the places I've never even heard of. Next to each town and city's name is the time, but it's in twenty-four-hour form and it takes me a while to work that sort out.

I'd better go and talk to the man in the ticket office. He's just sitting there, smiling at me from behind the glass sheet. I'm dead nervous.

'Uh, hi, hi. Uh, I need to, um, get to Peterborough? Is that OK?'

'Peterborough,' the man says. He's kind of old, with big, bushy eyebrows and fluffy white hair that sticks out as though he's been electrocuted. About, sixty, I'd say, but he's nice and smiley and he seems to want to help. 'Peterborough? Is that a single or a return?'

'Well, I need to get back into Spalding before tonight.'

'What time, do you think, my dear?' the man asks gently. I think he knows I'm an idiot.

'Well, uh, before six, I suppose, but it doesn't really matter.'

'That's fine. It's a return, then,' he says kindly. 'Trains run from Peterborough to Spalding until eleven at night. Well, the last one leaves the city at ten fifty-eight, so you've got plenty of time.'

'That's lovely, then,' I say. I can feel myself going red with embarrassment already, I feel so stupid. The ticket man prints out a ticket. I suppose it's how they get their name.

'That's four pounds fifty then, please,' the man says as he breaks into another smile. I slide him a fiver under the glass and he passes through the ticket, receipt and change. 'The next one to Peterborough is in about ten minutes,' the man says. 'It'll be on this side, Platform One, so there's no need for you to cross over the bridge. It's just straight through there,' he says as he points to a blue wooden door. He smiles at me once again as I thank him and walk off and out on to the platform. I'm glad that he told me when the next train was coming. Knowing me, because I'm not very clever, I admit that, I would have got on the train and ended up in Brighton or Manchester or some other faraway place.

The ground begins to shake. I look up, and a train is approaching in the far distance, rumbling slowly closer. As it pulls into the station, the train grinds to a halt, and all these people start spilling out on to the platform, carrying massive backpacks or dragging bulging suitcases. A man's voice crackles out over what must be an ancient PA system, but it's so muffled that I can't really tell what he's saying. I only catch the part that says '...to Peterborough...'

I run into the carriage nearest me and walk down the aisle. The train is nearly empty, so it looks as though I can sit where I want. I pick a seat with this table in front of it. In fact, there are four seats around the table, two sets of two facing each other, a bit like the breakfast bar we've got at home. There's no one in any of them, so I have the table all to myself. I've got nothing to use it for, like a newspaper or anything, but at least I'll have the space. There are a few other passengers dotted about the carriage, a lot of them in Peterborough United shirts. The Posh. They must be playing at home today.

A man stands up from his seat as the train trundles along. Earlier, he had given me a quick glance, and looked away. Now he's looking over at me properly, smiling. He's walking down the aisle towards me, holding on to the tops of seats to stop himself from falling. He stops at my table and begins to fiddle with his mobile phone. I don't really know what he's doing; perhaps he's trying to get a signal. I just keep staring out of the window and watch the speeding trees rocket by.

'Excuse me, little lady, but I was just wondering if I might be able to sit here,' he says in a low, rumbling whisper, pointing to the seat opposite me. I look up at him, and he smiles again, exposing large, slab-like teeth. 'It's just that, well, I've rather a lot of baggage with me today, and there's not quite enough room for it where I'm sitting, in a single seat. I'm awfully sorry,' he says, in a dead posh voice that indicates he's not from around Spalding way. I keep wondering why he can't put all of his stuff on some of the empty seats. I guess that some of them might have been booked up.

'That's fine, that's absolutely fine,' I say back to him. 'No trouble at all.' He thanks me with a little bow of his huge head and walks off back down the train. He returns with two rucksacks and one of them big, posh newspapers, the *Daily Telegraph*. There's nowhere near as much stuff as I thought there would be, and I'm a bit confused, but not really fussed. It's my first time on a train; perhaps stuff like this happens every day. Anyway, it's not as if I need this table for anything other than leaning on.

The big bloke squeezes himself into the seat opposite me, gives me another grateful smile, then buries himself in his massive newspaper. He's bald, perhaps fifty or sixty years old, but then again, I'm pretty rubbish at guessing ages. He has a big, straggly, ginger beard that swings from side-to-side whenever he moves his head. His beard is so large that it gets me thinking deep about stuff again. His beard must be so massive because the top of his head has no hair; he's bald. I mean, the beard has stolen the hair that was supposed to grow on his head.

This guy is, like, really fat as well. He can hardly fit in his seat, he's so round. It's probably not his fault, though. It could be genetic. I can see as he leans over the table, his hands under it as he struggles to cope with the giant paper, that he's wearing a pair of brown corduroys. He's also wearing a black shirt with a white tie, and a sleek suit jacket over the top. Pretty fashionable for a man of his age. I've seen blokes in their twenties that look really good in cords, and I think they're proper cool. This guy is an inspiration to old men everywhere.

The train keeps on chugging along. I'm getting really hungry. It doesn't help that the guy opposite is now eating a delicious-smelling bacon sandwich, sending me delirious. On the side of the train is a poster advertising the buffet cart, found on Carriage D. The trouble is, I'm not really sure which way Carriage D is, let alone how to open the doors, so I decide to wait it out until Peterborough.

The guy finishes with his newspaper, and puts it down on the table. I consider asking him if I can borrow it for a read; then I think of all the big words that'll be in there. I know I won't understand them, and also I know that I won't be able to hold the paper properly, so I don't bother. I look at him, and he's playing about with his phone again. It looks like one of them really cool posh ones, with a camera and video recorder and all that built-in.

By now, I'm getting well excited about going out shopping in Peterborough by myself. The shops and places that I can go to without being pulled this way and that by my parents and friends. I won't have to go into any rubbishy shops like Next or Dotty P's. It's going to be absolutely amazing.

Finding my feet. My independence.

I hear the very distinct sound of someone taking a photograph. It's the very same sound that you always hear in the films—

Click... bssssh.

I look around. I can't see anyone on the train with a camera, though. That's what's weird. Most of the people in the carriage are either reading a book or the paper, or listening on their iPods or whatever. It must be coming out of the speakers or something, I don't know. It doesn't matter. I just settle back into my seat, and think of some of the really cool dresses and tops I'm going to find in all the wicked shops.

I start daydreaming, thinking of the bright lights in the big city, then I hear that bloody camera noise again. I bolt straight up and look around like a demented snake, eyes picking out potential suspects. No one. WHO is taking photographs? Who? Where are they? No. Everyone is still reading or listening to their stereos. Some people are even asleep. The big old boy opposite is looking up to the roof of the carriage, his big, shovel-like left hand flat out on the table. He hasn't noticed me looking at him.

Click... bssssh.

The reality of what is happening hits me like an unseen tidal wave, smack in the face. Swallowing hard, I slowly look down into my lap, and notice the short skirt that I'm wearing, my legs slightly apart. Just beyond my knees, under that bloated bloke's side of the table, I see his fat fist, glistening with sweat, grasping the mobile phone, its camera lens aimed directly between my legs, its solitary eye leering at my knickers.

The dirty, filthy bastard. I slowly lift my head up to look at him. He's still looking away, looking out of the opposite window, sneakily pretending he's otherwise engaged. I feel my face, my neck, my back, then my whole body, just convulse with itches. My cheeks tingle as they flush into a flood of deep scarlet. This dirty pervert is going to take his phone home and wank over grainy pictures of my knickers. I bet that he's hoping he got lucky and caught a flash of my pubes that might have spread out from behind the lining. Then I'm thinking, perhaps it's too dark up there for his camera to pick anything up. I don't care if he can or not. That's not the point. The point is, he's a dirty fat bastard, trying to get pictures of my bits.

I look down to the floor of the carriage, my movements ever so slow in case he realises that I've clocked him. I'm upset and angry, but most of all I'm ashamed. Ashamed because I feel like a filthy object.

I just don't know what to do. The bastard still hasn't realised I've sussed him. I shuffle my feet, and uneasily wring my hands. I don't dare close my legs, because then he'll know that I know. That would be even more embarrassing. If I were to shout and scream then everyone would think I was a lunatic and he'd delete the photos and deny everything. I can feel tears forming at the back of my eyes as I hear the camera noise again, so I keep looking at the floor. I'm sure he sniggers to himself as his album collection builds.

Embarrassment is crippling.

I'm glued to the spot, frozen like I've been paused. Paused by his mobile phone. It's embarrassment that keeps me sitting here like a stupid plum, planted in this seat, too afraid to close my legs in case the lardy lensman notices. I try to raise a smile as I look out of the window, feeling a stab of happiness jutting into me with the sight of the great hulk of Peterborough in the distance.

An announcement from the radio speaker on the ceiling of the carriage: 'The train is now approaching Peterborough. Thank you for using Great North Eastern Rail. Be sure to collect all your belongings as you leave, and please do not open the doors until the train has fully stopped. To repeat, the train is now approaching Peterborough. Thank you for using this service.' The speaker buzzes for the end of the announcement.

It is a female voice coming from the speaker. I'm thankful for it; I found it kind of soothing in a certain sort of way. It makes me feel that everything is going to be all right, what with the Big Fat Photo Man sitting fatly across from me. I feel the train wheels slowing down from underneath me, and see the platform juddering into my eye space. He grunts and bellows as he begins the first of several attempts to shift his massive arse out of the seat. His laboured efforts eventually come good. His bald head, lashed with sweat, gleams in the sunlight beaming through the window. I try not to let my eyes wander into his, but it is dead hard for me. The train stops.

The bastard winks at me and then waddles off down the carriage.

I feel so broken. Hurt. The tears, welled up behind my eyes, begin to spill through the edges. Picking up my bag, I push through the rush of people trying to get on to the train and dart straight into the station's toilets. They are filthy,

SHANE ROBERTS

disgusting, but totally pristine when I think of that monster and his sickening grin as he took his horrid pictures. Perhaps that's why he does it, I think, as I pull down my knickers and try to wee, but can't. He does it because he can't get a woman, perhaps has never been able to. This is how he gets himself off. Easy to see why he can't get one, I think, as I stare down at a discarded syringe on the piss-splashed floor. I think I'd rather suck that needle than go anywhere near his vile piece. For a moment, I see his smiling face in my vision, and for a shorter moment still, I feel sorry for him, reduced to taking pictures of young women's knickers. The sentiment disappears when I think of what he might be doing now. I never saw where he went. He could be in the toilet block next to this one, looking at me.

I finally stop myself from holding it in, and let the tears flow.

I clean myself up and feel all the better for it. In my misery, I had almost forgot what I came here for.

Shopping.

SEX, IRAN, ROCK 'N' ROLL

narrative nonfiction by Roxana

I had just recovered from my night of doing the five *Kid Ego* boys and had just started to walk properly again when I got itchy, and it wasn't from an STD this time. Not unlike a scene from *One Flew over the Cuckoo's Nest*, I paced and jumped around, brittle and bitchy to get a new hit of action.

On Wednesday evening, Lucy and Coco were waiting in Euston station. I came up the escalators with my tour-weary bag, concrete-heavy in habit. They looked worn, like rag dolls hung limp from a peg. Coco from her recent tour around the country with *Towers* and Luce from working like a battery hen in some politician's office. She was still in her work clothes: navy trouser suit with an icing of white polyester blouse. We kissed and went to eat fried chicken in a Somalian takeaway around the corner.

Two men behind the food counter in traditional Muslim white cotton stood silent and blank as we ordered fast food. Their eyelashes thick as spider legs, they asked me where I was from. Just like every takeaway person, they were happy and proud I was from Iran. But the amore that I was automatically dished out with instantly became null and void as soon as Lucy, Coco and I opened our mouths. The three of us hadn't been together for a while so, as we sat facing each other around a table, our genetically modified chicken was served with verbal diarrhoea: words toppled out of our mouths to compete for space. Sentences about *Towers*, their cock sizes, their girlfriends, tour-bus stories and anal sex incidents all crashed into each other like a train wreck to pollute the Halal air. Those men looked at me with such disappointment after they heard the Iran girl talk in scientific fashion about how not to choke when deep-throating.

We seeped into the Wednesday night stuffed with manufactured chicken, aching for a band. Eventually we decided on *Brides of Destruction*. They were playing Camden Underworld, a place I called home number two. As I stood outside the venue making my grand plans of living arrangements there, complete with cutlery and a kitchen sink, the doorman told me that the gig had

259

already started and we couldn't go in.

'Let's go get a drink next door in The World's End and wait till they've finished... then we can go wait by the back door until they come out, *or* go back into the venue later, and try and get backstage to meet them.' Lucy had her usual military strategy.

My rock band bag was an extension of my hand, superglued to my skin like love. In The World's End pub I headed straight to the toilets to whore myself up while my friends swallowed alcohol fast. I missed drinking. That feeling of being floaty and warm like nestling in my mother's warm bosom had detached itself from me like a cold hard slap and all I was left with was not even cocaine any more. In the Victorian ladies' room, I started the process of bee-stung flesh pink lips, with eyes dressed in kohl and mascara. I entered into the safety of my skirt, thin as an anorexic belt and a jubilant slashed top. I did not care about the freezing weather breaking my body any more.

Around eleven pm we decided to penetrate the Underworld and its contents. The venue was packed to throttling. Even though the gig had ended, music boomed from the beatbox to blend in with voices into a milkshaked frenzy. Coco and Luce followed me on to side-stage, beating off little eyeliner boys, emo kids, and the wannabe groupies. The three of us together were like a Nazi force no one fucked with. By the stage, the guys from the band were having photos taken and signing limbs, asses, shirts, and posters. Luce and Coco started talking to various band members and I aimed straight for London, the lead singer.

'Could you sign my tits?' I had to be quick and direct.

'Yeah honey, but not here. Let's go to the dressing room.'

Backstage was a mess. Bottles and coats and people scattered everywhere. And I loved it. Holding my hand, London worked fast and methodically, hurriedly pulling me past people sitting around, playing guitar, smoking, play-fighting and screaming, to the back where there was a tiny room with a sink. He pulled me in there and clicked the door shut, clean as a surgeon. Squeezing into the tiny cubicle-like room, he pulled out a black marker pen just as I pulled my top down.

'You're not a talker, are you sweetie?' he said breathing close on my neck, placing kisses all over it and my chest.

'No, me and my friends are cool,' I whispered, pushing my breasts tight together for him to sign. I felt the cold rush of the marker pen soaking through my skin.

'You have fuckin' beautiful tits.' He said it breathily, dead serious, into my eyes and started to play with my breasts. 'The thing is we all have girlfriends.'

I knew what he was talking about. Websites like Metal Sludge and Groupie Central and www.ifuckedarockstar.com blah blah... where girls compared rock cock.

London didn't hesitate. He took off his coat and we started to kiss, fooling around and unzipping things. He slid his hand up in-between my thighs and his fingers found the slit in between my crotchless panties until someone knocked on the door.

Later on a fistful of us got a cab to Crobar. Crobar is the size of my hand and yet armies of people squeeze their bodies in there night after night to be soaked in putrid smoke and catch eardrum damage. The urine-yellow lights are hospital bright and you can't move unless you are comfortable being violent to people to get past. The Crobar makes me ill and every time I have gone there I have vomited from its virus. This particular time it was Scot the *BOD* drummer who had to be helped as his knees abandoned him. All I wanted was to be with London in the men's toilets but I found myself propping up Scot and aiding him in not passing out. London was downstairs with Coco anyway. He seemed to relish the knowledge that they looked like a circus act. Tiny chocolate milkshake Coco and seven-foot London with his top hat. The hot ringmaster and his lovely baby doll.

Right then, London was the one I had set my sights on; my project for the night. Maybe because it was his presence when he walked into a room, or maybe because he was the lead singer. But as I stumbled upon him in the toilets downstairs and once again locked myself in his body, I realised he was dull as paper. It was just his lead singer status I had wanted, and not him. I was disappointed and didn't know what to do. I decided to get Lucy and leave.

Many hotels in London – and one particular one in Cardiff – know my body intimately. I have spent a significant amount of my time in corridors running from one room to another half-naked trying to find people or a lost shoe. I have walked past one cliché after another: fists through windows; trashed rooms; girls patiently lined up outside the lead singer's room; people being hit and cut; tour managers losing it from lack of sleep; roadies having to go out in the middle of the night to find snacks and KY jelly. I always come out of it with inner thighs aching and soul flying.

I hadn't been to the Camden Lock hotel since the first time I met *Towers* and that had left me with a sour after-taste in my mouth. It wasn't a hotel that was my friend. It was hostile to me like an Indie crowd. I couldn't wait to get inside it and amend that by giving its heart and walls the best entertainment it had ever seen.

In the beginning, I was everybody's friend: helping little boy fans who stood outside the backstage area waiting for autographs, the family of the band, people, just people. And now I only cared for my own happiness. It had become a ravenous hunt to experience sweetness in my bitter salt rush of life. Rock bands' love had become my sugar. Week after week I went face-first through the nettle forest of raging rejection and their unpredictable moods, just to reach and touch the newborn yolk of love inside.

At the hotel Lucy and I showered in Scot's eggshell-white bathroom, slipping on the tiles and wondering which towels were appropriate for use. Our black make-up slid off like mud down marble and it reminded us of the many times in hotel room showers when we had had to scrub repeatedly to make sure we were clean 'down there' for girl/girl stuff. We didn't like this hotel soap. The best soaps had been at The Sanderson where Motley Crüe had stayed.

We stepped out from the bathroom nestled in plump white towels like two cream puffs. Scot, who had been lying on the bed sobering up, brought out a shiny camcorder. On automatic mode, me and Lucy positioning ourselves in the right lens angle, started to kiss and lick each other. Silent as a boy, he filmed Lucy and me 69-ing each other like two cats grazing on tender beef, kissing, going through the motions blah blah. But I didn't like it. I craved intimacy just for once with one boy without anyone else involved. Without a whole gang bang/porno scene. I wondered what that would be like, to be alone with someone that you were attracted to. Without a word, I stood up in mid lick, pushed Lucy away and walked up to Scot. I kissed him silent and deep, without permission. My insecurities were poison and they contaminated my friends' souls. My roaring beast of a desire for intimacy had reared itself like a hook-nosed paedophile.

The black carpets, stretched and taut over the frame of the stairs leading up to the BierKeller, feel like their skin. Years of beer-barrel stench staining the sea captain-worn bowels of the building. The same road as my gym and next to the club that used to hold Arabic nights where I did my belly dancing.

The walls are big hunks of granite rock, cave style, Seventies style. It is successful in being exactly what is says on the tin: a cellar. 'Please don't do drugs in our club,' it says on a piece of cardboard at the bar in neat thumb-thick letters of black. The bar: a wannabe star. It tries so hard. It's had Steven Adler inside it for god's sake.

It was here that I fucked up.

I recognised the signs that I was falling. That familiar honey gush that raised my heart right up to my throat like candy sickness. When I had just arrived and saw you backstage for the first time after a few days. You were surrounded by people, laughing and hips swaying. With your raven-black gleaming tresses, and soft kohl liner blazing your feline jewelled-green eyes that should have been illegal to be displayed and paraded around. Lips identical to mine; big with an obscenely perfect Cupid's bow. When you saw me, you suddenly stopped still. 'Hey baby,' you beamed and walked away from your crowd of people towards me. Right there, in that tight overcrowded backstage you hugged me hot and soft. I knew then that you were going to be 'that person' and fear was mine. Wednesday night had been so beautiful. My feelings were going to wreck me like a car crash, like mince meat. I should have left the scene right then.

I watched from the side stage while you played and I couldn't look at you, drummer boy. I danced to the music of the night, concentrating my gaze on London, Jamie and Tracii. I had worn a kind of bunny look crossed with the hooker look but I still looked innocent. Burlesque style corset with my pink-bow trousseau mini-skirt and thigh high leather boots. London, tall and rock starry with a mad scientist look, came over to me in the middle of one song, hugged me and smothered my face in salty sweaty kisses. My mango body-buttered skin became sticky and I panicked that you might hate the taste of London on my body. The venue was not full that night. It was receding and balding. Crowds of biker types, child-whore look girls and teen boys in emo gear. And hippy couples with identical lank hair and inoffensive thrift store clothing. It was a Sunday night.

I put Aerosmith on the back stage CD player. The room was packed with bodies, snacks, beer cans, dirty towels and luggage. Fans waiting around to get autographs and have their photo taken with the band; security people; a couple of girls from the London show dressed in purple. Wrecked jackets and leather accessories decorated the uniform-blue sofa, stained with white marks. The fridge in the corner, magic-marker graffitied with years of band names and lost people, had filled its square belly to bursting with useless lager. There was a girl showing her tits to Tommy and wearing a T-shirt: 'Fuck off, I'm with the band'.

I was dying to be with you so I danced to Aerosmith as I always did when I had ants in my pants, and let Jamie take pornographic photos of me. I know you hated that and I am sorry for acting like that. I just thought that all rockers would always be devoted to any behaviour that was wild and decadent. And anyway, I was determined to bury this rapidly intensifying feeling that was poisoning me. And I knew that I had to have a cigarette, because I loved you. You were brilliant, the worst thing that could happen to me. Backstage was chaos, and you held my hand and held my body, and it just was *not* going to happen to me. Even the pain of writing this disgusts me like rotten carcasses at a butcher's. Because I miss you.

Arriving in England – 1984

I was not scared of flying when I was ten.

Everyone came to see my grandmother and me on our last night. The whole neighbourhood, aunts, uncles and cousins, and a melting sea of unknowns. I was lost in a rainbow of lipsticked kisses and distant perfumes, tight hugs and constant photographs. The accurate aroma of the intricate dishes that my mother had cooked for the night danced around the neighbourhood to seduce the masses. I had cuddled and kissed my one-year-old sister's chubby dribbly mouth before she had gone to bed. In the early hours when everybody had gradually filtered out, my parents, my aunt and uncle stood around me and my grandmother and our suitcases. I took off my red nail varnish. I couldn't sleep because I was excited. I was excited because I thought I was coming back.

At 3 am my stepfather drove us to the airport. The air was thick with the mournful wail of an air raid siren and the dry heat retched over us. In the car the silence bubbled with unspeakable emotion as we glided past the sleeping neighbourhoods. I was already starting to miss playing with my friends and stealing from the pregnant trees' bursting fruits.

The varnish stain left a pink rinse on my freshly short-clipped 'good Muslim girl' fingernails. On the way to the airport I worried in case the officials noticed it. They interrogated us anyway. They took my grandmother and me into separate cubicles for a physical search. It tickled but the black *chador*-clad woman worked – hostile and silent. I got out and saw my grandmother sitting down on a chair in her cubicle. A few female officials were slicing out the inner sole of her shoes. I guessed it was to search for 'bad' things. Just in case my grandmother was a 'bad' person to be taken to prison.

I was ten years old and I was on my way to England, which meant being able to walk around in public without an Islamic headscarf and its matching martyr-themed long dark uniform and no fear of being stopped by the government's secret police. I was excited because going to England also meant that I would get to see blond blue-eyed English boys. That was all. I was trusting and optimistic. It was my last moments as me, the complete human. Stable and grounded, unfragmented. With sunshine thoughts and sweetened heart.

On the plane we had seats next to huge exit doors. I remember our secret giggling and joking about whether the ginger man sitting behind us was also ginger 'down there' as well. The instant I understood that we had entered British airspace, I unwrapped my tent-like Islamic uniform from my head and body and started working on my grand plans of applying the right shade of varnish to dress my nails in to fit with the glamour of England. Last night's colour, because I liked the instant glamour of its unforgiving red. The light cotton summer dress that my mother had bought for me a few days before bloomed and blushed from underneath the tent-like cloth. Cocky little me. Spunky street-smart spoilt princess. I *was* going to feel the air and the breeze of freedom on my skin. With my bright red finger nails, no one could stop me.

My bare arms, chest and back, my neck and legs went into shock as the outside air slapped my skin. I felt naked. Not since the age of seven had I walked outside without the compulsory Islamic cover. It was cloudy, about 3 pm and all was hush. I was so used to loud people all around me, talking, kissing, shouting, laughing and gossiping, berating each other for not coming to visit for dinner often enough. And colour. There was no colour. It was grey.

I was used to sunshine and flowers. Fruit trees and mountains. Orange taxis. It was barren.

My stepfather had given instructions on how to find a connecting flight to Manchester where my uncle and aunt lived. My grandmother and I were going to go and live with them. After the immigration, the escalators and brisk bodies wizzing past us like rainbow zebras, I ceaselessly whispered the words 'Gate tree, gate tree, gate tree.' A mantra, our salvation: gate three. We were now outside in the freezing August air with our suitcases placed all around us like decoration. I looked at my grandmother and she looked back. I suddenly saw that she was dying.

My grandmother had brought me up and to me she was my forever guardian. Everybody called her Anneh, meaning mother. What I loved most was climbing up against her fat tummy and warm bosoms and listening to the clutter of her insides. Her body had an undertone of Western perfume and secrets. I chuckled at the unusually large holes that hung from her earlobes, the ear piercings carved out by misguided beauticians when she was a little girl. I played with the weighty ruby ring that constantly sat on her violet-veined finger, hypnotised by the pools of its hard red colour. Her hair was always shoulder-length and toasted-brown with a wide side parting. She was known as a stylish woman. The beiges and caramels she wore matched her hazel eyes and tender white skin.

Anneh had decided that she was going to be at my side in a strange country. At the age of fifty-seven, she had left behind her home and security, her family and her life, and most of all she had made a choice to risk her health. For me. She was a high-risk asthma sufferer, and had flown from the sun to embrace England's damp cold climate.

The English air premiered on my exposure-hungry skin and poisoned my grandmother's lungs. Anneh stopped and clutched her chest right there, in public, with people all around, and us not speaking a word of English. Actually I could say 'apple', 'boy' and 'girl'. *All she needs is her inhaler*, I consoled myself. I dug out the feather-light blue lifesaver from the bottom of her cream leather handbag and watched as she pumped four neat puffs into her tightened lungs. *She'll be fine now*, I tried to comfort myself while I held on to the beat of 'gate three, gate three, gate three' in the back of my head. I had to remember to pronounce it the way the lady at the immigration desk had done, so that we could find our flight connection. I decided to sit Anneh down on the pavement because it would make her feel better.

'Sit down here while I go to find where the aeroplane is,' I heard my grown up voice say. Her round ashen face nodded as I dashed back into the terminal. Inside, I willed my eyes to spot a nice someone to ask about this wonderful place called gate three. The first people I stumbled upon were an elderly oriental couple. 'No English' came the instant reply. After that my rushed efforts to a blur of dizzy faces got no result. I ran outside to find Anneh sitting on the pavement. She was much worse. Dread froze my throat. Her soft cushioned cheeks were a violent purple. A strange mixture of loud whistles and wet crackling sounds came from her throat. She was struggling to breathe. Her wide eyes pleaded with me to help her. I turned my head away from her to dart my eyes around. People walking were scattered all over. No one would speak Iranian. I regretted skipping all those private English classes my parents had sent me to. She couldn't breathe and she was dying in front of me and no one could see it.

I went back inside the terminal. Somehow I associated going back in with finding all the solutions. I walked back and forth not quite knowing what to do. When I finally went outside again I saw an ambulance parked on the side of the road and a policewoman helping my grandmother to her feet. The policewoman had noticed my grandmother on the pavement and had called an ambulance. I loved that policewoman so much then. I thought her the kindest person in the world.

I remember climbing into the ambulance and then nothingness.

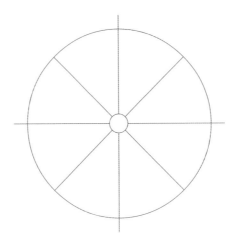

THE ROLLER OF BIG CIGARS

from the novel by Jennifer Russell

'I told you a thousand times. He's a runner,' said Shell's mother, prying open a hotdog bun. 'You want ketchup and mustard?'

Shell nodded.

'Relish?'

'Yeah. So, you never hear from him?'

Her mother sighed. 'Your Granny Ilse said she saw him a couple years ago. He was passing through Kent with his trailer. She said he didn't look that good. I figure the drugs are doing him in.' As she shut the fridge, condiment bottles clanked in the door's shelf. For a moment, Shell marvelled that a woman living alone could have such a full fridge. But then she knew the answer: you live in a neighbourhood, you feed a neighbourhood. Unlike her mother, Shell had never made herself part of her neighbourhood – she just happened to be lighting in a second-floor apartment for a few years.

She wanted to ask what her mother remembered about Farley, but changed her mind. The less they discussed him, the better. Her mother would see something in it, something sleazy about a man his age taking an interest in her daughter. Anyway, Shell didn't think she ever really liked him. Whether they had had words or whether her mother had no respect for him because he had been a cuckolded husband, she didn't know.

Shell was sitting at the yellow Formica table, rubbing her thumb over the label of a Tabasco bottle. 'Remember Mandy?' she chanced.

'What about her?'

'Oh, I just wondered what she'd be doing right now.'

'Sitting here next to you, I expect, eating a hotdog— '

'—just cheese.'

'God, that kid and cheese. I went to a flea market with her mom in Alhambra last weekend.'

Shell reared her head involuntarily and stared. She knew they still spoke to one another, but she couldn't imagine her mother's relationship with Cherie, after all that had gone down. 'How do you stay friends?'

Her mother shrugged. 'We don't think about it.'

'Huh.' She nodded. That was some heap of nothing they didn't think about – with Shell's dad being just about at the top of it. Just below Mandy, that was.

Her mother set a hotdog and a can of Diet Coke in front of her. 'Get some chips from the larder,' she said.

The larder was more like a coat closet, but it was stuffed to the gills with home-preserved pickles and jams, aluminium cans of every vegetable grown in America, soda, chips, and the usual foodstuffs. 'You want Fritos, Doritos, or Lays?' Shell asked.

'Fritos? Are you kidding? Take a case of that Coke home.'

'I can get my own Coke.'

'Don't get huffy, it was buy-one-get-one-free. Anyway, you're out of a job.'

Shell cleared her throat. 'Doritos?'

'You know I eat chips.'

She grabbed a large bag of Lay's, pulled it open and set it on the table. 'Why do you buy all this stuff if you're never going to eat it? The Fritos have been in there for maybe a year.'

Her mother bit the end off a hotdog and glared at her. With a full mouth, she said 'I got 'em for you. You eat Fritos.'

'I hate Fritos.'

'You used to eat 'em.'

'Yeah. Twenty years ago, before they invented Doritos.'

'Get rid of 'em, I don't care.' She popped open a can of Pepsi and took a long drink. Reaching into the bag, she caught a wad of chips in her cotton-candy-pink nails, and dropped them on her plate.

Shell took a large bite of her hotdog, wiping relish off the corner of her mouth and licking it off her thumb. 'Well, what is this box-lifting project? Spring cleaning?' She wouldn't mind seeing her mother sort through some of her junk, although she really didn't want to spend her days helping. That was one of the major problems of being unemployed – she had no excuse to refuse her mother's requests.

'Sort of.' She was studying the *TV Guide* magazine, one hand suspending the hotdog. Shell's radar went up; this was one of her mother's classic evasion tactics.

'So, what am I moving?'

She shook her head, still seemingly engrossed in the guide. 'Just stuff.'

'What? Old clothes, photo albums? Dead bodies?'

She made a derivative tssking sound. 'Books. A bunch of old books in the way. I got a wicker display case at the flea market, I'm going to put my china cups on it.'

'Ah,' said Shell, stifling a burp from the Coke bubbles. She got up and peeked into the living room to see if the stuff was boxed yet. Now that she bothered to look around, she did notice the wicker case and three boxes standing at the far end of the room. Her mother's house was like a museum of kitsch – cheap porcelain dolls, dried flowers, teddy bears, music boxes, china cups and photos of people Shell barely knew, all coated in dust. 'So I'm doing a thrift-store run.'

'Sort of.'

'Okay, I'll finish this and park closer to the house. Just those three boxes?'

She turned the page she was reading and curled it back. 'Mmm-hmm. Just put 'em in the Buick.'

'Your Buick?' Shell asked incredulously. Her mother had not driven for nearly two years, since the State of California revoked her licence because of her first epileptic seizure. She had practically left the Buick to rot, waiting for a miracle maybe. After eight months, Frank and Jody convinced her to rent it their youngest daughter, who had a job at a 7-11 and three kids by different fathers. Her mother went way back with Frank and Jody – Frank used to be the bouncer for her mother's house parties – so the deal seemed sensible to her. Why she couldn't just sell the car and move on was beyond Shell's understanding.

'It's in the alley. I knew I shouldn't have trusted Leah with it. It's totally trashed. The kids have spilled their pop in it and there's gum all over the back seat.'

'Hold on. Rewind. You've got your car again?'

'Yeah.'

'Are you driving it?' Shell glared at her.

'I told you. I went to Alhambra last weekend.'

'You drove? Isn't that a little illegal?'

Her mother stared wide-eyed at her. 'I told you I got my licence back.'

So this is what flipping the *TV Guide* was all about. To get her licence back, she would have had to be seizure-free for a year. 'Uh, no,' said Shell. 'What I remember is several panicky phone calls about minor seizures.'

'I wasn't panicky.'

'And you refusing to tell your doctor. Are you crazy? You can't drive.'

'I did go to my doctor. Will you listen to me?'

'When?'

'When I had to get my blood checked. Last February.'

'I drove you to that appointment.'

Her mother nodded as if the light had finally dawned in Shell's dim brain. 'They weren't seizures,' her mother said.

'You didn't tell me that.'

'I didn't know you were so scared about it.' She batted her hand in the air. 'They were just flashbacks.'

'Flashbacks?'

'Oh, don't give me that look. I haven't dropped acid since you were a kid.'

Shell took a deep breath. She remembered her mom and her boyfriend, Marty, standing on the back steps, feeding each other a smiley face of LSD. Marty had a parachute tattooed on his forearm and big, fat sideburns. The best thing about Marty was that when he and his friends stayed the night, Mom would cook pancakes, bacon and eggs for breakfast. 'And you found this out months ago,' she said. 'So I didn't really have to stick around this miserable, smog-ridden metropolis all this time.'

Her mother looked affronted. 'I could have had one.'

'But you didn't. And you conned me.'

Her mother yanked a cigarette from her long leather purse, lit it with a transparent butane lighter, and slammed the lighter on to the table. Exhaling a white plume of smoke, she said, 'I never told you I had a seizure.'

Shell nodded. 'Flashbacks.' She stared at a swirl in the Formica and felt her face grow hot. She never learned. How many opportunities did she lose because her mother had schemed to keep her nearby? She thought of the camping trips she had missed out on and that biology class weekend in the Mojave because her mother didn't trust the chaperones to do their job. She could have gone to an Ivy League college instead of staying in L.A. if her mother hadn't made her feel so guilty about leaving town. She could have backpacked around Europe and seen the places in the novels she had read. And now she had practically chained her here for two years with these seizures. OK, at least they started out as real. But flashbacks for an entire year? She wanted to chew her up one side and down the other, but taking on her mother in an argument was more than she could handle. She stood up, slammed her chair into the table, and grabbed her keys.

'Oh, for Christ's sake. Sit down.'

'I'm going.'

'I told you I was getting my licence before you packed off to Maui.'

'Bye.'

'Then take your damned Coke. I don't drink that crap.'

'Fine.' Shell snatched up the case, shoved a bag each of Doritos and Fritos into a plastic shopping bag, and left.

The Diet Coke reminded her that she needed to stock up on some basic groceries. Crystal had completely depleted the fridge during Shell's week in Maui. She swerved away from her mother's kerb and drove to the SuperShop, just down the street and around the corner. Still fuming from the conversation, she rolled her car into a parking spot and yanked the handle of the emergency brake.

She strode in through the automatic doors and took the first aisle. In spite of her black mood, the sight of the salad bar and the fresh fish counter made her smile. The old neighbourhood store had grown quite toney over the years. She used to come here with her dad when it was Jim's Mart. The beverage coolers had stood where they now displayed the freshly-baked bread. She remembered being four, maybe, on a summer morning, and her dad had lifted her up to see the soda bottles. 'Root beer or red Fanta?' he asked.

She pressed her finger against the glass and moved it back and forth. 'One potato, two potato, three potato, or more! Red Fanta.'

He set her down and reached into the cooler for a Fanta. Then he opened another cooler, grabbed a six-pack of Budweiser, and let the door clap shut. 'Yay. Are we going to see Mike?' asked Shell.

'If he's having a good day.'

'Let's get him some crackers,' she said, holding her index finger up like she was having a bright idea. She ran to the front of the aisle and stopped at the cracker section. The boxes came in so many colours, but choosing was easy. Mike's favourites were the same as hers – Ritz, in the red box.

At the checkout, her dad grabbed a packet of roasted sunflower seeds and set them on the counter next to the six-pack and the soda. She handed him the crackers. 'What are you getting, seashell?' He nodded to the metal rack of candy.

She giggled. 'Daa-ad, that's not my name.'

'Marathon bar?'

She shook her head.

'Bubblicious?'

'Uh-uh.'

'Well, hurry up, the lady's waiting.'

She pointed to the top of the rack.

He smirked, a small laugh-line framing his dark moustache. 'Roasted sunflower seeds? You're sure?' He shook his head and tossed a pack on to the counter.

'Good choice, sweetie,' said the checker. She winked at Shell, her eyes magnified by thick glasses. 'My, you're getting big.' The checker's hair was mostly brown, except where it was white at the top. It curled over the collar of her blue smock. Shell smiled at her and pressed herself against her dad's leg.

He nodded to the cigarette rack behind the checker. 'Pack of Zig-Zags.'

Outside Jim's Mart, Shell's dad held a paper bag in one arm and took her hand in his. The sun warmed her legs after the cool of the grocery store. She furrowed her brow. 'Why does Mike have lots of bad days?'

'He gets tired easily.'

'How come?'

'Um, he was in a war – that's when men fight with each other. Wars do real bad stuff to people. So now he's kind of hurt and kind of sick.'

Shell looked down at the sidewalk and stepped over the lines. 'Is that why he rolls around in his wheelchair?'

'Yeah.' They crossed the street and entered the school ground. 'Want to go for a swing?'

She ran ahead to the swingset, grabbed a pair of chains and shimmied herself on to the rubber seat. 'Push me,' she said, touching her toes to the tarmac.

He set the paper bag next to one of the lead posts. 'You don't know how to pump yet?'

'It's too hard,' she wailed. 'Push me.'

He stood in front of her, grabbed the chains, and gently pulled her toward him. She glided backwards. He held out his hands, palms down. As she swung toward him, he said, 'Kick my hands.' She extended a foot and tapped his fingers. 'Nope. Both feet, both hands.' At the next ascent, she threw out both feet and tapped his palms. 'Good. Scrunch your legs back.' Shell scuffed the ground with her shoes, wobbled, and continued backward. 'Another try,' he said, backing up slightly. 'Hold on tight.' She hit him squarely in the palms. 'Right on. Scrunch your legs.' It was as if she was a witch, pointing her broom. She could feel the swing buck and glide in the direction she poked her feet. She laughed.

Her dad sat next to her and began to swing. He could make his feet go higher than the bar above their heads. She wondered if a person could loop-the-loop over the swings. She didn't think she could hold on if she looped-the-loop. She let her legs go slack. 'I'm tired, Dad. Stop me.'

'Yeah?' he asked, scuffing his shoes on the tarmac. He jumped off his swing with a flourish, stood behind her and brought her to a halt. When he picked up his bag, they resumed their walk through the empty schoolyard. 'Did Grampa Weingartner teach you to swing?'

'Nope. Your grampa didn't teach me much of anything.'

'How come?'

He shrugged. 'Just didn't.' They walked down the lanes of the track and passed a jungle gym.

'Can Mike swing?'

'Not now.'

They reached the other end of the school and walked along a quiet street for a couple blocks. When they arrived at their corner, they turned and walked halfway down the street before they got to the yellow house where Mike lived. It wasn't really his house and he hadn't lived there for long. He was staying there with a grumpy woman and her boyfriend. They had day jobs.

Shell's dad didn't bother with the front door. If Mike were having a good day he would be on the back porch. Shell followed him along the driveway to the side of the house. A set of concrete steps led to a small landing and a door. Mike was alone on the landing, sitting in front of an easel, a round palette perched on the arm of his chair. The easel and his chair took up most of the landing; it was as if he were stranded on a tiny island. 'Hey, man,' called Shell's dad. 'How're you doing?'

'Danny! Hey, Shelly.'

Shell ran up the stairs. 'We brought your favourite crackers. Want some?'

JENNIFER RUSSELL

Mike and Danny exchanged a look. Mike grinned at Shell and said, 'Fantastic. Why don't you have some now? I'll eat mine later.'

'Did you know,' she said with wide eyes, 'the box is always red?'

He laughed. 'You painting today?' She nodded. Using his lighter, Danny popped the cap off a beer bottle and offered it to Mike. Giving anything to Mike was a slow process. Instead of hands, he had metal hooks. Each hook split in the middle so he could open and close it like a pincer. After he rinsed his brush, he swivelled it lengthwise and laid it on the ledge of the easel. 'The paper's just inside the door, man,' he said, clamping the bottle and taking a long drink.

'Got it.' Danny removed the canvas, set the pad of paper on the easel and opened it to a clean page. 'You sitting or standing, seashell?'

She shot him a playful look. 'Dad, don't call me that.'

'Why?' interjected Mike. 'That's your name, isn't it? Seashell, my belle?' He nipped a pincer-hook at her.

She wrinkled her nose and laughed. 'You're a silly head.' Then she studied the brushes jutting out of Mike's shirt pocket. She was looking for the one with the blue handle. When she found it, she pulled it out and flicked it in her hand as if doing warm-up exercises. Danny checked the brakes on the wheelchair and set the palette on the ground before settling Shell on to Mike's lap. He handed the palette to Mike. 'Remember to sit back, Shelly. Your mom will have me on a platter if you both tumble off this porch.'

Shell dipped her brush into the red and began to paint a butterfly the way Mandy's older sister had shown her. Danny gave Mike another beer and opened one for himself. He leaned against the house and crossed one leg in front of the other. 'How's the home front?' asked Mike as Shell painted antennae.

'Can't get any worse. Remember her brother I was telling you about?'

'Came home in a box?'

Danny pulled a pack of Camels out of his pocket and lit one. He exhaled the smoke through his nose. 'I'm told I'm not fit to wipe his tombstone.'

'What's a tombstone?' asked Shell.

'They're the signs in cemeteries,' Mike said. 'You need more spots on the wings.'

'Guess I was supposed to go over there and get shot at.'

'Jesus. You think she'd be glad.' He finished his beer and handed the bottle to Danny.

'You'd think so, but...' He shook his head. 'According to her, I'm not half the man he was.'

Mike glanced over his shoulder at him and arched a brow. 'She said that? Does she want me for a night?'

Danny coughed and laughed at the same time. 'Shut up. You're more real than any of us.'

Mike shifted the palette. Shell was dabbing her brush in the blue paint. 'You know what my sergeant used to tell us 'Nam was? "Man" spelled backwards – 'cause that's what it makes you.' Shell began filling in the wings. 'Good job, Shelly.'

Danny got another beer for Mike and opened it. He fished something from the pocket of his cut-offs and dropped it into the grocery bag. Mike took a drink and stared at him. 'What are you gonna do?'

Danny shrugged.

'You know what's the most important thing,' he said, nodding toward Shell.

'Yeah. The only thing.' He and Mike watched Shell smear blue across the red lines of her wings. She leaned back against Mike's chest. 'It's finished.'

'I think we'd better autograph a painting that beautiful.' He gently clamped the back of the brush. Together, he and Shell signed her name to the bottom. Danny carefully tore the page from the book, replaced the canvas and lifted Shell from the wheelchair. She wiped her hands with a rag from Mike and took the sunflower seeds her dad handed her. Danny tucked the cracker box under his arm.

'Oh no. We forgot to eat the crackers,' she said.

He winked at her. 'You take those with you. I'll pick up some more.'

Danny set the grocery bag next to Mike's chair. 'I left you something in there. Rolled and ready.'

'Thanks, man. What do I owe you?'

'It's on the house. You know it is.'

'Hang in there, brother.' But her dad hadn't hung in there – he had left Shell and her mother just after Christmas and skipped town a couple years after that. Shell jangled her keys and peered at the soda cans and bottles in the cooler. She wondered what he was doing and where he was living. The man she remembered was quiet, sweet, somewhat guarded – not the careless, self-centred man who had been branded responsible for Mandy's death. She wished she were brave enough to ask Farley about it all – he would tell her the truth.

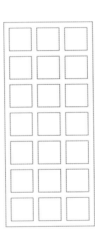

THEM STORIES MY DADDY USED TO TELL

a short story by Richard Scott-Ashe

Before my daddy got killed, he used to tell us stories on long family car trips. I can't for the life of me remember any of them.

My friend Jim came along sometimes, and if we start getting into his potato moonshine he says he remembers them stories fine. Jim started drinking that evil stuff a lot more after he got married. I can never get him to tell me none of them stories he says he remembers. All he talks about are things about his wife that I can't imagine anyone ever wanting to know. She's a pig-farmer from Hungary. When they met through the bridal agency, it turned out she had some kind of power over old Jimbo. She had him pinching pennies, saving up his state checks for her plane ticket. Since the mine closed, Jim's been making do on government handouts, which are none too generous. Once she got over here, she gave up pig farming and started studying hat-making. She holds that lumpy chin of hers up and says her school's one of the finest hat-making schools in the county. I can't say I've heard of any others. She was already in her mid-thirties when she finally convinced Jim to marry her. When I drove Jim to pick her up at the airport in my truck, I could've sworn I heard her biological clock ticking in the back seat like a bomb.

I try to push my brain back into corners and remember them stories when I'm driving. Being that I make my money by trucking these days, I get a lot of time to try. I turn off the radio and listen to the cars swish past; I watch the yellow line run. Thing is, usually all I come up with are real things that happened. My sister Jenny once started laughing at my granddaddy's funeral. She's younger than me, and she was then too. She whispered, 'Wake up, Granddaddy!' to me and burst out laughing. She rolled over in the pew with tears in her eyes. Daddy smacked her on the backside and I remember the sound echoing in the church. Then Mamma started with the tears too.

Sometimes I think I get a grip on a memory of one of them old stories, but it always gets away from me. It's like a song you can only remember a couple words to, but no tune. My granddaddy was a man who could remember a tune.

He was a damn fine banjo player before his accident. He was a miner, my granddaddy, just like my daddy. Thing was, he handled a lot of dynamite for a guy who smoked so many cigarettes. People were pretty evenly split about which one would finish him off. It was the dynamite, but since the cigarettes were what set it off, no one really felt like they'd won anything by being right. If he'd lived after the accident, he would've been no good at the banjo no more.

See? One minute I'm trying to remember them stories my daddy used to tell, the next I'm at my granddaddy's funeral. Now's I think about it, my daddy's funeral was in the same church. It's against the hill down by the mine. The railway tracks coming out of the mine run right through the graveyard, and sometimes coal used to spill out of the leaving cars on to the graves. The relatives of the dead folks were none too happy with the mining company when that happened, but I can't remember the company ever not doing something because it made folks unhappy. Mamma used to make me and Jenny go down there on Sundays and brush the coal off Granddaddy's grave. Sometimes we even took a bit of it home to burn, even though the company put a sign up in the cemetery saying that was illegal.

Some stories do come into my mind on the road. Especially if it's raining and the windows fog up on the inside. But who knows if those're stories I made up myself or if they're really what my daddy used to tell me. Hell, they could be true things that happened, or something I saw on TV and forgot about. I once saw this show about a fashion designer woman who was making fur clothes out of road kill. They showed her out on the street with a snow shovel, scraping some poor dead thing off the tarmac. She went on and on about how fur was bad in principle, but how waste for no reason was even worse. I only remember because Jim's wife got the idea to make a hat out of squashed squirrels from that show. Funny how some things catch on.

You could tell when my daddy was getting ready to tell a story. It was usually when my sister got to whining about having to go to the bathroom, or when I got to hitting her because she wouldn't stop whining. He would turn down the radio and clear his throat and say, real loud, 'Once upon a time!' Sometimes he'd have to say 'Once upon a time' a few times before you could hear him over my sister's crying. I could hit pretty hard as a kid, and Jenny was no slouch at loud crying. It's strange: I remember the beginning of them stories clear as day, but then everything he'd say after is kind of misted over, just like the insides of the truck windows on rainy days.

I can't think where those stories've disappeared to, but I've been trying to remember them for a long time and I ain't gotten nowhere. My brain just blocks me out. Hell, sometimes I even catch myself making up fake stories just to fill in the gaps. I figure when you start trying to cheat on your own memories, it's a good time to quit.

Daddy knew a thing or two about cheating, or at least he thought he did. Especially at cards. Thing was, people got to know that he was good at cheating and that's one thing it's no perk to be famous for. For a while, at the end, when everyone knew he was cheating, he kept it up just because he couldn't resist showing how good at it he was. Mamma said it'd be all right, on account of folks pretty much knowing him for what he was and knowing not to bet too heavy on games he was involved in. Even so, one day Daddy somehow got started playing against the mine boss. On nights that Daddy didn't come home, the light in the office on the hill stayed on all night. Me and Jenny used to watch it through our bedroom window until we fell asleep.

I guess Daddy proved Mamma wrong in the end about everything ending up all right. Jenny used to take walks along the tracks, starting from behind our backyard and following them through the graveyard around the hill into the valley. So she was the one who found Daddy's body, all bent up in a weird shape down the valley bank. If I'm honest about it I'd say she's never quite been the same since. She says that sometimes she tries to lie down in the position she found Daddy, but she can't because it hurts too much to bend like that.

In their big report, the police wrote down that he'd fallen off the train. They never tried to explain how he had a full pack of cards stuck up his ass. Maybe they thought there was a deck just laying by the tracks for him to fall on, but I'm personally of the impression that they didn't care enough to find out what really happened. Maybe sometimes only rich folks can afford the truth.

After they found his body, the mine closed up within a couple of weeks. Folks were too worried about what was going to happen to the town to notice how strange it was for the company to be packing up shop so soon after Daddy's death. The train tracks still run back behind the old yard, but now they're covered over with grass. People came and took all the coal that was left stacked up in the company yard, and once that was all gone they started to leave town. I got my trucking licence and now it feels like I'm always leaving somewhere.

I tried to get Jim to come get the licence with me, but he said that once his wife graduates from hat-making school and starts selling hats, he's going to have it made in the shade. Lately, when I try to get him to remember Daddy's stories, all he talks about is the stuff he's going to buy with his wife's hat money. If you ask me, that's as good an example of counting your chickens before they're hatched as I can think of.

I guess I'm going to stop trying to dig them stories up one day. I just end up remembering things it don't do me no good to remember.

CLEAN

from the novel by Sarah Sims

Tom desperately needs a glass of water. His throat feels tight and dry from the bleach fumes. But there is a complication. To get to the kitchen tap – sorry, Maddy, *faucet* – he will have to walk over the freshly scrubbed lino. Then it will need to be washed again. That will be another hour gone and he hasn't even started on the living room. Usually he plans it through, has his glass of water waiting for him outside the kitchen door. But today he forgot.

Sweat starts to trickle between his shoulder blades. He stands frozen in the kitchen doorway, staring out of the window at the Detroit River. The November wind has whipped the water into a broiling mass. There'll be another tanker passing within the hour. Sometimes they come so close that sheet metal blots out the sky. Tom has started to avoid the kitchen window when they pass. He is convinced that one of these days the captain will make a false turn and the tanker will plough straight into the apartment.

Imagine the mess then, eh? He starts to laugh. Then he stops, because the sound of his laughter in the empty flat is absurd and frightening.

He can feel his heart swoop and dip, as if it wants to escape his chest. It has become hard to breathe. He crouches on the floor in an effort to calm himself. His mind starts running in its familiar circle. Why doesn't he leave the flat? He hates living here. The stairs stink of piss and the lift never works. The hallways are daubed with graffiti: *Suck My Dick. Fuck You Kenny.* As Tom walks past, he always feels a pulse of sympathy for Kenny.

This is the sort of place people end up in only because they're too poor or too unlucky to go anywhere else. He should move back to Oxford, where he belongs. Find a place in a decent area, a modern place, without all those unnecessary spaces where the dust can gather. When he thinks about it, it's an insult to the other inhabitants, living here, when he has his teaching certificate, his options.

Only he doesn't have options, because he can't leave the city whilst Maddy still lives here. Not when there is the chance that he might see her at that awful mall. Or at least catch a glimpse of her smart little convertible driving across downtown to somewhere better.

It has been two years since she asked him to leave the house in Dearborn, and he hasn't seen his wife once.

Anyway, he can't afford a better place now that he doesn't work. He can't possibly hold down a job when there is so much to do at home. And he doesn't really belong in Oxford any more; he knows that. Maybe he has lost the right to belong anywhere. Tom's thoughts loop from Dearborn, across the Atlantic to Oxford, and then back again, as his feet start to cramp from his crouched position outside the kitchen door. *Water. Come on.* He pinches the skin on the back of his palm and releases it, pinches and releases it, concentrating on the little eddies of pain. Then it comes to him. Rather than ruin the clean lino, he will buy a bottle of water from the shop across the way. Yes.

He goes to the hallway, pulls his shoes out of their plastic bag, slips them on and reaches for his jacket. Then he remembers he's left his wallet on the bedside table. He walks to the bedroom.

Halfway across the bedroom floor, he realises he hasn't taken his shoes off.

In the silence, he hears his wife's voice: *Jesus, Tom, you never think, do you?*

He presses the heels of his hands into his eye sockets and takes a deep breath. *Come on, man. You've got to look.* You've got to look. He takes his hands from his eyes, the blood singing in his ears, and bends down to inspect the damage. No marks, thank god. But he'll have to wash the whole carpet, just to make sure.

The thought of dragging the heavy carpet cleaner out of the hallway cupboard makes him feel sick. He stands listening to the steady tick of the bedside clock.

The alarm is set for six. He wakes at 5.45, at 5.30. These are the worst times. Being asleep is safe, so long as he doesn't dream. Being awake is safe, so long as he gets straight out of bed and starts the chores. But in the unscheduled, in-between moments, his mind can't be trusted. This morning he awoke a full hour before his alarm to find his body curved around the empty space where Maddy used to be.

Lying on the cold sheet, he could see the morning stretching ahead of him: hours of kneeling on the floor, head bowed over mop and bucket, the bleach stinging his nostrils. He scrubs his way to atonement as outside his window the tankers slip past and the gulls swoop and cry. What does he expect? That one day there will be a knock at the door and Maddy will come in, see the purified lino, the scourged carpet, the shelves innocent of dust, and say, *Tom, I understand, I see you love me, I forgive you, come back home to me?*

Tom goes to the wardrobe and pulls out the blue shift dress he bought for her, the new dress to replace the one that was damaged. The new dress she never wore. He sits on his single bed and wraps the material around his fists tighter and tighter until it hurts. He is so tired.

One

That Neil O'Connor had been at it again, Tom would put money on it.

The brick wall behind the swimming pool had been doused with red. *Call Suzy 4 Free Sex*, followed by a mobile number. Well the Head should be pleased that the kids were adapting to new technology. Someone had confiscated a can of spray paint from the O'Connor lad only last week. He'd even used the same colour, the little bugger.

'I've got enough to do without clearing up this filth.' The caretaker shook his head.

'I know. I'm sorry to call you out, Ted.'

The older man pulled out a handkerchief and wiped his forehead. 'Hasn't anyone had words?'

Tom sighed. 'Yes, of course.' You could make them sit through PSHE twenty-four hours a day but you still wouldn't eradicate the instinct for cruelty.

Which poor kid was Suzy, anyway? At the start of his second week, he was still struggling to put faces to names, but he taught a Suzanne, didn't he? Yes. His Wednesday afternoon class. Small, stocky girl. Painfully tidy, her hair stretched in a low plait, her brilliant essays written in minute script. Sat with her arms wrapped around her, as if afraid something might escape. Always chose a desk near the teacher's. That was the sign. Confident kids didn't want to sit under the teacher's nose, they wanted to hunker down with their mates. It was only the ones who needed safety that ended up at the front.

Ted zipped up his overalls jacket. 'Well, I'll put it on the list, Mr Braithwaite.'

Tom had a sudden image of the other kids gathering around the wall, staring at the naked words, the laughter bubbling up. 'Can't you do it now? I – We don't want anyone to see this, do we?'

Ted frowned and looked at his watch. Hell, the old codger probably held Suzanne responsible as the only named party.

'We're out of cleaning fluid. I can pick some up tomorrow night.'

Tomorrow night. So it would be there all day. Tom made a quick calculation in his head.

'Look, Tesco's will still be open. How's about I pop down and pick some cleaning stuff up? You'll be here until sevenish, won't you?'

He knew his voice had taken on a slightly pleading quality, but he wasn't going to give up now. He coughed hard. 'I'll give you a hand.'

'Well, I can't see what all the fuss is about. But if it's that desperate.'

Tom smiled with relief. He'd only been in Oxford for two weeks but he'd already discovered a short cut to the supermarket on his runs. As the last of the day's light faded from the school yard, the two men scrubbed at the bricks until not a trace of red remained.

'So, what do we learn about Romeo from this passage? Peter?'

The following day: his Wednesday afternoon lot. Tom paced up and down in the empty space between the kids' desks. The carpet, the exact colour of leaf-mould, was sticky with generations of can spillage. He'd spent the Sunday night before his first day dragging the desks from their rows into three tiers around a central square. It had seemed like a great idea at the time; more egalitarian, more open. Today, the square felt less like a democratic forum and more like a bullring.

In the silence, there came a thud and a shout. A couple of lads were kicking a football against the Sixties prefab opposite.

Tom passed Natasha Woodville and caught the glint of a mobile phone. At his glare, she thrust it back under the desk, but he could still sense her fingers tapping.

Peter stared at the text in front of him, as if trying to decipher a code. 'Um. He seems angry.'

'Angry.' Tom rapped the desk in front of him, startling Liam Pascoe out of his usual turbid adolescent daze. 'Angry. Is that as far as we can go? Liam?'

'I don't get it, Sir.'

'OK, OK. Did anyone else?' The headache that had been threatening to break all morning started to beat a dull rhythm below his left temple. *Hang on, it might not be them, maybe you didn't explain it. One more go–*

'Anyone?'

He scanned the faces and came to rest on Suzanne Watts. He was startled to see her on a seat a few rows back with a group of girls. Her hair fell loose over her shoulders and she had the afterglow of a giggle about her. Something had clearly happened to Suzy.

Well, good for her. The memory of her latest essay, clean and taut as fresh linen, came to mind.

'Suzy?'

She looked up at him. He detected a shimmer of eye shadow.

'Help us out here. What did you make of this passage?'

She glanced quickly at her neighbour, Haley, one of the lesser stars in 3B's universe, and looked down at her desk. 'I don't know, Sir.'

Tom sucked his breath in sharply.

'Nothing at all?'

She gave a little shrug, her face flushing. 'Sorry, Sir.'

Tom felt his own face flush. He turned his back on the class and started attacking the whiteboard.

'Right. Let's take this line by line, then.'

He tried for ten more minutes. These were the worst days. The days when it felt like pounding nails into hard wood. Turning away from the board, he tossed his pen in the air and caught it neatly.

'OK, that's your lot for today. Off you go.'

There was a startled pause as the clock ticked loudly, a full five minutes short of the bell, then a scramble for the door. Suzy kept her head down as she passed.

Tom sank into his chair and stared at the empty rows. The pain in his head was piercing now. *After all he'd done for her.* He crumpled the sheet of paper in front of him. Come off it. Why should Suzy owe him anything?

Now he was feeling let down, and guilty for feeling let down. Laura was right, sometimes he was worse than a bloody girl. Forget it. He gathered his papers together. A pint would be the thing now, but he wasn't on those terms with any of the other teachers yet. No matter. Marking and a run, then. A long run.

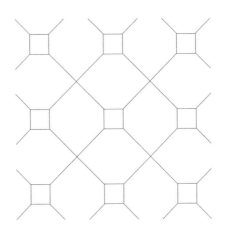

NAMING THE BABY

from the novel The Island by Madeleine Tobert

On the day after his birth, Amalia Matete officially named her baby Ioane after his father, but Ioane was far too adult a name for the little wrinkly-faced creature she held in her arms. Ioane was a man's name, a rough name, a violent name, and the perfect little baby was none of those things. She looked at her son and tried to find traces of her husband in him, but his little hands would never beat her and his tiny legs could not pin her down. She looked into her son's eyes and wondered whether the light brown in them, that was so different from the darkness in hers, was his father's colour; but she could not remember Ioane's eyes and so chose to believe that her mother had looked like that instead. It wasn't entirely true.

'You look just like your grandmother,' she told her child, and he gurgled back at her. 'If you were a girl I would name you after her. I'd name you Temalisi Matete. But you're not a girl and you're not an Ioane, not yet. Not ever,' she thought. 'Don't be like him. Be you. But what are you?'

Amalia's child had been born with a full head of curly hair, curls that the baby, as a boy and then a man, would hate and shave off, but which his mother delighted in.

'Shall I call him Curly?' she asked the doctor's wife, Whinney Moala, who had moved into her house to help her during the first couple of weeks.

'No,' came the definitive reply. 'These curls will fall out soon. A baby that is born with hair loses it quickly. Your baby may not end up with curls at all. Besides, what kind of name is Curly? Honestly Amalia, think of the child.' And the old woman tutted and fussed and shook her head. She picked up the broom and began sweeping the floor of the wooden house. 'Amalia, this house is a disgrace. You need to put something down on this floor, and the walls need repainting. In a few months the baby will eat everything that peels off them, and as soon as he crawls he'll get splinters.'

Amalia Matete did not reply.

'Are you listening to me?'

But the mother was too absorbed in her child to notice anything else. 'Have you smelled him, Whinney?' she asked. 'He smells wonderful. Like coconuts and mangos and earth all mixed in together.'

'He'll smell like his own shit soon if you don't change him,' replied the doctor's wife. So Amalia cleaned him, found a new cloth to wrap the baby in and threw the old one out of the window into a tub full of water.

Amalia's baby hardly seemed human to her. He was like a curious little fish, floundering out of water. He rasped for breath and she worried he was drowning.

'He's asking for milk. Feed the poor thing,' said the doctor's wife. So Amalia lowered her simple brown dress to her waist and offered her breast to the baby. With nothing to hold them up, her clothes fell to the floor. Amalia watched as her son's mouth searched for her nipple, found it and began to drink.

'You shouldn't wear dresses while he's young. You'll spend half your life naked or taking clothes on and off. I'll bring you over some plain tops. Do you have material for a new *lavalava*?'

'Yes, I've made some out of my mother's old things. Look at him drinking. It tickles a little.'

'Soon you won't even notice it.'

'I like noticing it. Should I call him Fish? He looks as though he's been in the water for too long.'

Whinney Moala sighed.

Amalia Matete had a permanent trickle of visitors coming over to see the baby. All of them had different ideas about what she should call him.

'Name him Vete after my relatives,' suggested an elderly Zeno Tatafu.

'No, call him Tamatoa, after your father,' said the doctor.

'Josea is what we'd call a boy,' confided the Havealetas.

'How about Vete?' another Zeno said.

'I like Simione,' Grandmother Unga added.

'No!' exclaimed her pregnant daughter-in-law, 'that's what I want to call my son.'

'Vete?'

'No, Simione.'

'They can have the same name. Anyway you might have a girl.'

'All us Unga wives have sons!'

'That's true enough,' said Grandmother Unga.

'Anyway, you've already named him Ioane, haven't you?' someone else asked.

'Yes,' replied Amalia. 'But I can't call him that. It's his father's name, not his.'

'Why not just call him Baby while he's little until another name sounds right?'

'Because Baby sounds so wrong! And what if he never becomes Ioane? I couldn't call him Baby for more than a few months.'

'Maybe he's not supposed to be named,' said Ana Havealeta quietly, thinking of her own dead children.

'Don't say that, please,' said Amalia growing fearful. 'I'll think of a name.'

When the midday sun drew her visitors back to their houses for an afternoon sleep, Amalia Matete took her baby down to the beach. It was low tide, so she was able to sit in the shade of her house and look out at the waves. The day was hot, but sitting there on the damp sand she felt cool enough to stay awake. She didn't want to sleep. Closing her eyes meant looking away from her son, meant missing precious seconds of his life, and she wasn't ready to do that just yet. She held him in her arms so that he was facing the sea, and pointed out the gentle waves that lapped on the sand.

'Look at the sea, baby Matete,' she said, and her little son moved his mouth into what might have been a smile. 'We belong next to the sea,' she told him. 'We are sea people. You'll be a fisherman one day. Like my father was. He used to spend most of every day out at sea. "You don't know anything about an island," my father would say, "unless you can feel the movement of the sea around it. It's where people find their souls, though they don't all know it." He sat me on his knee as he rowed, and I moved forward and backwards with the boat.

'Ever since they were married, my parents would row all the way around the island each year. I was born in my father's boat. The lull of the sea was so relaxing that my mother's labour began right here. She said I swam out of her. She said I was so desperate to see the sea that I swam right out into the boat. My father had to drop the oars and try to grab me, but my mother fainted overboard and I followed her into the waves. The sea looked after us. You'll never drown unless it wants you to, but it loved my parents, and I think it loves me. "Now that you're born, little one", my father said, "there's no need to go home." I was three weeks' old before I spent a day on land. Whinney thinks

I'm going to drown every day and she'll probably tell you the same thing. But you mustn't listen to her. You'll swim.' She looked hard at her son. 'I'll show you.'

Amalia Matete stood up and waded with the baby into the sea. When she was up to her chest, she took a deep breath and knelt down, submerging her head below the waves, holding her baby firmly in her hands facing her. She let out a steady stream of little bubbles to keep her head below the surface. She opened her eyes and looked at her boy. He was staring back at her, his thick black curls floating above his head, his mouth wide open. She smiled at him, but couldn't quite tell if he was smiling back. Maybe he was, or maybe he was upset. She began to worry and rose up quickly. As she broke the surface, she heard a sweet sound that could have been his first laugh, or a gull calling out to its mate. She looked at him delightedly.

'You looked like a sea urchin,' she said merrily. 'Shall I call you that?' But she knew that she wouldn't. It wasn't quite right.

The following day was a Sunday, so Amalia Matete took her baby to the service that was held on the far side of the beach from her house. She joined the rest of the villagers lolling on the sand and watched the children stand up and sing for the adults. They were all dressed in their finest Sunday clothes, white shirts and white sarongs, with palm-weaved waistbands decorated with different-coloured cloth. Most were barefooted. They sang enthusiastically and Amalia wondered which of these children her son would most resemble. She could hardly wait to see him standing there, singing, and grinning with the rest of the little boys. One of the Tatafu children sang particularly loudly and badly. The adults smiled.

Amalia found herself surrounded by other young mothers. She cooed over their babies, and they over hers. They talked about the children and only half listened to what was being said. Tom Havealeta was talking about angels. She heard sentences about being half way between a man and god. About the devil being a fallen angel. About them being everywhere. She heard something about them helping mortals. But when she started to listen properly, he had moved on to other things.

'God created the countries,' Tom said, 'and then the seas. And He made this ocean huge so that there'd be enough room for the whales, enough room for the fish to swim in peace and enough room for coral to stretch out over its floor. But when God had finished with the oceans, He needed to get back to the other countries because He still had to add trees and grass to feed his animals. So He stepped across the water, and wherever He put down his foot, land rose up to meet him, so that He did not get wet. And He was so thankful to the ocean for keeping him dry that He gave his footprints the best plants and the best weather. His footprints are these islands, and that is why we live in paradise.'

Amalia Matete looked around her as she sang and realised that the island really was paradise. She loved the turquoise blue of the sea on a calm day, and the rough brown of the coconuts standing out against the clear sky. She loved that she always heard only one bird singing at a time, but could never see where it was. She loved the faces of the other villagers as they shut their eyes and let the sun caress their eyelids as they sang. She wondered about the other countries that she knew so little about, countries that had not been given the best of everything. And she felt sorry for the people who lived there.

'We're lucky to be islanders,' she whispered to her son, and later on in his life he claimed to remember her saying this.

The next evening Amalia Matete and her baby were sitting on the beach, when the doctor came stumbling out of the Ungas' house, saw the young pair and came to join them.

'I am too old for so much *kava*,' he announced. 'But Zeno Tatafu is pouring today, and she always gives everyone a full cup.'

Amalia laughed at the bloodshot eyes of her old friend. 'When I used to pour, you demanded I fill them up,' she told him.

'I was younger then, and considerably more foolish. A full half coconut shell, each round – it is too much for me now.'

'It wasn't too long ago,' Amalia said.

'Long enough for you to grow up though,' he replied, 'and long enough for me to grow old. Excuse me a moment.' And he walked into the trees, either to pee or to be sick; Amalia did not want to know which. He returned a few minutes later and sat back down again.

'Look at that tree, Amalia,' he said to her, pointing at a coconut palm tree a few metres from them. 'That tree is an angel.'

Amalia looked at him, waiting for the explanation. He shut his eyes, then forced them open again.

'That tree is what links the islanders to God. It is not God, but it contains the spirit of the island.'

Amalia looked at it, and then back at the doctor.

'That tree saves us,' the doctor continued. 'Where would we be without coconuts? A coconut is the finest thing. It is more than food. It is spirit.'

'I think I know what you mean,' Amalia said, thinking of Lave Unga and the tattoo of a coconut world on his leg.

'A coconut is fun!' the old man shouted, raising his right arm triumphantly, 'And life, Amalia, a good life, should be fun. I love coconuts, they are a treat. Whinney puts one in the fire for me every Sunday. I make her burn them. I love them burnt. So coconuts, burnt coconuts, are my religion! They make me smile and that is an angelic thing to do.' The doctor laughed.

'I think *kava* might be angelic as well, then,' Amalia said.

'It might well be! I must go and drink some more. Goodbye.' And he stood up and swayed back to the Ungas' house.

'The doctor is mad this evening,' Amalia told her son. 'And one day *kava* will make you mad too. It will make these crazy curls of yours stand up straight,' she said, as she played with them. The baby squirmed in her arms, trying to wriggle out of her grip. 'You don't like it when I play with your hair,' Amalia cried out delightedly. 'Already you're the man of the house!' she said and laughed at his cross little face. 'I think you might be my angel,' she told him, and then she said it again: 'My angel.' It felt right. And so the baby became known as Angel Matete.

SKY DANCER

from the novel by Louisa Tomlinson

Kate is a twenty-eight year old harpist who lives in London. Recently, strange things have started happening to her and she is worried that the line between her imagination and reality is becoming too blurred.

Kate ran her hands lightly over the harp strings. Deftly, her fingers found the sounds she was seeking. As she played, she found herself woven back into the strange fabric of her dreamworld. She felt herself move beyond clock time into the rhythm of the music, and concentrated on its pathway of sound, letting it wind her through a high white gate into a tunnel of pale pink light.

The narrow tunnel was lit by the gossamer glow of hundreds of fireflies. She pressed her fingers into the pockmarked walls and felt them yield to her touch.

The tunnel sloped down ahead of her. She looked up at the ceiling and it seemed to be breathing. She looked closer. It was hung with bats, all soft fur and leathered membranes, their pointed faces closed in sleep. The tunnel smelt of old excrement.

At the bottom of the slope, the passage widened into a bright white corridor lined with doors. She opened the second door and it led her on to a high shelf that hung over an airless afternoon sky. There was only empty space beneath her and she stepped quickly back into the corridor.

She walked on until she came to an old oak door with a brass handle. She turned its heavy weight with both hands and pushed the door open.

Darkness. She groped around the floor on her knees until she found a wire. She took the wire in her fingers and followed it until she found a lamp, which she turned on.

She was in her bedroom. It was bare but for her bed and side table, a pile of books and a glass of water. She walked over to the full-length mirror. Its frame was decorated with stickers of pop stars and butterflies.

An eight-year-old child stared back at her with green catlike eyes full of fear. She was dressed in dungarees, her long brown hair tied loosely back in a ponytail. Her grubby cheeks were streaked with clean lines where her tears had travelled.

The child wrapped her arms around herself and looked beyond her reflection to the room behind her. In the mirror, the sheets of paper taped to the wall were just paper. Her gaze rested on each one. Reading the words this way was not so bad.

DEHSINUP EB OT EVRESED SLRIG ELTTIL GNIYL

SEIL YM ROF LLEH NI NRUB LLIW I

NEES EB OT TIF TON MA I

She stopped. It was no good; she knew what they said. She had written them.

A scream rose in her throat, but the thought of her father pushed it down again. She swallowed its bitter taste.

She wanted to leave this body. It was broken, she was sure.

She walked back to the mirror and willed Tenzinmonk to come soon. She had been waiting for two days. He had always come before.

Downstairs, a door slammed and her body trembled with the violence of it.

Only her reflection looked back at her. How long would she have to wait before she was big enough to leave this place?

She sighed. She had tried to help her parents, but it had only made them angrier. They could not believe that Tenzinmonk was real.

She searched the mirror anxiously. Where was he?

Outside her bedroom, the floorboards creaked. She froze, then ran to her bed. She pulled a pillow on to her lap to cover herself.

The key turned in the lock and the door was pushed ajar.

She gulped.

Her mother's head appeared round the door, then the rest of her. She looked thin and old, like she had been ill for a long time.

Kate's relief made her dizzy and she lay back on her bed.

Her mother tiptoed over to her and pushed Kate's seal into her arms.

Kate breathed in the washed smell and let its white fluffiness rest against her cheek. Its shape in her arms calmed her.

'Just make sure he doesn't see it,' her mother whispered, and for a second, their eyes met. Her soft fingers stayed to stroke Kate's tears into her daughter's cheeks.

Kate breathed in the hint of her mother's perfume. It held out a promise of other worlds, better worlds than this one.

Her father's voice rose up the stairs. She could not hear his words, only his fury.

Her mother scuttled to the door without hesitation. She closed it quietly behind her and locked it again.

Kate clutched her seal and waited for the shouting downstairs to turn into silence.

There was a movement in the corner of her eye, and she turned to see Tenzinmonk in the mirror. He beamed and beckoned her closer.

She loved his face and told him so. He was always smiling and wore big red blankets because he was a monk and didn't have any clothes.

'Hello Katie-la,' he said in his voice that sounded like music.

'Hello Tenzinmonk.' She settled herself in front of the mirror.

'I am sorry to keep you waiting, great one. I could not be here before.'

'That's OK. I knew you would come.' She paused. 'Tenzinmonk, please can I come and live with you?' The words came out in a rush.

He smiled sadly. 'Ah great one, this is my supreme wish, but your parents would never allow it.'

'They'd be happier if I went away.'

'This may be so, but still they would not give you up. This is the way of parents.'

'You could take me?'

'Katie-la, this is hard for you to understand, but when you died in the last life, you chose these parents to come back to. You chose the lessons and the opportunities they would give you for this life. We must have patience and trust that this is for the best.'

'They don't try to believe anything I say. They are frightened of me.'

'They are ignorant of much. This is not your fault, Katie-la.'

She sighed.

'You will learn to be strong,' he whispered. 'Because one day, you are to do great things and you need strength for that.'

'I just want to help them.'

'I know. Your heart is immense, and you forgive a thousand times. But you cannot change them, Katie-la. Try to put this energy into your thinking, your speech and your actions. If these can be pure, then this is enough.'

She watched him carefully, remembering his face for later.

'How old are you?' she asked suddenly.

Tenzinmonk chuckled. 'Younger than you, Katie-la. But in this life, I am forty nine.' He leaned forward in the mirror. 'I want you to do something for me. I want you to imagine a small box that you can put all your magic in, and only you can open it. You can put anything in there and it will be safe.' He tapped his chest. 'Keep it here.'

Kate nodded seriously.

'And when finally we meet,' he continued, 'we will open this box together, and look at all that is in there.'

She put her hand to the mirror and he put his up to meet hers. She could only feel the glass, but she imagined that they were touching.

Slow awareness entered Kate's mind and she realised her whole body was aching. She stretched out her legs and listened to the silence.

She replayed the memory she had just revisited. She had done what Tenzin had said: imagined a box and put all her magic in it. But then had come the pills and the doctors and later the ECT... and now she couldn't find it. What else had she lost? Fucking ECT, she thought, and opened her eyes.

The truth was that Kate still missed the monk. Seeing him again in the mirror had brought back just how much. She knew it was better to be sane than mad, but she also knew that something precious had been lost.

Her buzzer was pressed and its shrill sound jarred Kate back into the present.

Bloody Jehovah's Witnesses, she thought and rolled her eyes at their persistence. She waited for them to leave, but instead, her buzzer was pressed again.

She jumped up from the stool. This was absolutely the last time they would try to convert her. No more nice. She picked up the intercom phone and yelled down it.

'What?'

There came a chuckle at the end of the line, and a deep throaty 'Ha!'

Kate's anger morphed into curiosity.

'Hello?' she tried more tentatively.

'Hallooo!' The voice boomed back.

'Can I help you?'

'Ha!' came the response again, followed by a snuffling that sounded like laughter.

'Who is this?' Her skin was already starting to goose bump from the draft coming through the doorframe.

'All is good question. Quite. Yes. I come now.' The voice was thick with foreign inflection.

'Where you come?' Kate shook her head as she caught herself copying his syntax.

'UP!' the voice roared with enormous enthusiasm, and in spite of herself, Kate giggled.

'Can you wait please? Sorry. One moment.'

She skipped to the window and opened the curtains, her eyes briefly closing as they adjusted to the light. Pulling the window open, she leaned out to see the street below.

Her heart jolted as if it had left the starting blocks too quickly. She could see red robes. The figure below looked up at her.

It was Tenzinmonk.

He beamed and waved.

Kate stepped back from the window as if she had been slapped by what she had seen. Fear opened something in her heart which had been locked away.

She made herself lean against the wall and slow her breathing. This is not happening, she reminded herself.

She walked towards the front door, and stopped halfway to steady herself by the harp.

'You're imagining things,' she announced aloud. 'You're tired and off the pills and some old stuff is just coming up. We're just going to have a nice cup of tea and it will go away.'

The buzzer sounded again.

Kate wondered if the best thing was to humour her hallucination: trick her mind into sending its creation away.

She went to the intercom phone. 'Hello? Could you come back another time, please. I'm very busy.' She waited.

'Halloooo!' the voice bellowed heartily back.

'Did you hear me? I said I'm busy.' She drew her words more clearly this time.

The singsong voice replied rapidly. 'Yes yes. Always busy. Round and round never stopping. Why you running from, Katie-la?'

At the sound of her name, Kate's heart lurched again. This was too much, even for a hallucination.

'OK, I'm going now. Byeeee.'

Her breath was quickening again. She hung up the phone and curled up on the sofa. The opened box in her heart had released something horrible, something sharp.

She clutched her head as long-hidden images started to form in her mind: a locked box where her heart should have been; a child's seal discarded in the corner of a room, cold pads pressed against her temples as doctors measured the strength of her electric extinction.

She was losing herself again.

Images of her mother's reedy despair, her father's toxic rage, and her quivering child self. All rose up with querulous voices and pointed faces.

'Go away', she whimpered. She was filling with her family's despair. A drop will drown me now, she thought, as she pushed down her tears.

All the fury of those lost years: to be told she was wrong, damaged, broken. The pillow beneath her knees. The cold steel of the injection.

What if they had broken her?

'Stop!' She screamed out.

Silence.

Kate lay stunned. There it was in techinicolour, as if no time had passed and she hadn't changed at all. She would never escape it. She could not outrun herself.

She forced herself to breathe deeply. She was still here.

Her gaze wandered to the window and her unshed tears washed through her. She thought of the man who had died last week in the hospital, and of the light she had seen running through him. She thought of the tramp in her dreams, prophesying her death. She thought of the pills, poured into her as a child. The same pills that, a month ago, she had finally thrown into the bin. She thought of her friends' concern for her. She thought of her childhood friend, Tenzinmonk, and how she'd sworn never to stop believing in him.

The monk was waiting for her on the low wall opposite her building. He looked up when she came to the window again, and smiled at her in that sad way she remembered.

She listened by the door to the heavy steps that climbed towards her, and then the spy-hole was filled with his eye, looking back, winking at her.

Kate started to open the door, before she remembered with a jolt that she was naked.

'God! Sorry. I'm... Wait there!'

She ran to her room and pulled on some clothes.

Back at the door she took a deep breath and flung it open before she could change her mind.

Before her was the monk in the mirror, the man she knew so well from her childhood. She had lost everything for insisting he existed. And now, for the first time, he was here.

Kate's eyes ran over his golden skin, the red robes wrapped round his plump middle. That face, which managed to be full of concern and the comedy of life at the same time.

The monk placed his hands together and bowed to her.

Kate mirrored his action, secretly glad no one was watching.

The monk wagged a finger at her. 'You hard to find. All buildings here looking same same.' His voice carried the cadence of an eastern melody.

'Please come in. Can I make you some tea?' Kate felt deeply moved by his presence.

'Thank you, thank you so much.'

As he passed her, Kate poked his arm, just to see whether he was really in her flat, or whether she had achieved new levels of psychosis.

Her fingers found solid flesh.

'Please sit down.' She gestured to the sofa.

The monk gathered his robes around him, and sat back into the cushions, his feet nodding above the floor. He grinned at Kate and settled his bag beside him.

She stood, mesmerised by this manifestation of her childhood hallucination.

His eyes fell on the harp, which was standing in the centre of the room.

'You play?' he asked.

'Everyday', Kate replied seriously, grounded by its solidity in this sea of unknowing.

'So this is your practice', he observed. 'This is good. Practice takes person long way.'

Kate smiled nervously, and went into the kitchen. She busied herself around the kettle, taking out her favourite elephant cups and the milk from the fridge.

She realised that she was shaking and forced herself to watch the steam start to rise and evaporate into the air. She wondered, *do monks take sugar?*

She poked her head round the door to ask.

The monk had moved to the edge of the sofa. His eyes were closed, and he sat with the poise of a dancer, despite his bulk.

He had a quality of shimmering stillness like the Buddha statues in the Battersea Peace Pagoda. Fear pricked her with the otherness of this man. She had an overwhelming sense that she could not contain him within her understanding. But at the same time, he was so familiar to her. So dear to her. She drew back, feeling like a voyeur to her own memory.

She held the cup steady as she poured in the boiling water, and wondered what her father would say to her now.

Anger flashed through her and she yelped as pain spread across her hand. Water was flowing over the cup, on to her hand, over the work surface and on to the floor.

The monk appeared at the door and, seeing what had happened, started to laugh, louder and louder until he was roaring: 'You very full! No room! Empty empty!'

Kate had an urge to scream, but held herself together for fear that she too would spill all over the floor.

'It *hurts.*' She eyed him furiously, incredulous at his laughter.

'Sensation only. Watch. Pain passing.'

Kate's hand started to throb and she thrust it under the cold tap. It didn't help, and she felt the fury of an accident that shouldn't have happened.

The monk spoke again: 'Attention. Always attention. This way, no surprises!' He touched her shoulder and looked at her solemnly. 'Do you know who you are?'

'No,' she whimpered. She knew nothing.

The monk looked at her hand, reddening raw, and beckoned Kate back into the sitting room.

Sitting her on the sofa, he rested her hand in his calloused clasp and looked at her kindly.

'Do not worry about all that is happening. The mind needs time.' He smiled and closed his eyes. Still holding Kate's hand, he began to chant; his voice moved to such a deep register that it vibrated through her.

She closed her eyes and let the waves wash through her. Delicious energy started to tickle up her spine, and her breathing slowed as she felt herself lighten. She was losing feeling in her limbs and her hand seemed to dissolve as she merged with the sound. Fear left her body, and she was pinpricks of light in the deep, like constellations showing their shape at dusk. She had no name for any of it.

From the depths, there was a ringing... A bell underwater...

Kate opened her eyes with a start, her head numb as if she had stayed in the water too long.

The monk did not move.

Kate hastily removed her hand from his and picked up the phone.

It took her a few seconds to remember how to speak.

'Hello?' she managed, already regretting it.

'You OK? You sound kind of spacey.' A voice full of concern.

'*Zac?*' Kate glanced guiltily at the monk.

'Hey you, what are you up to?'

'Oh, just stuff.'

'Yeah? What kind of stuff?' His voice was like liquid.

'Umm...' Kate raised her hand to her head. 'Just some cleaning.'

'*Cleaning?* It's a beautiful day out here.' Zac laughed. 'I thought we could meet, practise some Tai Chi?'

'Yeah, sounds good. Let's meet in the park. Give me an hour, would you?'

'Meet you by the statues.'

'Great.'

'Kate?'

'Yes?'

'I look forward to it...' He hung up.

Kate tingled and looked up to see Tenzin watching her thoughtfully.

'This person, on the phone. He makes you unsteady.'

'Yes,' she snapped. 'But that's the way it's supposed to be.'

'Ah, yes. Love.' He smiled kindly and patted her hand.

Kate's irritation dissolved as she realised with a start that her hand no longer hurt. She looked back at him wonderingly. 'Who are you?'

The monk put a finger to his lips. 'First, let us see who *you* are.'

His hand dived into the bag and brought out an old looking bell, placing it carefully on the coffee table.

Kate watched fascinated as the little table quickly filled with strange and ancient looking objects. The monk sat behind it, like an antiques dealer revealing his wares.

She stretched out a hand and fingered the carvings on the bell before picking it up with her left hand to ring it. Its sound reminded her of the sea. Seeing that the monk was watching her, she replaced it on the table.

She spotted a wooden beaded necklace, and instinctively rubbed the beads and brought the sweet smell of sandalwood to her nose.

As the monk pulled out a battered wooden bowl, he glanced at her once more. Kate held out her hands and took it from him. It filled her with unbearable sadness, though she only realised she was crying when a tear dropped into the bowl and was quickly absorbed by the grain.

She heard a sniff and looked up to see the monk gazing at her.

His own tears were falling freely over his papery cheeks. He stood up awkwardly and then, to Kate's horror, fell to his knees and prostrated himself face down in the carpet.

Kate knelt over him.

'What happened? Are you ill?'

She could hear a muffled string of sing song sounds trying to escape through the carpet and wondered wide-eyed if he was saying his last rites. She raised a hand to her mouth, and then stretched it out to touch him.

The monk wheeled round on to his back and sat bolt upright.

Kate screamed.

The monk roared with laughter. 'I am well. Now very good!' he bellowed. 'Ha! You disappear!'

She folded her arms in front of her.

The monk softened his laughter to a chuckle.

'You experience fear. It is natural. No need fear! No need completely!'

Kate pulled back.

The monk tried again: 'I Tenzin Norbu.' He smiled eagerly.

'I know your name. I remember you.' She hesitated. 'But I don't understand who you are, *what* you are.'

She quietened her voice to a whisper. 'No one else can see you.'

The monk seemed unfazed by this. He chuckled again. 'You remember me from before?'

'Yes, when I was a child. You were my friend.' My only friend, Kate thought wryly.

'No no no. *Before*,' he insisted.

'*What* before?' Before my childhood? What was he talking about?

'Last life. Yes. Good life.'

Kate went cold.

'So you don't remember,' the monk said, softer now. 'That is the way. You Bodhisattva. Very powerful. You come back.'

Kate stared at him in incomprehension.

'You *very* hard to find.' He continued. 'Sky-dancers not like monks. You live alone. Many secrets.'

'I don't understand.' Kate shook her head, though something in her broke – a sweet splintering.

'You great teacher. You *my* teacher.' He beamed at her.

Kate looked at him suspiciously: 'I'm sorry but I don't know what you mean.' She stood up.

There was something in the monk's containment that made her feel scattered. His single bag made her flat seem ridiculous: a museum of memories arranged to give substance to her life.

The monk nodded. 'There is no hurry. I already wait twenty-eight years!' He laughed as if this was something very funny. Then he shook his head and sighed as if suddenly old.

'Something happened to you,' he looked at Kate directly. 'Many years back, your heart closing. I lost you.'

Kate shivered. She could not go back to that time. She would not.

DITCH

a short story by Richard Walsh

Two boys dressed in school uniform stumbled along a path that ran through a 307 wasteland of knee-high grass, rubble and twisted metal. Tower blocks and the backs of terraced houses framed the field on three sides, but, apart from the boys, the only movement was the dots that circled high above Heathrow in the late afternoon sun. The boys walked in file, the taller behind, twisting the left arm of his slightly-built companion behind his back.

Andrew started to trot, forced by Patrick's longer stride. Andrew was twelve, with pale, undefined features and a thatch of untidy brown hair. Mud and dust streaked his trousers, and the pocket of his shirt was ripped. His shoes scuffed along the path, kicking loose stones into the long grass and weeds. Both boys appeared composed, and they proceeded without a struggle, in silence.

Freckles and sunburn had merged into a band across the broad face of the larger boy. Patrick was thirteen. Sweat glistened in his shaved hair, soaking into the blue-and-gold tie wrapped around his forehead. He gave a sudden tug to the left, and the two turned into the tall grass, towards the open side of the field. In the distance was a wire fence, and beyond that, a railway line. Grasshoppers whirred ahead of the boys as they forced their way through the undergrowth. A tube train, running overland, clanked its way past and was gone. Old cans and crisp packets, half-buried in the mud, gleamed and were lost again. There had been rain, a summer downpour, that morning and the air was rich with the smell of earth and wet grass.

They both knew where they were going. The ditch was Patrick's latest favourite. Patrick's growing boredom with torturing Andrew had been banished by the discovery of the ditch the previous week. It was only a short distance from the school, an easy detour to drag the smaller youth. He made it a point of pride to know the areas in which he lived better than the locals.

Patrick was a traveller, and had been at Andrew's school for three months. Travelling kids did that, mysteriously appearing, staying for half a year, a year, a month, and then disappearing again. For two of those months he had tormented Andrew, relentlessly hunting him in and after school.

They reached an area of scrub and small trees where the ground rose and fell like the barrows of ancient kings. Butterflies took off as they approached a clump of buddleias, their pink flowers glowing in the late sun. At the brow of a low rise they stopped.

They stood at the lip of a ditch, about twenty metres long and three deep, with steeply sloping sides that were a patchwork of grass and weeds and treacherous blue-grey clay. Tyres and broken timbers protruded from the black water that filled the bottom. Set into the ends of the ditch were the dark mouths of concrete pipes, half a metre in diameter, into which the water disappeared. One pipe was sealed with a rusted iron grille. The other was open.

Suddenly, Andrew leapt, kicked his legs and tried to dart away. But the older boy's grip was strong, and he forced Andrew's arm even further behind his back.

'Owww! Owww! Sorry, sorry!' squealed Andrew.

Patrick gave a high laugh of delight. 'You done that before – I don't forget. You sly little prick.' He twisted Andrew's arms, forcing him to his knees. 'No use, Williams. You're shit, so why try?' Patrick's voice was light, relaxed, with a faint Irish accent. 'You know what's coming. You know it, don't you?'

'Please, Pat, please. I don't want to do it. You've seen me do it before, not again.'

Patrick laughed again. 'You were cheeking me in school today, boy. You were cheeking me.'

'No, Pat, that wasn't me. You know it wasn't me.'

'And you're calling me a liar to my face are you?'

'No.'

'So you're either cheeking me, or you're calling me a liar, ain't yah?' Patrick grinned at his cleverness.

'Pat!'

'Look at the ditch today!' said Patrick.

'Please.'

'Down you go!' A high, singsong voice.

'Please!'

'Do you want a push or do you want to go down yourself? It's gonna happen, so you might make it easy,' sang Patrick. 'Show-some-brains-Will-iams-you-shit.'

Patrick pushed Andrew to the very edge of the ditch and released him, letting him turn to face his tormentor. Patrick took a step forward, forcing Andrew back. Andrew dropped to his hands and knees and extended a foot behind him, trying to feel for a foothold.

'Ooh, no hands I think,' said Patrick, kicking at his wrists.

'Fuck,' said Andrew and he started to slip. His foot caught in a tussock of grass.

'Lick my boots and you can come up.'

Andrew stared up at Patrick. From his angle, Patrick filled his vision, the blue sky wrapped around him. There was wink of light over his shoulder, as a plane turned and caught the lowering sun.

'Lick it,' said Patrick. Patrick balanced on one foot, holding out a dusty black shoe in Andrew's face. There was a smear of brown on the toe. He waved it in front of his nose. Andrew could smell the dog shit.

'Lick it. One lick and you can come up.'

Andrew said, almost to himself: 'Fuck off.'

'Excuse me?'

'Fuck off.'

'Fuck off? Fuck yourself, then.' Patrick pushed the sole of his shoe in Andrew's face. Andrew felt his toe-hold go; he almost stopped himself, but then fell utterly, tumbling down the slick flank of clay.

His back cracked against a tyre and he gasped for breath. He sat waist deep in the inky water, shocked at the pain in his ribs. He didn't know you could be winded by being hit in the back, and he felt angry at his body, obscurely betrayed. He plucked at his soaked and filthy shirt. His mother couldn't miss this. Normally, with a few grass stains, he could slip into the flat and stuff his clothes in the washing machine without her noticing. The pills she took slowed her down. If she did ask, the bruises were from football or rugby; sometimes he would even change into his games kit before he came home.

Something exploded into the water by Andrew's face.

'You fucking animal, Williams!'

Patrick was dancing. He whooped and sang, and rained handfuls of clay down on Andrew, spattering his body and the water around him. A strong boy could have climbed the bank, gouging handholds with debris from the ditch. Andrew wasn't strong, and, anyway, Patrick would have joyfully stopped any attempt.

The only way out was through the pipe. He had done it twice before; two hundred metres of stinking slime, of animal bones and faeces, until he emerged into a ditch with sides shallow enough to climb. The first time, Andrew truly thought he was going to die. Forced into the tunnel by the jeers and stones of Patrick, he had found himself shaking with fear, unable to move forward or back. Now, despite his dread, he knew the crawl was possible. But the previous times the ground had been almost dry, with only a trickle of water in the tunnel. Today, it was half full. He shivered and looked up. The war-whoops and catcalls had stopped. Patrick stood with hands on hips.

'Do something, then!' shouted Patrick.

'It's too small,' he called back, contemplating the pipe. 'The water's too high.' He looked up. Patrick had gone; but, a moment later, reappeared, cradling something in his arms.

'You better watch out, Williams!' He threw a brick high over the ditch. It fell a body-length from Andrew, dousing him and the ditch sides. Andrew didn't move.

'Go on! Go on! I'm not going to stop. I got plenty more!' He bent down and hefted another brick. It flew over Andrew's head and thudded into the clay. Too close. Andrew scuttled on his hands and knees towards the hole, his body tensing like a soldier expecting a bullet.

Without a final glance, he ducked into the pipe.

Water slapped at his chest and cast pale reflections on the curved surface above his head. Patrick's calls, weirdly distorted, echoed from the smooth coldness of the concrete. For a minute Andrew paused and peered into the darkness. There didn't seem any option. He pushed forward.

His fingers probed through the soft mud, touching twigs and gravel, wire and bone. Patrick's taunts receded and disappeared with the last of the light. The world shrunk to touch and sound. Andrew closed his eyes and listened to the loud rasp of his breath.

The pipe wasn't entirely horizontal. There was a gradient; not large, but enough to force his face closer and closer to the water. The wave he created as he inched forward would suddenly slosh back, forcing its way into his nose and mouth. He lost sense of time, its meaning leached away, until he didn't know whether he had been crawling for ten minutes or an hour.

Eventually there was no space left above the water and he had to press his cheek against the roof to breathe. Fear threatened to overwhelm him, and he had to fight to stop himself from retching. He paused, trying to work out how far he had come. He had just passed a point he thought he remembered, where the tunnel kinked to the right. He thought it was no more than thirty metres from the end. For a long time he crouched, motionless, debating whether he could shuffle backwards and beg Patrick for mercy, or try and find some impossible strength and haul himself from the ditch.

He made a decision; he started to take deep, fast breaths, and then, just as he began to feel light-headed, he plunged his face into the water and forced himself forward, counting as he moved. Once his trouser leg caught on something, but he calmly reached behind and plucked it free. On the count of thirty-seven, with his blood and lungs screaming, he found there was space above his head again. He surfaced and promptly vomited. Through the pain and blurred eyes, he could see the half moon of the end, ten metres away. He didn't stop to catch his breath. There was always the horror that Patrick might block the other opening.

The light of the early evening was soft and forgiving, and there was no sign of Patrick. This ditch was shallow, with crude wooden steps running up one side. With his last strength Andrew pulled himself to his feet, and stumbled up and out of the ditch and into the field. He looked around. The waste was empty and Patrick was nowhere to be seen.

Andrew rolled in the long grass like an animal, trying to get rid of the filth that covered him. He could taste it. He could feel it inside him. Tears of disgust and shame sprang to his eyes. He squatted and convulsively pulled clumps of grass from the earth, putting the roots in his mouth, tasting the leaves, stems and soil.

When he looked up, an old man was watching him from the other side of the ditch. Andrew coughed and retched and a ball of half-chewed grass fell from his mouth. The man was white, although his skin was as brown and fissured as a walnut. Thick, dishevelled grey hair almost touched the collar of a tweed jacket. He was slightly stooped, but still tall, and the breadth of his shoulders was apparent. His eyes, so deep set as to be almost black, were fixed on Andrew.

'I saw it all,' said the man in a flat voice. He started to walk towards the head of the ditch, above where the pipe emerged from the earth. Andrew scrambled to his feet.

'I saw it all,' said the man, still walking.

'I gotta go,' said Andrew, half-turning to look at the field. It was still deserted.

'Wait.' The man stopped walking. 'I saw it all.' A faint, sickly-sweet smell, of alcohol and aniseed, drifted across the ditch.

Andrew didn't think there was much he could say. He nodded, and again glanced behind, judging the distance to the path.

'I was wondering if you'd make it.' The man plucked the head from a tall stem of grass, and rubbed it in his hand. 'You'd like to get him, yes?' The man's voice was educated, unaccented, but strange. Each word was painfully enunciated, as though forced out at a cost.

Andrew stood still. He slowly nodded.

'Do you hate him?'

'Yes.'

'How much?'

Andrew shrugged.

'How much?' repeated the man, his voice lifeless. He held his arms apart, as though boasting of a record fish. 'This much?' It could have been a comical gesture, but it wasn't.

Andrew shook his head. The man raised his eyebrows in a gesture of surprise, and held his arms further apart. 'This much?'

Andrew shook his head again. 'No,' he said, and held his arms as wide as he could. 'This much.'

The man tilted his head to one side, his eyes suddenly gleaming like split coal.

'I could get him for you,' said the man.

'What?'

'I could get him for you. Shall I?'

'Get him?'

'Yes. Do you want me to?'

'Yeah. Get him,' said Andrew, quietly. 'Fucking get him.' Without waiting for an answer, he turned and fled across the field. Brambles tore at his trousers, but he didn't slow down. Only when he reached the path did he look back. The man had gone.

The next day was a Tuesday. Andrew wondered whether Patrick would be at school. He was. He spat on Andrew in the playground at lunch, and then went back to playing football. As though they were something private and intimate, the events of the previous evening went unmentioned.

But, after school Patrick didn't come searching in the cloakroom for him. Patrick didn't fall in step with him as he sneaked out of the gates. Patrick wasn't at the shops, or at the bus stop. Andrew walked home scarcely able to believe his luck. Only when his mother opened the door of the flat did he allow himself to sag with relief.

Patrick wasn't at school the next day, or the next. By Thursday evening, a dull, mysterious ache had appeared in Andrew's lower stomach. The relief of each day untouched was beginning to be replaced by something else. Had he misheard the man, misunderstood him? Had he even been real? On Friday, Andrew asked a boy who played basketball with Patrick whether he'd seen him. The boy looked at him with contempt.

'What? No, haven't seen him. Fuck off.'

At the weekend he almost managed to forget what had happened. But, shopping with his mother, he found himself constantly watching the crowds, scanning for Patrick. He knew that on Monday the basketball team were receiving an award in assembly, for winning the borough championship. Patrick was on the team, one of the top scorers. He would be there, thought Andrew, he wouldn't miss that.

Monday came. Andrew sat in the hall, his stomach churning, waiting for the familiar, swaggering figure to appear. He didn't. No mention was made to explain his absence. After assembly he approached Patrick's form tutor.

'Sir, what's wrong with Patrick Duffy?'

'Don't know.' Mr Mitchell kept on walking, a stack of exercise books balanced in his hand. 'Why?'

'Nothing. He's been away. Just thought that—'

'I've heard nothing,' said Mr Mitchell and strode away.

Three days later, he tried again. Mrs Cross was both Patrick's and Andrew's English teacher. Andrew waited until the class had filed out.

'He's a traveller,' replied Mrs Cross. 'He must have gone.'

'Oh. Do you know that? Did he tell you?'

'What? No. They never say when they're going.'

'Oh. OK.'

Mrs Cross looked closely at Andrew.

'You should be glad. I've seen him around you.'

Andrew nodded. 'Yeah. Course.'

As the days went by, fear and hope became tangled and indistinguishable in Andrew's chest. He didn't ask the teachers again, wary of linking his name to Patrick's. Like a problem in maths class, columns of possibilities stacked themselves in his mind. The man was old. What could he do to Patrick? Patrick could handle himself. But Patrick had never talked of leaving. The man was big, imposing, frightening.

On a Saturday, twenty days after the encounter, Andrew spotted the man, dressed in his tweed jacket, walking slowly along a street near Andrew's house. The man swayed as he walked, leaning against garden walls for support. For half an hour, Andrew trailed him, trying to pluck up the courage to approach. He seemed to be following no particular route, taking streets at random, sometimes doubling back. Eventually, when walking beside a main road, the man suddenly turned and went into a basement flat on a crumbling Victorian terrace, slamming a brown front door behind him.

Andrew crouched on the pavement, face pushed against the iron fence that surrounded the small, overgrown front garden. The curtains of the flat were drawn, and the flats above appeared to be abandoned, with several smashed windows and a large water-stain, like a port-wine mark, spreading over the front of the house from a broken gutter. Although bordered by a busy road, the street had few pedestrians; some quirk of town planning had cut it off from the hustle of city life like an oxbow lake from a river. He crept on quaking legs from his hiding place to the door, and pressed his ear against the wood. Over the noise of the traffic, he thought he could hear hammering. He ran.

One month later, on a Wednesday evening after school, he went back to the house. Patrick's name hadn't been mentioned at school for weeks. Andrew squatted outside, his hands gripping the sun-warmed railings as though resisting the buffeting wind of the traffic, puzzling at the pile of objects on the grass of the front garden; two stacked plastic chairs, a sewing machine, bulging bin bags, a stained mattress.

The front door was open, showing a dark, wood-panelled hallway. A middle-aged woman, large and white, with her blonde hair scraped tight into a bun and forehead glossy with sweat, appeared in the open doorway and walked heavily up the steps. Andrew moved further into the shadow of the bushes. She deposited an armful of books on the growing pile. The women disappeared down the steps, but re-emerged a moment later with a brown-haired woman, also large and white, carrying a long cream-coloured table between them. Both were dressed in white polo shirts and dark blue aprons with Swiburn's Cleaning Services printed in gold letters. As they climbed the stairs, the plug connected to the table uncoiled and caught under the door. The blonde-haired women called back into the hallway:

'Grace!'

There was silence from the house.

'Grace! Gracie!'

A younger woman, with coffee-coloured skin and hoop earrings appeared. Like the others she wore a polo-shirt and apron. She looked bored.

'The plug?! Get it, yeah?'

'What is it?'

'Tanning-bed, isn't it?'

'What's an old man want with that?'

'I dunno! The house is full of crap.'

'You don't want it do you?' said Grace, and sniggered. 'Can you imagine!'

'Shut up and help us move it.'

Gracie helped them lift the tanning-bed into the garden. She kicked the mattress, and it slithered off the pile in a cloud of dust. Andrew caught the faint smell of decay and mould.

'Don't do that!'

'It all wants burning, I say.'

'Probably will be, love.'

They went back inside. Gracie and the woman with brown hair emerged again, carrying a Hoover and plastic boxes filled with cleaning cloths and bottles. They lit cigarettes and sat on the steps.

'All done,' said the older woman.

'Creeps me out.'

'You get used to it. First day and all that.'

'I wouldn't have believed the shit you can find.'

'This one's not the worst. This one's fine.'

'So that's it? All finished.'

'Yeah. Leave it in the yard. It's not gonna rain is it?'

'No, not tonight.'

'Council will pick it up tomorrow. No relatives. Nothing else to do.'

The blonde-haired woman came out and locked the door behind her. The others flicked their cigarettes away and walked up the path. Andrew followed at a safe distance. They loaded a small white van parked on the next street and drove off.

In the garden, Andrew started to pick gingerly at a bin bag, and then he realised he didn't know what he was looking for. He stared at the pile for a long time, and then turned and walked out of the garden and down the street. There was nothing else to do.

THE WALLED GARDEN

from the novel The Castle *by Kathryn Whinney*

Ella had never been in this room in the evening. During the day, while cleaning, she and Jenn had killed a long time pointing out the sloppy, tacky aspects of the decoration to each other. The way the bamboo stencilled around the wall was smudged in places, and also didn't line up properly. The way the round, Chinese style lampshade was a garish magenta colour that was incongruous with the rest of the colour scheme. Jenn was particularly disgusted by the generic Chinese pictures that hung on the walls.

'What was she thinking?' Jenn had cried out, flinging a hand towards a black and white print of the Great Wall of China. It looked ridiculous, hanging off-centre between the doors to the en suite and the closet, but when they took it down to see whether its absence improved the aesthetic, a massive stain was revealed on the wall. After some speculation, and the agreement that if there had been a murder they would have heard about it, they concluded it must be a coffee stain, hurled by the girlfriend of a best man who had discovered he had slept with the bride.

The blue was definitely the worst of the three Chinese rooms. The other two, pink and yellow, were pretty bad, but the staff all agreed that the blue was the worst. The Chinese rooms were for third-tier guests: younger brothers, great aunts, anyone who wasn't paying for themselves.

In the day – in the day it was the worst room. At the moment, now, in the night time, it was the damn best finest room any of them had ever been in. By the time she, Jenn and Josh crept upstairs the lights were softened to the point that the smudgy walls and tacky fabrics were lit so dimly they weren't noticeable. With the champagne, followed by the minibar whiskies, the room was the height of glamour. One of the more braying of the men described it as 'early nineteenth century opium den'. It sounded impressive, even if the men weren't. They seemed to be mostly from the same mould: braying, boasting. She was fairly sure some of the boys at her school would grow into these men. Still, they were generous to a fault.

Five of the younger guys from the wedding were there, in various states of disarray. It was the groom's youngest brother's room, and the others were hangers-on with nowhere else to stay. And there was the Werewolf – sitting quietly in one of the armchairs. He looked even more dishevelled than he had at the wedding, where they had last seen him trying to chat up Louise. They had thought he had gone home. On seeing him, Ella stopped in the doorway, and Josh ran into her back. She gave Jenn a *look*, inclining her head in the Werewolf's direction. Jenn made a 'relax' face, and waved Ella in. There was also a woman, looking to be in her mid-twenties, slumped against the side of the bed, apparently asleep already. Ella had seen her at the reception, in a white minidress, dancing crazily with anyone who came along. She was barefoot now, and someone had courteously laid a jacket over her lap and legs.

The conversation drifted around, only occasionally pulling Ella into its webs. Jenn was making up to one of the more handsome of the men, and he was responding, though Ella was sure he'd mentioned an absent girlfriend earlier in the evening. Not that Jenn would be too bothered about that. They had withdrawn themselves a little from the general circle, leaning back against a wall, turning inwards, keeping the rest of the group outside. Ella couldn't hear what they were saying, and from their body language she was quite glad she couldn't. She kept her gaze firmly fixed away from them, though unfortunately she kept catching things a little out if the corner of her eye.

It seemed like she was the only one with such feelings of modesty and privacy. The Werewolf was watching Jenn and the guy with a leer on his face. Ella couldn't help glancing in their direction to see what he was leering at. Jenn's skirt had ridden up fairly high, and the guy's hand was wandering up her thigh.

A glimpse of the digital clock read 2.12 – hours since she last checked it. Where had the time gone? A stumble as she got up to go to the bathroom received a cheer.

Later still. Jenn had disappeared with her guy. Josh had also gone off somewhere. She knew she should be mildly annoyed that he'd buggered off without her, but she knew he would say she was old enough to look after herself.

Blinking didn't clear the blurring from her eyes. The lights were definitely dimmer. She'd missed something, some joke. The girl in the white dress was awake now, and was lounging on the canopied bed, waving at the guys to worship her.

'Peasbottom, Mustardseed – pass me some champagne.'

They laughed with her, one of them applauding her cleverness and rushing for the drinks. She clambered to her feet, dragging a sheet with her, which she wrapped around her waist into a long skirt.

They were tripping over each other to serve the silly bitch. Hopefully she would get tangled up in the sheet and fall flat on her face. She kept one hand raised in the air, winding it round and round in a drunken approximation of regal behaviour. Mincing on tiptoes she approached Ella's spot on the floor and stood over her.

'Come and join the dance dah-ling.'

Her hair was falling out of its chignon, creating bouncy tentacles around her face.

'Where is Bottom... where? Ah, you must be Bottom.'

She swung away from Ella, bearing down on the Werewolf instead, who had so far sat in his armchair, not joining in with the fairy game.

'What you sayin'?'

Unlike the others' posh accents, his was deepest mockney.

'Come now dah-ling, I am Ty-tay-nea, these are my servants,' annoyingly, her sweeping arm took in Ella as well, 'and we need someone to be Bottom.'

Had she thought this through? Bottom did, after all, go to bed with Titania, and the Werewolf, with his crappy beard and sneering expression, wouldn't have been Ella's first choice.

'Didn't 'e 'ave a donkey 'ead?' Was she imagining the sharpness in his voice?

'An asses head!' crowed one of the other lads, not yet feeling the change in the atmosphere. Ella shifted in her spot on the floor; was it the drink making her feel antsy and wanting to move? The Werewolf had sat up in his chair and leant forward a little, one hand clenched tight around a heavy whisky glass in his hand.

'Yes, Ty-tay-nea, under a spell, falls for the donkey-headed Bottom.' The girl had not noticed the way the Werewolf's face had flushed red, and his eyes were flashing.

'What?' It was impossible not to hear his anger, and the atmosphere in the room had definitely shifted as quickly as his mood. Titania dropped back from him, subconsciously pulling her makeshift skirts further up her body, holding the sheet to her chest. This action revealed a lot of her legs but the Werewolf refused to be swayed and continued to fume.

'So, you're sayin' that I'm so ugly that I practically 'ave a donkey 'ead? And that the only chance I'd 'ave with you would be if you were under a spell?'

One of the lads realised the danger and heroically put himself between the Werewolf and Titania.

'Now then mate, what did'ya think? That you were in just 'coz she danced with you? Is that why you've been hanging around all night?' His plummy accent had taken on a twinge of the Werewolf's mockney. All the better to fight you with.

Unfortunately, that was apparently what the Werewolf thought. With a 'fuck you mate' he'd stood quickly, surprising the lad. Titania backed away, unsure what to do. Suddenly she swung back to Ella, who had been keeping out of things as much as possible. 'It was a joke. You know that, right?'

Her hair was crazier than ever, and she had a sheen of sweat on her skin. Mascara smudged under her eyes made them look sunken, and Ella suddenly had a flash of a skeleton looming over her, shouting at her. Behind her two of the other guys had weighed in – one of whom looked like he might be on a rugby team. They were trying to back the Werewolf into the chair without actually fighting him.

At the same time the Werewolf was trying his hardest to get past the lads and was yelling at Titania again. His face was screwed up, his mouth spitting words Ella couldn't quite make out. Skeleton Titania was screeching back, a block of suits moving in between. The cigarette smoke was making her eyes water, and unable to think of anything else she stood, walked over to the door as quickly and unobtrusively as possible, opened it, and without even a glance behind her, slipped out into the corridor.

Rather than going the long way, through the main castle, and risking running into Nick or Fran, she headed towards the back stairs. She could still hear the noise from within the blue Chinese room, muffled by the door but sounding no less vicious. As she reached the fire door at the end, she heard the clunk of a door opening and the volume of the argument increased again. Not wanting to risk getting further involved in the fight, she ducked through the fire door and pulled it closed behind her. She would go down the old spiral stairs, through the kitchen, and out the kitchen doors. Jenn must have gone out that way when she'd left with her guy. She would have had to take him back to their bungalow.

The twists of the stairs, combined with alcohol, meant that by the time she reached the bottom she was swallowing her stomach back down her throat. She leant against the wall briefly, and only then became aware of the sound of the fire door above her closing, and the sound of footsteps coming unsteadily down the stairs.

The Werewolf. It had to be. He probably wasn't following her, just lost and drunk. She didn't fancy having to deal with him, though, so she made for the kitchen door.

Locked.

And she didn't have the key. Options: go through and try to sneak out the front way. Or go back up, down the side stairs, along the passage and try the door that lead out to the walled garden. It was usually locked but as they'd been out there that afternoon the key might still be in the door. Even Sheryl usually never bothered to check it, as the outer gate to the garden was kept locked, so it was almost certain that Fran wouldn't have bothered. Or was even aware of the need.

Most of the castle doors were fairly new, on account of health and safety regulations. But the door out to the walled garden was an old wooden door, painted green on the inside, with six panes of glass in the top half. She knew this from memory alone, as it was pitch dark in the passage. She felt for the key, and luckily found it sitting snugly in the lock. She turned it as gently as possible, waiting to feel the bolt turn. She edged it round, not wanting the thud of the lock to attract the Werewolf in the darkness. She felt, rather than heard, the lock slide across.

She could slip out into the walled garden, wait long enough for the Werewolf to go back into the main castle and find his room, then sneak back through and out the front way. The door clicked gently as she closed it behind her, but she was sure he wouldn't have heard it. There was no reason for him to head off down a side staircase and a dark corridor.

The night air smelt of roses and cut grass, and although there was still some light coming from the room she had left above, she couldn't see much. It was lawn in front of her, and it was damp under her bare feet. Damn, she'd left her shoes upstairs.

Before she'd gone more than three steps, she was suddenly bathed in the bright, sulphurous lights of the security system. Shit. Was this area alarmed? Instinctively, she threw herself off to one side, landing heavily in some bushes.

There she froze, waiting for a siren, followed by her sacking for waking everyone up in the night. The siren didn't come. Instead, she heard the voice of the Werewolf behind her.

'Is there someone there?'

Fuck. Instead of escaping, she'd just lured him with the lights. What was wrong with him? Why didn't he just go to bed? Now she was stuck, and chances were he would see her. She had the advantage that while he was standing just outside the door, she was in the darkness next to the trees, and if he wasn't really looking he might not see her.

The wind was blowing fairly hard, throwing the branches around above her. She took advantage of the noise to crawl closer to the wall and duck behind a tree.

The Werewolf huffed around a little, and in turning around, noticed the lights on in the room, two floors above. The wind dropped and Ella heard him muttering to himself about 'tossers'. He then reached for his trousers, unzipped, and starting pissing on the lawn.

Next, he took out a cigarette, and after a few false starts, managed to light it. He sauntered over to the bench next to the castle wall, and sitting down heavily, seemed quite content.

His comfort unfortunately coincided with something pollen-like flying up Ella's nose and starting it itching. She pinched her nostrils together, willing herself not to sniff or sneeze.

Too late, before she knew what was happening her immune system had let her down (again) and caused her to sneeze. Although she stifled the noise as much as possible, it coincided with a stillness in nature so immediate that she could have sworn that the world around her was deliberately betraying her.

The Werewolf, living up to the nickname he didn't know he had, pricked up his ears at the sound, and after a moment pushed himself up from the bench and started to prowl around the garden.

Luckily for Ella, he started to walk away from her and the wind had started up again, masking the sounds of her push through the greenery. Thinking desperately for a way out of the situation, she began to edge behind some scrubs, her back scraping the garden wall a little. Sneaking around the outside, making it to the door and getting back inside without him seeing her would be the ideal solution, but she was fairly sure it was a pipedream. What else? Stumble out on to the lawn pretending to be as drunk as him and hope he didn't recognise her as the girl from upstairs.

That was probably the best. Claim she was going to be sick so headed outside and then passed out momentarily and therefore didn't hear him. After all, she was still pretty drunk, even though adrenaline had given her some clarity. The bushes in front of her were fairly dense; she would need to go round further in order to get through.

The Werewolf continued to try to sniff her out. He called out 'hello', then started a fit of hacking coughs. She used this as cover to move to the edge of the shrubbery, ready to fall out. Bracing herself against the wall behind her, she prepared to push herself out on to the lawn.

Only to find herself falling backward as the wall behind her gave away. It wasn't the wall, of course, but the heavy door that led out on to the main lawn. Although her head seemed clearer, her arms and legs hadn't received the message that she was feeling soberer. They refused to work quick enough to stop her falling and she tumbled over, shrieking slightly. She landed on her side, at the feet of a large figure. Before she could register much more, the Werewolf, drawn by her cry, could be heard.

''o'se there?'

The large figure stepped over her and into the archway in the wall, blocking the glow from the security lights. He didn't speak, and when the Werewolf's voice came again he sounded nervous:

''Ello mate. Where'd you come from?'

'I work here, mate. You shouldn't be out here you know. Time for bed, aye?' Ever calm, but sounding more authoritative than she had ever heard before, Iolo's quiet voice contrasted immensely with the 'wolf's drunken slurring.

'There was a girl – one of the waitresses. She said to meet 'er out 'ere.'

Had she not been so lost for words at this claim, Ella would have protested vehemently. She couldn't believe he had actually been following her. He must have known she was there all along. Why hadn't he said that he knew she was there? The unpleasantness of the situation dawned on her, and she was even gladder of Iolo's broad back standing between them.

'Don't think so mate, they would have all gone home long ago. Drove the last ones home in the minibus myself.'

Unable to see the Werewolf, Ella couldn't judge his reaction, but after a pause she caught the sound of the old door into the castle closing. Iolo didn't move for a long time, until the security light inside the castle clicked off. Then silently he pulled the heavy gate towards him and presumably locked it. There was only one light mounted on the outer wall of the garden, and in its dim glow she saw a large key with a ribbon attached disappear into the pocket of his fleece. He looked at her for a long moment, but it was too dark to see what he was thinking, even if he had given anything away. He then threw himself down on the lawn with her.

'Watch out if you're running with Jenn,' he said, surprising her. 'She's a great girl but she looks after herself and expects everyone else to be able to.'

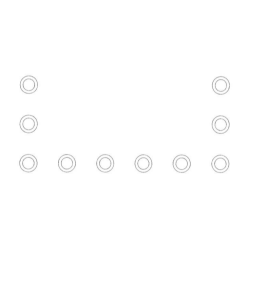

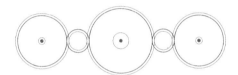

CONTRIBUTORS

Jessica Barnecutt (page 3) was born in Cornwall in 1979. She moved to London in 2001 to study English literature and creative writing. Before taking the MA at Bath Spa University, she spent ten years working in Michelin-starred restaurants. Write to jessica@springanthology.com.

Amethyst Biggs (page 9) is that quiet one in the corner, drinking wine and making sarcastic jokes. She was born in 1979 and grew up in the US. She did not vote for George W. Bush. In addition to short stories, she also dabbles in poetry and – though it's against her better judgment – might one day consider a novel. Write to amethyst@springanthology.com.

Rachael Bloom (page 19) is thirty-one. *The Child at the Window* is loosely based on her experience with her own family. She lives near Oxford with her three children who are a continuing source of inspiration and exasperation. Write to rachaelb@springanthology.com.

Alexandra Bockfeldt (page 29), born in 1982, is originally from San Francisco and grew up in Norway, France, the UK and Germany. She has a BA in International Studies from the University of Oslo and, after completing the MA and having a baby, she hopes to finish her novel and return to Bath to live. Write to alexandra@springanthology.com.

Val Bridge (page 39) is more Latvian than not. Once upon a time a Vicar's wife, now married to a racing driver, she has OTT offspring, a BA (Hons) in Russian, runs a small-holding, and rescues injured badgers. *Lost Property* is her third novel; her poems are published in small presses. Write to val@springanthology.com.

Pj Buchanan (page 49) lives in Bristol with her partner. Her alter ego is Poetry Jack. When she isn't performing poetry on stage she rides a motorbike and knits, though not at the same time. Write to pj@springanthology.com.

Stephanie Cage (page 53) wrote her first poem aged four and went on to tackle a variety of forms, including business writing, literary essays, science fiction and romance. Her work has appeared in magazines from *Woman's Own* to *AlienSkin*. To find out more visit www.stephaniecage.co.uk or write to stephanie@springanthology.com.

Neil Callender (page 61), a moderately handsome male, twenty-six, seeks a female for relationship and good times. He likes naps, stewing in inner-turmoil and toasted-cheese sandwiches. His perfect woman will be aged eighteen to thirty, will enjoy listening to turmoil, and know her way around a sandwich toaster. Write to neil@springanthology.com.

Judith Cameron (page 71) became a freelance journalist after a career in education. She writes regularly for the *Guardian* and contributes to other publications including the *Daily Telegraph* and *Good Housekeeping*. She is keen to write novels about difficult family/life issues and admires the work of Anne Tyler and Jodi Picoult. Visit www.judithcameron.co.uk or write to judith@springanthology.com.

Vincent Cassar (page 81), forty-three, has had a short story collection published, *Now Please Don't You Cry, Beautiful Edith* (Halfacrown 2001), and won the Theatre West Search for a Script playwriting competition, 2001. He is the editor of the forthcoming *Bloomsbury Good Reading Guide to World Fiction* (A & C Black, 2007). Write to vincent@springanthology.com.

Kristin-Marie Combs (page 89) was born in Blue Earth, Minnesota and raised in Minneapolis. She attended DePaul University, in Chicago, graduating early with honours in English literature. She immediately tore across the pond to develop her writing at Bath Spa University. Currently she roams, debating where home should be. Write to kmc@springanthology.com.

David Craik (page 99) is a freelance journalist who writes a range of articles for national newspapers and magazines. A Scotsman living in London, he is writing a novel celebrating Scottish working class life both in Scotland and elsewhere, and how this survives the ups and downs of an unforgettable World Cup and the Falklands War. Write to david@springanthology.com.

Caroline Dawnay (Foreword) runs the book department at PFD, Europe's leading literary and talent agency.

Tara Diamond (page 107) was a teenager in the last years of the South African apartheid. She witnessed the impact that politics of fear had on her generation, and believes these accounts once again hold truths in today's climate. Having settled in England with her partner and two children, she now writes novels and radio plays on this subject. Write to tara@springanthology.com.

Lindsay Flynn (page 117) was a lecturer in further education before deciding to do the MA. She now teaches creative writing at Evesham & Malvern Hills College. She has been a prizewinner and on the short and long list in a number of short story competitions, including *Real Writers* and *Fish*. She is writing her third novel, *All That Remains Is*. Write to lindsay@springanthology.com.

Richard Francis (Introduction) is a biographer, historian of American culture, and novelist. He was an American Studies Research Fellow at Harvard University, and taught American literature at the universities of Missouri and Manchester. He is now Professor of Creative Writing at Bath Spa University, where he has taught since 1999. His most recent book is *Judge Sewall's Apology: The Salem Witch Trials and the Forming of a Conscience* (Fourth Estate, 2006).

Sally Gander (page 127) has been writing for twenty years, while bringing up her two children and working in a variety of jobs that include recruitment consultant, chef and laboratory technician. She lives in Frome and teaches creative writing at Norton Radstock College. *The Staymaker* is her third novel. Write to sallyg@springanthology.com.

Lorien Hallama (page 135) has been writing short stories since she was seven years old, the first one being about a treasure troll and a money tree. After completing her MA from Bath Spa, she plans to return to the US in order to pursue her teaching certification, and, as always, continue writing. Write to lorien@springanthology.com.

Sally Hare (page 145) lives in Bristol. Teaching belly dancing when nine months pregnant has been her most sensible choice of career to date. Write to sallyh@springanthology.com.

Lucy Hewitt (page 155) was born in 1978. Before the MA, she worked as a secondary school teacher in Oxford. 'Apenti's Luck' is part of a short story cycle, set in and around a leprosarium and child-care centre in Ghana. 'St Anne's Leprosarium' – also part of this cycle – was published in Issue 31 of *Mslexia* magazine. Write to lucy@springanthology.com.

Carole Humphreys (page 165) was unjustly disqualified from a national children's poetry competition at the age of nine for submitting a poem 'which must have been written with the aid of an adult'. Her time is usefully spent sticking pins into voodoo dolls, bearing a remarkable resemblance to the bastards concerned. Write to carole@springanthology.com.

John Kefalas (page 171) is a composer and sound artist. His output includes opera, orchestral and multimedia works which have been recorded and performed in the UK, Europe and the USA. In 2005 he kept an election weblog for the BBC Radio 4 Today programme and hasn't stopped writing since. Write to john@springanthology.com.

KM Kernek (page 181) grew up in Oregon, USA, but has travelled to Japan, Australia, New Zealand and Belize, and now lives in Yorkshire, England. At twenty-two, she won the Provost's Literary Prize for Outstanding Fiction in 2004 for her short story, 'All By Myself'. She is currently completing her first novel *Shark Bait*. Write to kmk@springanthology.com.

Rachel Knightley (page 189) lives in London. In 2005 she won the Promis Prize for her short story, 'The Existence of Tim'. She edits a theatre magazine and her other roles in the field have included administrator, marketing officer, judge, duckling and wicked fairy. Write to rachelk@springanthology.com.

Carin Lake (page 199) was born in Devon in 1961. She graduated from Oxford University with a First in Modern Languages and then worked as a media lawyer in London. She now lives in Bath and tries to avoid libeling anyone she knows. Write to carin@springanthology.com.

Emma London (page 207) lives in Bristol but was born and bred in the Capital. Her youth was spent working as a theatre stage manager and deciding whether she was a punk or a hippie. In 2004 she gained a BA (Hons) in English at UWE. This extract is from her first novel, *If The Shoe Fits*. Write to emma@springanthology.com.

Kate McEwan (page 215) left Cape Town in 1975 to scrape a living as a copywriter, sub-editor and freelance journalist in the UK. She has published a successful non-fiction book, *Ealing Walkabout*, and hopes *Learning to Swim* will be the first of many novels. She would like to live and write in a tree-house by the sea, and grow a beard. Write to kate@springanthology.com.

TRC Martin's (page 223) first feature-length screenplay, *The Acid Army*, is currently in post-production. She is collaborating on two further scripts, one a Hawthorne adaptation, the other a remake of *Superchick*. She lives in Berlin. This is her first novel. Write to trc@springanthology.com.

Lawrence Pettener (page 227) grew up in Liverpool, but now lives in Bristol. He's been doing readings and getting published since 1980. A varied life gives him material, including Liverpool-Irishness, Asian overland hitching, living in Nepal, life-modelling and teaching yoga. His poetry varies between children's, humorous/bizarre and emotionally resonant. He gives readings and workshops in London and the South West. Write to lawrence@springanthology.com.

Christopher Pilditch (page 239) was born in Bermuda in 1956. He has variously worked as a bowling green attendant, dispatch rider, teacher and faceless bureaucrat. He has published occasional poems and short stories and won a prize in the 1991 National Poetry Competition. *Paradise Alley* is his first novel for teenagers. Write to christopher@springanthology.com.

Nazalee Raja (page 249) obtained two law degrees and worked in housing law before realising it was impossible to evade the pull of her first love – writing. She has had poems published in an anthology, and was chosen to read her work at the Bath Literary Festival. Write to nazalee@springanthology.com.

Shane Roberts (page 253) is a twenty-two-year-old aspiring novelist, born and hand-reared in Spalding, Lincolnshire, the town that serves as the primary location for his novel-in-progress, *English Machismo*. He has had short stories and poetry published in various magazines, including *The North*. Write to shane@springanthology.com.

Roxana (page 259) prays every night for her wild heart. Born in Iran before the revolution, she came to England during the Iran–Iraq war when she was ten. She now plays with American rock stars. She loves animals and deconstructing socially understood meanings. Roxana does not give a fuck. Write to roxana@springanthology.com.

Jennifer Russell (page 269), a professional journalist, hails from the Starbucks Territory of the western United States. Her features, ranging from fly-fishing to Sandinistas, have appeared in American magazines and newspapers. She lives with her family in Bath, where she is currently working on her second novel, *The Coffee Geek*. Write to jennifer@springanthology.com.

Richard Scott-Ashe (page 279) grew up in Vancouver, Canada, with stints in Europe, Asia, and the Wiltshire countryside. He speaks fluent French, and some Korean, Spanish and Japanese. He's worked as a sailing instructor in the Bahamas, a teacher and writer in Vancouver and is currently a broadcaster in Seoul, South Korea. Write to richard@springanthology.com.

Sarah Sims (page 283) has worked as a nursing auxiliary, an accommodation officer, a publisher's assistant and, most recently, in a university. *Clean* is a novel in progress. She also writes short stories and runs. Write to sarah@springanthology.com.

Madeleine Tobert (page 289) was born in Scotland in 1982. She travelled in Asia, Latin America and the South Pacific before graduating in Spanish and English literature from the University of Durham. She began writing her current novel on the island of Tonga and hopes to return there soon. Write to madeleine@springanthology.com.

Louisa Tomlinson (page 295) has had poems, short stories and journalism published. She is twenty-nine and lives in London. This extract is taken from *Sky Dancer*, the first novel in a series of Buddhist adventures. Write to louisa@springanthology.com.

Richard Walsh (page 307) travelled around the wilder areas of South America and London after graduating from Bristol University in 2003. He now lives in Bath where he is currently completing his first novel. Write to richard@springanthology.com.

Kathryn Whinney (page 317) was born in 1980 in the south of England. Write to kathryn@springanthology.com.